The Concept of Spirit

A Study of Pneuma in Hellenistic Judaism
and its Bearing on the New Testament

by
Marie E. Isaacs

HEYTHROP MONOGRAPHS
1
London, 1976

To

ERIC W. HEATON

PREFACE

'Spirit' is a major category by which New Testament writers chose to express their faith. It is a term used by early Christians to articulate their own personal experience of the power and presence of God, which they believed had arrived with the dawning of the Messianic Age, and which was the principle at work in the life of the church.

So much is clear. However, why did they choose to express this experience and conviction in terms of 'spirit'? With the exception of the Qumran Covenanters, it played scant part in the language of the eschatological expectations of Palestinian Judaism in the inter-testamental period. There, *ruach* was more a term of popular demonology than of theological hope. Similarly, in pagan Greek thought πνεῦμα cannot properly be described as a theological term. Rather it was part of the terminology of the natural sciences. Only in Stoicism was πνεῦμα used of the divine, and then not of a transcendental, immaterial being, but of a deity pervading the physical world and sharing its material properties. So who 'spiritualized' spirit? This study examines the contribution of Hellenistic Judaism to the process.

It began life as a doctoral thesis submitted to the University of Oxford. During that gestation period the patience and wisdom of my supervisors, the Very Reverend Dr Henry Chadwick of Christ Church, Oxford, and Dr Morna D. Hooker, Lady Margaret's Professor of Divinity in the University of Cambridge, played no small part in its completion. I gratefully acknowledge their valuable comments and criticisms. However, the person who originally stimulated my interest in the subject was my former Tutor, the Very Reverend Eric W. Heaton, who, many years ago told me to 'go away and write a bell-ringing book on the Spirit'. The result is, I suspect, hardly what he had in mind! In spite of which I hope he will accept its dedication as a tribute to an outstanding teacher.

London, August 1976   *Marie E. Isaacs*

CONTENTS

TEXTS AND TRANSLATIONS

The following texts and translations have been used throughout:

The O.T. and Apocrypha:
ed. A. Rahlfs, *Septuaginta* (8th ed. Stuttgart, 1935);
ed. R. Kittel and Co., *Biblia Hebraica* (7th ed. Stuttgart, 1961).

The N.T.:
ed. G.D. Kilpatrick, Ἡ Καινὴ Διαθήκη (British and Foreign Bible Society, 2nd ed. London, 1958).

The English Translation of the O.T., N.T. and Apocrypha has been taken from *The New English Bible with Apocrypha* (Oxford and Cambridge, 1970).

The only alteration to the above texts is the non-capitalization of 'spirit'. This has been done to avoid any pre-judging of issues of classification.

The Pseudepigrapha:
ed. R.H. Charles, *The Apocrypha and Pseudepigrapha of the O.T. in English* (2 Vols. Oxford, 1913).

The Sibylline Oracles: ed. J. Geffcken, *Die Oracular Sibyllina* (Leipzig, 1902). *Fragments in Théophile D'Antioch, Trois Livres à Autolycus*, ed. G. Bardy (Sources Chrétiennes, Paris, 1948).

The Letter of Aristeas: ed. H.St.J. Thackeray in H.B. Swete, *Introduction to the O.T. in Greek* (2nd ed. Cambridge, 1902), pp. 499–574.

3 Baruch: ed. M.R. James, 'Apocrypha Anecdota II', *Cambridge Texts and Studies* Vol. V, No. 1 (Cambridge, 1897).

Philo Judaeus:
ed. L. Cohn, P. Wendland, S. Reiter, *Philonis Alexandrini Opera* (6 Vols. Berlin, 1896–1930), Vol. 7, H. Leisegang, *Index Verborum*.

J.R. Harris, *Fragments of Philo Judaeus* (Cambridge, 1886).

F.H. Colson, G.H. Whitaker, J.W. Earp, *Philo* (Loeb Classical Library, 10 Vols., London and Cambridge [Mass.], 1928–1962).

R. Marcus, *Philo Supplement:* Questions and Answers on Genesis and Exodus (Loeb Classical Library, 2 Vols., London and Cambridge [Mass.], 1953).

The Cohn, Wendland, Reiter section divisions are used throughout.

Josephus:
ed. B. Niese, *Flavii Josephi Opera* (editio major, 6 Vols., Berlin, 1887–1889).

H.St.J. Thackeray, R. Marcus, A. Wikren, L.H. Feldman, *Josephus* (Loeb Classical Library, 9 Vols., 1926–1965).

The Niese section divisions are used throughout.

The Dead Sea Scrolls:
G. Vermès, *The Dead Sea Scrolls in English* (Revised, Harmondsworth, 1968).

The section divisions follow those used by T.H. Gaster, *The Scriptures of the Dead Sea Sect* (London, 1957).

ABBREVIATIONS

General

ET	English Translation	MT	Masoretic Text
LXX	The Septuagint	NEB	*New English Bible*

Books

V. Arnim	H. Von Arnim, *Stoicorum Veterum Fragmenta* (4 Vols., Leipzig, 1904–1924).
Blass, Debrunner	F. Blass, A. Debrunner, ET and Revised by R.W. Funk, *A Greek Grammar of the New Testament and other Early Christian Literature* (10th ed., Chicago, 1961).
Diels	H. Diels, *Die Fragmente der Vorsokratiker* (5th ed., 3 Vols., Berlin, 1934–1935).
Müller	C. and T. Müller, *Fragmenta Historicorum Graecorum* (4 Vols., Paris, 1885).
Strack-Billerbeck	H.L. Strack and P. Billerbeck, *Kommentar zum neuen Testament aus Talmud und Midrasch* (4 Vols., Munich, 1922–1928).
TWNT	*Theologisches Wörterbuch zum Neuen Testament*, ed. G. Kittel and G. Friedrich (Stuttgart, 1933–1973).
TWNTE	*Theological Dictionary of the New Testament*, ET of TWNT, (Amsterdam and Grand Rapids, 1968–1974).

Commentary Series

BNTC	Black's New Testament Commentaries	MNTC	Moffatt's New Testament Commentaries
CB	Century Bible	PGC	Pelican Gospel Commentaries
EB	Etudes Bibliques		
ICC	International Critical Commentaries	TBC	Torch Bible Commentaries
		WC	Westminster Commentaries

Periodicals

BJRL	Bulletin of the John Rylands Library	NT	Novum Testamentum
		NTS	New Testament Studies
Expos	The Expositor	RB	Revue Biblique
Exp.T	Expository Times	ZNTW	Zeitschrift für die Neutestamentliche Wissenschaft und die Kunde der älteren Kirche
HTR	Harvard Theological Revue		
JBL	Journal of Biblical Literature		
JTS	Journal of Theological Studies		

Classical works

Aen.	Virgil, *Aeneid*	Pers.	Aeschylus, *Persae*
Def. oracl.	Plutarch, *De Defectu Oracularum*	Phaedr.	Plato, *Phaedrus*
		Phys.	Aristotle, *Physica*
De nat. deo.	Cicero, *De Natura Deorum*	Prom.	Aeschylus, *Prometheus Vinctus*
Diog.Laert.	Diogenes Laertes		
Enn.	Plotinus, *Enneads*	Rep.	Plato, *Respublica*
Od.	Homer, *Odyssey*	Stob. Ecl.	Stobaeus, *Eclogae*
Or.	Euripides, *Orestes*	Tim.	Plato, *Timaeus*

Works of Early Church Fathers

C.Cels.	Origen, *Contra Celsum*	Praep. Ev.	Eusebius, *Praeparatio*
Const.Apost.	*Apostolic Constitutions*		*Evangelica*
Hist.Eccl.	Eusebius, *Ecclesiastical*	Strom.	Clement of Alexandria,
	History		*Stromateis*
Philostorg. E.H.	Philostorgius, *Ecclesiastical History*		

Works of Philo Judaeus

Abr.	*De Abrahamo*	Leg. ad Gaium	*Legatium ad Gaium*
Aet.	*De Aeternitate Mundi*	Migr.	*De Migratione Abrahae*
Agr.	*De Agricultura*	Mut.	*De Mutatione Nominum*
Cher.	*De Cherubim*	Opif.	*De Opificio Mundi*
Conf.	*De Confusione Linguarum*	Plant.	*De Plantatione*
Congr.	*De Congressu Eruditionis Gratia*	Post. C.	*De Posteritate Caini*
Decal.	*De Decalogo*	Praem.	*De Praemiis et Poenis*
Det.	*Quod Deterius Potiori Insidiari Soleat*	Prob.	*Quod Omnis Probus Liber Sit*
Ebr.	*De Ebrietate*	Prov.	*De Providentia*
Flacc.	*In Flaccum*	Qu. Ex.	*Quaestiones in Exodum*
Fug.	*De Fuga et Inventione*	Qu. Gen.	*Quaestiones in Genesin*
Gig.	*De Gigantibus*	Sacr.	*De Sacrificiis Abelis et Caini*
Heres.	*Quis Rerum Divinarum Heres Sit*	Sobr.	*De Sobrietate*
Hyp.	*Hypothetica*	Som.	*De Somniis*
Immut.	*Quod Deus Sit Immutabilis*	Spec. Leg.	*De Specialibus Legibus*
Jos.	*De Josepho*	Virt.	*De Virtutibus*
Leg. Alleg.	*Legum Allegoriae*	V.Contempl.	*De Vita Contemplativa*
		V.Mos.	*De Vita Mosis*

Works of Josephus

Ant.	*Antiquitates Judaicae*	B.J.	*Bellum Judaicum*
C. Ap.	*Contra Apionem*	Vit.	*Vita*

The Dead Sea Scrolls

CD	*The Damascus Rule*	1QM	*The War Rule*
1QH	*The Hymns*	1QS	*The Community Rule*

PART ONE

The Concept of Spirit in Hellenistic Judaism

1
INTRODUCTION

What is Hellenistic Judaism?

The answer to this question must be established before we can ask 'What did Hellenistic Jews understand by the term Πνεῦμα?' We must first determine to whom we are referring when we speak of Hellenistic Jews. Scholars are by no means agreed in their definition of Hellenism. It can be used broadly to describe a historical period, i.e. from the third century B.C. to the first century A.D., when Alexander the Great and the successors to his Greek empire politically dominated the world. Such a definition can be, and usually is, extended to include a cultural perspective. Thus Hellenism can be 'a term used to describe the epoch of Greek dominance of world culture after the time of Alexander the Great'.[1]

If this were to be the starting point of our investigation, it would involve the examination of Jewish literature which reflects such 'Hellenistic' cultural influence. However, this is easier said than done, for we would first have to establish what constituted Hellenistic culture, and once again, we would find ourselves in an area of considerable controversy. If by Hellenistic we mean Greek, which Greek thinkers are to be taken as normative or definitive? The philosophy of Plato and Aristotle was no more typical of Greek thought in the Hellenistic period than was Pauline theology of early Christian literature. Greek culture was neither homogeneous nor static; it developed and was influenced by other cultures — notably by those on the eastern boundaries of Alexander's empire. Thus Hellenism cannot simply be equated with 'Greek', that is if by Greek we mean the culture of the Classical period of Greece's history. That culture was but one element in a highly syncretistic society, which absorbed oriental ideas foreign to earlier Greek writers.

Furthermore, even if an agreement were to be reached as to what exactly constituted Hellenistic culture, far from indicating at the outset what was to be regarded as the literature of Hellenistic Judaism, it would form the major conclusion of our studies. We should have to examine all Jewish literature of the period, and only at the conclusion of such an examination, having determined which works reflected such influence, would we be able to define our area of investigation.

---

1   H. Conzelmann, *An Outline of the Theology of the New Testament* (London, 1969), p. 10.

Needless to say, such a procedure could prove highly subjective; one man's 'Hellenistic' is another man's 'Jewish'. Although value judgements are part of the business of scholarship, such judgements must be arrived at via an appropriate and valid methodology. All too often, when applied to Judaism, the term 'Hellenistic' has carried with it overtones of 'heretical', or even 'contaminated'. Not only are such value judgements unhelpful; they can distort the evidence and confuse the issues. To take Rabbinic theology as 'normative' of Judaism[2] and to see Hellenistic Judaism as a kind of heretical deviation, is, no doubt, to echo the sentiments of later Judaism, but it hardly reflects the true state of affairs in the period with which we are dealing. At that time Judaism was far from being homogeneous in its approach or its beliefs. It was only from the second century A.D. that Jewish thought was tightly laced into the shape in which we see it in the Talmud and Mishnah. In this later period Talmudic Judaism ruthlessly attempted to destroy the culture of its Hellenistic brothers – and with considerable success. That any of the literature of Hellenistic Judaism has survived is largely a result of its preservation by the Christian Church. The Church, of course, only bothered with those works which it found useful for its own purposes. Even granted that what is extant has gone through this highly selective process, it is plausible to assume that what has survived represents but the tip of an iceberg, and that originally the literature of Hellenistic Judaism was both extensive and influential.

The evidence of excavations, inscriptions and papyri would certainly seem to bear this out. Even if we adopt a cultural definition of Hellenism, the extent of Hellenistic influence was obviously far greater than has been assumed in the past. No longer is it possible to assume that such influence was confined to the Diaspora; Palestine itself was not immune.[3] V. Tcherikover has reminded us that some thirty Greek cities were established in Palestine in the Hellenistic period.[4] I Maccabees[5] bears witness to the presence of Hellenism in the very heart of Judaism – Jerusalem. Whether with E. Bickermann we interpret the events which led up to the Maccabean revolt as an attempt on the part of the 'hellenizing' party to reform Jewish religious practice by abolishing its current exclusiveness,[6] or whether we accept Tcherikover's contention that the

---

2   As does for example G.F. Moore, *Judaism in the First Centuries of the Christian Era,* Vol. I (Cambridge, 1927), p. 125.
3   See M. Hengel, *Judaism and Hellenism,* 2 Vols. (London, 1974), which attempts to assess the degree of Hellenization in Palestine from the third century B.C. onwards.
4   V. Tcherikover, *Hellenistic Civilization and the Jews* (Philadelphia, 1961), p. 105.
5   I Macc 1:11–15.
6   E. Bickermann, *Der Gott der Makkabäer* (Berlin, 1937), p. 132.

'hellenizers' were political rather than religious in their aims,[7] the fact remains
that Hellenistic culture had reached Jerusalem and that it had gained a number
of supporters. This movement came to a head in the reign of Antiochus IV and
led to the Maccabean revolt. Such Hellenistic influence must have been at work
before the crisis of 167 B.C. It is also unlikely that it was banished forever with
the Maccabean victory. Hellenism obviously continued to influence Palestine.
Therefore, it would be an over-simplification to confine Hellenism to the
Diaspora, or, on the basis of such an assumption, to make a rigid distinction
between Palestinian and Hellenistic Judaism.[8] Both were open to the same
cultural influences, although by virtue of their very situation, the latter group
were more so. Furthermore, we must not forget that there were frequent con-
tacts between both groups. The Jews of the Diaspora made regular pilgrimages
to the Temple in Jerusalem. Moreover, exchange between Dispersion and
Hellenistic Jews was not limited to the annual levy of Temple dues; Palestinian
literature was widely read in the Diaspora, as is borne out by the fact that most
of the Hebrew and Aramaic literature of the period was subsequently translated into Greek.[9] It would seem improbable that the exchange of literature
was only a one way process.

Although one cannot, therefore, confine Hellenism to the Diaspora, undoubtedly Dispersion Judaism was more open to its influence. The settlement of
Jews outside their homeland has a long history, stretching back to the time of
the Assyrian Exile, and gaining in impetus during times of political and economic pressure. Strabo said that Jews 'were to be found in every city and that in
the whole world it was not easy to find a place where they had not penetrated
and which was not dominated by them'.[10] Even allowing for the exaggeration
of such a statement, it is undoubtedly true that, by the Hellenistic period, the

---

7 V. Tcherikover, op. cit., p. 81, argues that this dispute within Judaism was over the
   Hellenizers' attempt to change the constitution of Jerusalem, in order to make it a
   Greek polis. Therefore, the difference between the Hellenizers and their opponents was
   essentially a political rather than a religious one. He maintains that the Hellenizers, contrary to the account given in I Maccabees, were not proposing any change in religious
   practice. The defence of the Law of Moses was merely the war cry to which the Hasidim
   rallied the masses. Cf. especially pp. 187–191.
8 M. Friedländer, *Die Jüden in der vorchristlichen griechischen Welt* (Wien, 1897) is a
   typical example of a previous generation of scholars, who maintained that Dispersion
   Judaism was entirely different from that of Palestine.
9 E.g. *Psalms of Solomon, Book of Adam and Eve, Jubilees, I Enoch, 2 Baruch, 2 Esdras,
   Martyrdom of Isaiah, Apocalypse of Abraham, Assumption of Moses.* For an introduction which includes this translation literature, as well as the original Greek works of
   Dispersion Judaism (although omitting the LXX, Philo and Josephus) see A-M. Denis,
   Introduction aux Pseudépigraphes Grecs d'Ancient Testament (Leiden, 1970).
10 Quoted by Josephus, Ant. XIV.115.

Jewish Diaspora was both large[11] and widespread. Papyri[12] and inscriptions[13] point to particularly large settlements in Egypt, Babylonia and Asia Minor. It was these Jews, scattered throughout the Graeco-Roman Empire, who were most open to Hellenistic influence.

The main vehicle of this influence was the Greek language itself. The need for a Greek translation of the Jewish Scriptures is a reflection of the Diaspora's adoption of Greek as its predominant language.[14] R. Marcus has pointed out that 'the mere use of the Greek language by the Jews in the Diaspora could not fail to produce some measure of assimilation, although the process may have been quite subconsciously effected'.[15] However, we should remember that the influence was a two-way process. The Greek language not only constituted the means whereby Jews were influenced by Hellenistic ideas; its adoption by the Jews, and especially its use in translating the O.T., enabled them to communicate their religious thought to the pagan world. It is the very dynamic of this cross-fertilization, which produced the creative thinking of Hellenistic Judaism. The Jews of the Dispersion had a sense of being *in* the Hellenistic world, although not *of* it. This created the tensions which are evident in their thought, and out of which their distinctive contribution to Judaism emerged.

For the purposes of this study, Hellenistic Judaism is defined as the Greek-speaking Judaism of the Diaspora. This definition does not prejudge the issue of how far 'Greek' influence was paramount. Neither does it assume that such influence was absent from Judaea itself.

The data examined will be Jewish literature originally written in Greek, together with the Alexandrian text (K) of the Greek translation of the O.T. (i.e. the

---

11 H. Lietzmann, *A History of the Early Church* (2nd ed. London, 1949), Vol. 1, p. 76, estimates that the Jews constituted some 7% of the total population of the Graeco-Roman Empire.

12 Cf. V. Tcherikover, A. Fuks, M. Stern, *Corpus Papyrorum Judaicarum,* 3 Vols. (Jerusalem and Cambridge [Mass.] ,1957–1964). The Elephantiné Papyri also provide evidence of an Aramaic speaking settlement in Egypt in the fifth century B.C.

13 Cf. J.B. Frey, *Corpus Inscriptionum Judaicarum* (Rome, 1936).

14 *The Letter of Aristeas* (c. 100 B.C.) maintains that the Greek translation was made for the benefit of Ptolemy II Philadelphus (285–245 B.C.), as an addition to his library at Alexandria. However, as with other elements of Pseudo Aristeas' story of the origin of the LXX, we may assume that apologetic motives played a dominant role in his writing. It is far more probable that the translation was primarily intended for the use of Jews in their worship. The discovery of second-century A.D. Jewish prayers, embodied in a fourth-century Christian work (Const. Apost. 7, 33–38) furnishes further evidence of the use of Greek in Jewish worship. See W. Bousset, 'Eine jüdische Gebetsammlung im siebenten Buch der apostolischen Konstitutionen,' *Nachrichten, K.G.W.* (Göttingen, 1915), pp. 435–485.

15 R. Marcus, 'Divine Names and Attributes in Hellenistic Jewish Literature', *Proceedings of the American Academy for Jewish Research* (1931–1932), p. 44.

LXX). Although, strictly speaking, the latter comes into the category of translation literature, it has been included for two reasons: a) because of its unique influence on Hellenistic Judaism, and b) because much of the translation is by way of paraphrase and interpretation, and as such is a work in its own right. 'Anyone who translates interprets at the same time. In a translation there appears not only the underlying text, but also the translator's own apprehension of it'.[16] Therefore, just as the Authorized Version of the Bible rightly constitutes a proper area of study in English literature, so the LXX may be studied as part of the culture of the Diaspora.

Exactly which Jewish works were originally written in Greek is still open to debate.[17] For our purposes the following have been examined,[18] although not all have provided data about the use of πνεῦμα: *I Esdras* 3:1–5:6, the *Rest of Esther*, additions to Daniel (i.e. the *Prayer of Azarias*, the *Song of the Three Holy Children*, the *History of Susanna*, and *Bel and the Dragon*), the *Prayer of Manasseh*, the *Book of Baruch*, the *Epistle of Jeremiah*; various works extant only in fragments,[19] e.g. Demetrius, Eupolemus, Artapanus, Aristeas, Cleodemus, Philo the Epic Poet, Theodotus, Ezekiel the Tragic Poet, Aristobulus, *Sibylline Oracles* III.98–808, Pseudo-Hecataeus, Pseudo-Phocylides; together with the larger extant works of *2 Enoch*,[20] *3 Baruch, 2 Maccabees* (incorporating Jason of Cyrene's work), *3 Maccabees, 4 Maccabees, Pseudo-Aristeas, Wisdom of Solomon* and the writings of Philo Judaeus and Flavius Josephus.

Although much of it is fragmentary, this material covers a wide range, both in time (from the third century B.C. to the first century A.D.) and literary *genre*, including within it history, legend, fable, poetry, drama, mantic, propaganda and philosophy. This must be borne in mind if we are to avoid sweeping statements about 'Hellenistic Jewish Literature': in period or *genre* it is not all the same; neither does it reflect one point of view. Hence, we must beware of imposing upon it a homogeneity absent from the material.

---

16 E. Würthein, *The Text of the O.T.* (Oxford 1957), p. 33.

17 The Epistle of Jeremiah, Baruch, the Prayer of Manasseh, the Song of the Three Holy Children and the History of Susanna have all had a Semitic original attributed to them. See R.H. Pfeiffer, *History of N.T. Times with an Introduction to the Apocrypha* (N.Y., 1949), pp. 413, 423, 426–433, 444–455, 457–461.

18 For a classification of this literature see Appendix A, pp. 147–149.

19 Collected in C. and T. Müller, *Fragmenta Historicorum Graecorum,* 4 Vols. (Paris, 1885). Many of these fragments are also to be found in Eusebius, Praep.Ev. IX.17–39, where they are quoted from the historian Polyhistor (80–40 B.C.).

20 Extant only in Slavonic versions. See A. Denis, Introduction, pp. 228–29.

Purpose

The purpose of this study of Hellenistic Jewish literature is a) to ascertain what Jews of the Dispersion understood by the term πνεῦμα, b) to determine whether any development took place in their ideas of πνεῦμα, and c) to attempt to explain how and why such changes took place. Only when this has been accomplished can we examine the question of its bearing on the N.T.

Previous studies have tended to be confined to listing the occurrences of πνεῦμα or to labelling the various uses 'Greek' or 'Jewish'. Obviously such source criticism has provided the essential basis for any further work. However, we are concerned primarily with an understanding of the uses which Hellenistic Judaism made of its various sources. Furthermore, we shall attempt to see the concept of πνεῦμα in Hellenistic Judaism in the light of the *Sitz im Leben* which influenced its uses.

As we have seen, recent trends in scholarship have inclined to the view that the basic similarities between Palestinian and Hellenistic Judaism far outweigh their differences. 'The difference between Palestinian Jews and the Jews of the Diaspora was not a difference of principle but only of degree.'[21] What united them was their belief in the One God, a fidelity to the Mosaic Law (with its ensuing ritualistic and ethical obligations), and an awareness of inheriting a common history. However much later generations may have underestimated the links between the Diaspora and Palestine, the Jews of our period were very much aware of them. They thought of themselves as Jews, and as such were primarily regarded by their Gentile neighbours. It was this very awareness of their distinctive character as a people which made them the object of attack and ridicule.[22]

The Jews of the Diaspora were internally weaker and more exposed than their Palestinian co-religionists. They were particularly vulnerable, not only to persecution, but to something more subtle, i.e. to the attractions of the culture which surrounded them. Wherever they lived, the Jews were granted the right to practise their religion. However, the tensions inherent in attempting to maintain their own traditions in a Hellenistic *milieu* were more acute for the Jews

---

21 V. Tcherikover, *Hellenistic Civilization and the Jews* (Philadelphia, 1961), p.344. Cf. also R.H. Pfeiffer, op. cit. p. 183, and D.S. Russell, *The Method and Message of Jewish Apocalyptic* (London, 1964), p. 23.
22 For the general dislike of Jews, and its various manifestations in the ancient world, cf. I. Heinemann in Pauly-Wissowa, *Realenzyklopädie des klassischen Altertumswissenschaft,* new ed. by W. Kroll, K. Mittelhaus, Supplementary Vol. 5, cols. 3–43. See also R.H. Pfeiffer, op. cit. pp. 174–178 and H. Lietzmann, op. cit. Vol. I, pp. 83–86.

of the Diaspora. Their political institutions, judicial framework and education were undoubtedly influenced by the Gentile models which they saw around them.[23]

The basic question the Diaspora had to face was 'What was to be the relationship between the Jew and his pagan neighbour?'[24] There would appear to be no common answer to this. Some Jews solved the problem by becoming totally assimilated and thus apostatizing from Judaism. Perhaps the most notable example of this is Philo's nephew Tiberius Julius Alexander, who rose to high office in the Roman administration.[25] Such total assimilation would appear to be rare. At least, there is very little evidence of wholesale apostasy in the literature of Hellenistic Judaism. This is not surprising, since it reflects the viewpoint of those to whom such apostasy was anathema.

Others, in their attempt to deal with the Gentile world, went to the other extreme. They became aggressively nationalistic, and even more exclusive in the claims which they made for Judaism. For these particularists, the pagan world had nothing to offer Judaism, except the potential weakening of her faith. However, the glorification of Israel was not the sole prerogative of this group; it is the predominant note in all Hellenistic Jewish literature, even that which betrays some sympathy with the Gentile world. Of course, the option of 'withdrawal' was not entirely open to the Diaspora. However much her nationalists wanted to remain unsullied by Hellenistic culture, and indeed may have made this their conscious aim, they could not remain entirely free from its influence. Thus some of the most anti-Hellenistic of the Diaspora's authors betray marks of that influence.[26]

Between the apostates and the nationalists were the Jews who attempted to relate their traditions to those of Hellenism. Their efforts to reach some kind of *rapprochement* were as much for the benefit of their fellow Jews as for the Gentiles. Their works thus reflect a dual aim: the attempt to reconcile their fellow believers to the culture of which they were now a part, and the interpretation and commendation of Judaism to the Hellenistic world. This involved a re-thinking of the doctrine of election, so that they could acknowledge both

---

23 Certainly in Egypt this is borne out by the papyri. Cf. V. Tcherikover, A. Fuks, M. Stern, op. cit. For the evidence of such influence inside Palestine, see M. Hengel, op. cit. pp. 6–57.

24 This question was not confined to the Diaspora, although it was more acutely posed there. Thus the various parties within Palestinian Judaism (i.e. Pharisees, Sadducees, Essenes and Zealots) can be seen as representing different answers to this question.

25 Cf. also the reference in 3 Macc. 1:3 to the apostate Dositheos.

26 Thus most scholars recognize Stoic and other Greek philosophical influence in Sap Sol. Cf. C. Larcher, *Etudes sur le livre de la Sagesse* (Paris, 1969), pp. 181–236.

the presence and activity of God outside Israel, and yet allow a unique place for the Jewish people in God's revelation. This attempt is particularly evident in the works of Philo and Josephus.

Their effort has been variously assessed by subsequent scholars. Some have seen in it nothing more than an indiscriminate syncretism. They would judge them to have failed in that they do not retain their Jewish heritage. Thus H. Leisegang maintains that Philo totally departed from the spirit of his forefathers' religion.[27] If this judgement is correct, then Jews such as Philo were basically no different from anyone else in the Hellenistic world. They simply introduced the worship of Jahweh as one more element in the syncretistic amalgam which we call 'Hellenism'.

However, not all scholars share this evaluation of the work of Philo. Some see it as a genuine and largely successful attempt to relate Judaism to the Hellenistic world, without jeopardizing the main tenets of the former. The very exercise was naturally hazardous, whereas the extremes of total assimilation or particularism were naturally less complex. However, it can be maintained that those who did try to span the two cultures by and large succeeded in retaining the integrity of their religious beliefs. Obviously, the very nature of the task meant that they were prepared to be open to foreign influence. But their borrowing was not indiscriminate.

Judaism was in need of translation: not only into the Greek language, but also in terms of the culture in which it was living.[28] This was necessary if its own adherents were not to relinquish their faith. It was also essential if Judaism were to win the understanding and respect of its foreign neighbours and if it were to make converts. Inevitably, such a translation would not necessarily be in terms appropriate to the Judean situation.

Theological questions could not be avoided. Bombarded as they were by the various philosophical questions of the Schools, Diaspora Jews were obliged to speculate about the nature of their God, if they were to face the accusations levelled against their beliefs. For those who were not content to rest on mere assertion, the defence of Jewish beliefs and practices needed to be couched in the terms of their opponents. Hence the form of much Hellenistic Jewish apologetic was that of rational, critical and logical argument. Judaism needed its own champions, who could defend it in philosophical terms.

---

27 H. Leisegang, *Der Heilige Geist* (Berlin, 1919), especially pp. 266–267.
28 So E.R. Goodenough, *Jewish Symbols in the Graeco-Roman Period* (N.Y., 1953–1968), Vol. 12, p. 5, 'Only by finding Greek ideas in the Torah could Judaism have taken Hellenism into itself and have survived as Judaism. It would have lost itself in the syncretistic mixing bowl of Hellenistic civilization if its center of gravity had shifted from the Torah to the Sibyl'.

The defence of Jewish ethical monotheism was their major task. They were obliged to re-think and re-state their belief in a God who was both transcendent and immanent. They had to defend the moral nature of the Deity, whilst taking into account the existence and origin of evil. In an environment riddled with fatalism and determinism, they asserted not only the moral nature of the Creator, but the moral nature of His creation – man. Finally, in a culture which possessed its own wise men and philosophers, the defendants of Judaism had to argue the superiority of their own sages, lawgivers and prophets. Thus Hellenistic Jewish apologetic was both defensive and attacking; conciliatory and uncompromising.

Any study of the history of ideas has to take into account the social, political and cultural backgrounds in which these ideas circulated. A study of the concept of πνεῦμα is no exception. Ideas do not exist *in vacuo*. Therefore, we shall have to consider how far the questions posed by the Hellenistic *milieu* are reflected in the Diaspora's understanding of the term πνεῦμα.

2
ΠΝΕΥΜΑ IN THE SEPTUAGINT

Procedure

The 'Septuagint'[1] translators normally use πνεῦμα to translate the Hebrew *ruach*. Of 378 occurrences of *ruach* in the Hebrew O.T., 277 appear in the LXX as πνεῦμα. These include all the various uses of the word to be found in Hebrew: breath, wind, life principle; human disposition, mood, thought or determination; and the spirit of God.[2]

To determine whether πνεῦμα is used in any different sense from *ruach*, it is necessary to examine those passages where *ruach* is not translated πνεῦμα, together with those in which πνεῦμα is introduced into the text where *ruach* is not part of the original. In this way it should be possible to see whether the meaning of *ruach* has undergone any change as a result of the process of translation from Hebrew into Greek. A comparison of the LXX usage with that found in pagan Greek literature should also reveal how far the Greek concept of πνεῦμα has itself been modified or extended as a result of its adoption by the LXX translators.

Where *ruach* is not translated πνεῦμα

Of the 117 instances of *ruach* meaning wind in the Hebrew, 65 are rendered πνεῦμα by the Greek translators. In the other 52 cases the alternative word ἄνεμος is employed.[3] Thus the LXX reflects common Greek usage in regarding πνεῦμα as a synonymous term for ἄνεμος. This is evident in the Greek rendering of Job 13:25:

Ἦ ὡς φύλλον κινούμενον ὑπὸ ἀνέμου εὐλαβηθήσῃ, ἢ ὡς χόρτῳ φερομένῳ ὑπὸ πνεύματος ἀντίκεισαί μοι;

---

1 Strictly speaking the term 'Septuagint' should only be applied to the translation of the Pentateuch. However, here it is used loosely to refer to the Alexandrian text (K) of the whole of the O.T. For a discussion of the origins and transmission history of the Greek O.T. see S. Jellicoe, *The Septuagint and Modern Study* (Oxford, 1968), pp. 29–171.

2 For a complete statement of the use of *ruach* in the O.T. see C.A. Briggs, 'The Use of *Ruach* in the Old Testament', JBL 19 (1900), pp. 132–145. Cf. also W.R. Shoemaker, 'The Use of *Ruach* in the O.T. and of Πνεῦμα in the N.T.', JBL 23 (1904), pp. 13–67.

3 E.g. Ex 10:13; 14:21; 3 Kgdms 22:11; Jer 5:13; 28(51):1; Isa 41:16; 57:13; Ps 1:4; 34(35):5; Ezek 5:10; 12:14; 17:10; 19:12; Hos 13:15; Job 15:30; Dan 8:8; Prov 11:29; 25:14; 27:16 etc.

When *ruach* means breath it is also normally translated πνεῦμα. Occasionally it is rendered ἄνεμος,[4] and sometimes πνοή is employed.[5] However, the fact that the alternative Hebrew word for breath *(neshamah)* is also translated πνεῦμα[6] is a further indication that the LXX used πνεῦμα to mean breath. The association of breath with life – indeed the realization that respiration is essential for its continuity – is evident in the translation of Isa 38:12:

τὸ πνεῦμά μου παρ᾽ ἐμοὶ ἐγένετο ὡς ἱστὸς ἐρίθου ἐγγιζούσης ἐκτεμεῖν.

So far we have seen that the LXX rarely departs from rendering *ruach* πνεῦμα, and where it does the changes are insignificant. However, it is when the O.T. speaks of man's *ruach* to indicate human emotion, inclination, thought or determination that the translators obviously had most difficulty. This is understandable, since the term πνεῦμα was not used in this 'psychic' sense in pagan Greek literature. Although it would seem that ψυχή and πνεῦμα were synonymous in early Greek literature,[7] from the sixth century B.C. onwards it was ψυχή, rather than πνεῦμα, which became applied to man in this way. The poet Hipponax[8] described the part of man affected by emotion as ψυχή, although most subsequent authors confined emotional activity to θυμός, and attributed intellectual activity to ψυχή. Thus Heraclitus confined ψυχή to a noetic function, and firmly distinguished this faculty of thought from the part of man which feels (θυμός).[9] Therefore, by the time the O.T. came to be translated, the normal Greek vocabulary employed would be θυμός for man's emotions, and ψυχή when indicating his thought or determination.

It is not therefore surprising that this normal Greek usage is reflected in the vocabulary of the LXX. Thus *ruach* is rendered ψυχή in Gen 41:8; Ex 35:21; Ecclus 7:11, and various compounds of ψυχή are also to be found.[10] *Ruach* is also translated by θυμός[11] or one of its compounds,[12] and on one occasion by ὀργή.[13] Isa 40:13 has the translation νοῦς, Josh 5:1 φρόνησις,[14] and Ezek 13:3 καρδία.

---

4 E.g. Jer 5:13.
5 Isa 38:16; Ezek 13:13; Prov 1:23.
6 3 Kgdms 17:17; Dan 5:23 (Theod. πνοή).
7 Homer, *Iliad* XXII.417, speaks of ψυχή as a kind of breath, which resides in the body and is exhaled at death. This is how πνεῦμα would normally be used.
8 Hipponax (42D), 'I will surrender to misery my much-lamented ψυχή'.
9 For the history of the development of the word ψυχή see T.B.L. Webster, 'Communication of Thought in Ancient Greece', *Studies in Communication,* ed. A.J. Ayer (London, 1955), pp. 130–137.
10 Cf. ὀλιγοψυχεῶ in Ecclus 4:9; ὀλιγοψυχία in Ex 6:9; ὀλιγόψυχος in Isa 54:6; 57:15; Prov 14:29; 18:14; and ἡσύχιος in Isa 66:2.
11 Cf. Job 15:13; 6:4; Zech 6:8; Ezek 39:29.
12 Eccles 7:8; Prov 14:29; 17:27 have μακρόθυμια, and in Prov 16:19 πραΰθυμος occurs.
13 Prov 16:32.
14 Cf. ταπεινόφρονας in Prov 29:23, and κακοφροσύνη in Prov 16:18.

This tendency to refrain from describing man's *ruach* in terms of πνεῦμα is nowhere more evident than in Proverbs, where the translators use a wide range of paraphrases instead.[15] Similarly, 3 Kgdms 10:5, in describing Sheba's reaction to Solomon's glory, translates the phrase 'there was no more *ruach* in her', by καὶ ἐξ ἑαυτῆς ἐγένετο. 1Kgdms 1:15 and 2 Chron 21:16 solve the problem of ascribing *ruach* to man by omitting the phrase altogether.[16]

Although the tendency of the LXX is not to apply the term to man's spirit, the translators are not entirely consistent in this. There are occasions when they remain faithful to the Hebrew text, in using the same term, not only for wind and breath, but also for human emotion and thought. To cite but a few examples, Judg 9:23; 8:3; Eccles 7:8; Num 5:14 and Deut 2:30 all use πνεῦμα in this 'psychic' sense. In 3 Kgdms 20:4 (MT, 21:4) πνεῦμα has been introduced where there was no reference to *ruach* in the Hebrew text.[17] Therefore, it would not be true to assert that there is any major shift in the Hebrew concept of *ruach* in its 'psychic' sense in the LXX translation. The most one can detect is a tendency to assimilate to normal Greek usage in preferring such terms as ψυχή or θυμός.

Where πνεῦμα is introduced into the text

We have already seen three instances of πνεῦμα being introduced into the text in its 'psychic' sense where there is no reference to *ruach* in the Hebrew.[18] In one of these, i.e. 2 Kgdms (2 Sam) 13:21, it comes in the context of the story of Amnon's rape of his sister Tamar. Here the translator adds the interpolation καὶ οὐκ ἐλύπησε τὸ πνεῦμα Ἀμνὼν τοῦ υἱοῦ αὐτοῦ,ὅτι ἠγάπα αὐτὸν, ὅτι πρωτότοκος αὐτοῦ ἦν. It is evident that the translator was embarrassed by the lack of reference to any kind of punitive action on David's part and hence introduced this phrase as an explanation of his inactivity.

Perhaps the most significant introduction of πνεῦμα into the text is with reference to prophecy. In Num 23:6, when translating the story of Balaam, the LXX adds: καὶ ἐγενήθη πνεῦμα θεοῦ ἐπ ' αὐτῷ. A similar interpolation is to be seen

---

15 E.g. Prov 15:13; 16:1f; 16:18; 17:22; 17:27. For a list of these alternative terms employed for man's spirit see Baumgärtel and Bieder, 'Πνεῦμα in the LXX', TWNTE ed. Kittel and Friedrich (Vol. VI, 1968), pp. 367–372.

16 Cf. also Prov 16:1f and Isa 40:7 where *ruach* is also omitted.

17 3 Kgdms 20:4: καὶ ἐγένετο τὸ πνεῦμα Ἀχαὰβ τεταραγμένον. A similar introduction of πνεῦμα can be seen in 2 Kgdms 13:21, and in Job 7:15 where πνεῦμα is used to translate *nephesh*. The MT of this verse reads, 'So that my soul *(nephesh)* chooseth strangling and death rather than my bones'. The Greek rendering is: Ἀπαλλάξεις ἀπὸ πνεύματός μου τὴν ψυχήν μου, ἀπὸ δὲ θανάτου τὰ ὀστᾶ μου.

18 3 Kgdms 20:4 (1 Kgs 21:4); 2 Kgdms (2 Sam) 13:21; Job 7:15.

in the addition of the phrase ἐν πνεύματί to Zech 1:6.[19] The association of spirit with the prophetic activity was common in post-exilic Judaism,[20] and these LXX interpolations seem to reflect this tendency.

It now becomes important to consider how far the LXX reflects any change in the Hebrew concept of *ruach*. Has the meaning or meanings of the word altered in the process of translation? So far the evidence would seem to indicate that all the various uses of *ruach* can be paralleled by the use of πνεῦμα in the LXX, although we have noted a tendency to avoid πνεῦμα of man's spirit, since it did not have such a 'psychic' connotation in contemporary Greek.

However, W. R. Shoemaker[21] has suggested that, in some passages, the LXX introduced a new nuance of meaning, absent from the Hebrew, and having considerable theological implications for the future development of the concept of spirit. He asserts that a belief in 'non embodied, personal spirits, both good and bad', arose out of the translators' 'misinterpretation of the old Hebrew conception of the function of the spirit of God'. He claims that, not wishing to ascribe evil to God or His Spirit, the LXX introduced a plurality of spirits. As evidence of this, he cites the Greek version of 1 Sam 16:16, 23 (1 Kgdms 16:16, 23), which translates the Hebrew 'the spirit of God for evil' as πνεῦμα πονηρὸν. Also Shoemaker regards the absence of the definite article in these two verses, together with the same change to the anarthrous use in 3 Kgdms 22:21, as a further indication of the same theological motive, i.e. the multiplication of spirits surrounding the throne of God, to whom can be attributed evil – thus avoiding the attribution of anything which smacks of the unholy to *the* spirit of God.

Shoemaker's attempt to base his argument on the absence of the definite article in 1 Kgdms (1 Sam) 16:16, 23, would appear to be untenable if the whole passage (1 Sam 16:14–23) is examined. The anarthrous use of πνεῦμα in these two verses becomes insignificant in the light of the fact that it is also indefinite in the Hebrew of 1 Sam 16:14f.[22] In other words, the translators are merely adopting the usage of the previous two verses. It would be more plausible to explain the change in terms of uniformity of style, rather than to look for apologetic motives.

---

19 Zech 1:6: ὅσα ἐγὼ ἐντέλλομαι ἐν πνεύματί μου τοῖς δούλοις μου τοῖς προφήταις.
20 See Ezek 2:2; 3:24, Isa 61:1, Joel 3:1f, Zech 7:12.
21 W. R. Shoemaker, 'The Use of *Ruach* in the O.T. and of Πνεῦμα in the N.T.', JBL 23 (1904), pp.37–38.
22 Note also that 1 Sam (1 Kgdms) 18:10 and Judg 9:23 speak of 'a spirit'.

Far stronger is Shoemaker's contention that the LXX translation of Num 16:22; 27:16 would seem to indicate that the 'hosts of angels which surround the throne of God were called πνεύματα'.[23] Here the Hebrew 'God of the spirits of all flesh' has been translated θεὸς τῶν πνεύματων καὶ πάσης σαρκὸς. The Hebrew referred to human beings, whereas the translators seem to have understood πνεύματα to refer to disembodied beings – probably the angels who act as God's agents. Certainly this understanding of πνεύματα was common in later Jewish literature.[24] It is possible that this later description of angels as πνεύματα has its beginning in the LXX.

David Hill[25] has tentatively suggested that there is a tendency for spirit to become thought of as independent from God, when *ruach* is translated into Greek. He believes that, in adopting the Greek word πνεῦμα, its Greek connotation of substance would inevitably also be conveyed. Hill suggests that Ps 50(51):11: καὶ τὸ πνεῦμα τὸ ἅγιόν σου μὴ ἀντανέλῃς ἀπ᾽ ἐμοῦ, together with Isa 63:10f: ποῦ ἐστιν ὁ θεὶς ἐν αὐτοῖς τὸ πνεῦμα τὸ ἅγιον, implies a distinction between the spirit and God and the source of the spirit. However, Hill himself admits that the language alone cannot furnish proof of the introduction of such a notion. The Hebrew O.T. itself uses language which could suggest that the spirit was thought of as a separate agent. We have already noted the passage in 1 Sam 16, which speaks of 'a spirit of God for evil'. One could find even stronger evidence in 1 Kgs 22:21f, where God and the spirit appear to be separate beings – holding a conversation about the proposed deception of Ahab. However, it would be extremely dangerous to postulate a separate hypostasis, based on foundations which may well be no more than poetic imagery. That the LXX introduces the idea of a separation between God and His spirit remains unproven.

It would appear, therefore, that attempts to detect a significant change in the meaning of *ruach*, resulting from its translation in terms of πνεῦμα, are unfounded.

23 W.R. Shoemaker, op. cit., p. 37.
24 Cf. *Ethiopic Enoch*, which frequently uses the expression 'Lord of the Spirits', instead of 'Lord of Hosts'. E.g. En.39:12; 41:10 etc. R.H. Charles, *The Apocrypha and Pseudepigrapha in English* (Oxford, 1913), Vol. II, p.209, lists 104 instances of this expression in 1 En. See also 2 Macc 3:24.
25 D. Hill, *Greek Words and Hebrew Meanings* (Cambridge, 1967), pp. 218f.

The introduction of Hebrew ideas of *ruach* into the pagan Greek concept of πνεῦμα

What is far more apparent is that Hebrew ideas have been introduced into the Greek concept of πνεῦμα.[26] Like *ruach*, the most common meaning of πνεῦμα in pagan Greek literature was 'wind'. From the time of Aeschylus it occurs frequently, in both poetry and prose, as a synonym for πνοή or ἄνεμος.[27] It is also used of breath, [28] and in this sense, is an important term in medicine from the time of Hippocrates (being regarded as essential for bodily health). From the metaphor πνεῦμα βίου understandably developed the use of πνεῦμα to indicate life itself.[29] In all these senses πνεῦμα is parallel with the O.T. idea of *ruach.*

Occasionally we find πνεῦμα used to indicate ψυχή,[30] but we have already noted that the Greek view of the soul developed in terms of ψυχή rather than πνεῦμα.[31] Thus πνεῦμα could be used, both of an element in the composition of the body, and also, since it was separated from the body at death, in contrast to σῶμα. In the latter sense it is synonymous with ψυχή.

Via its metaphorical use, πνεῦμα also came to have the transferred meaning of spiritual reality. Greek literature does associate it with the process of inspiration,[32] although but rarely. Plato prefers the term ἐπίπνοια, retaining πνεῦμα for an element in natural science.[33] For him the highest form of inspiration occurs when man is totally passive and becomes possessed by frenzy (ἐνθουσιασμός),[34] while the task of νοῦς, φρόνησις, or φιλόσοφος, is to evaluate this ecstatic inspiration. Most mantic literature is similarly anti-noetic in its view of inspiration. Thus, although Greek writers certainly had a concept of inspiration, they did not usually associate πνεῦμα with the process. The only evidence of πνεῦμα being used with reference to divination is in the descriptions of the Pythia at Delphi, and then, only in the Roman period.[35]

---

26 For the occurrence of πνεῦμα in Greek literature cf. Kleinknecht, 'Πνεῦμα in the Greek World', TWNTE ed. G. Kittell and G. Friedrich, (Vol. VI, 1968), pp. 334–359, and G.H. Liddell, R. Scott, S. Jones and R. McKenzie, *A Greek English Lexicon,* (9th ed., 1940).
27 Aeschylus, Prom. 1086 ἀνέμων πνεύματα.
28 Euripedes, Or. 277 etc.
29. Aeschylus, Pers. 507.
30. Zeno, Fr. 136 (V. Arnim, I.38.6–9), Fr. 140 (V. Arnim, I.38.30–33) etc.
31 Cf. W.W. Jaeger, *Die Theologie der frühen griechischen Denker* (Stuttgart, 1953), pp. 88–106.
32 Cf. Euripedes, Fr. 192, which speaks of πνεῦμα as playing a part in the inspiration of poets and priests. Cf. also Democritus, Fr. 18.
33 Yet Phaedr. 265 B does ascribe all inspiration to the divine πνεῦμα.
34 Phaedr. 244A.
35 H.W. Parke and D.E.W. Wormell, *The Delphic Oracle* (Oxford, 1957), Vol. I, p. 23.

Spiritual realities were more usually described in terms of δαίμων or its cognates. This was used by Greek writers to indicate gods or divine powers.[36] It could also be synonymous with τύχη,[37] the power controlling the destiny of men and nations. Sometimes it referred to the good or evil genius of a person. Thus δαιμόνιον was applied to the genius of Socrates.[38] Since fate could be for good or ill, it could be described as εὐδαίμων or κακοδαίμων.

Popular belief regarded the δαίμονες as personal, intermediary beings, controlling, supervising, and indeed possessing man.[39] Sometimes they were thought of as the spirits of the departed. Since they were supernatural and capricious, they needed to be controlled by magical means. Some philosophers attempted to refute such popular beliefs. Thus Epicureans denied their existence,[40] and Posidonius claimed that they had no power over men.[41] The later Neo-Pythagoreans incorporated the idea of δαίμονες into their philosophical system. As intermediaries, Neo-Pythagoreans gave them a spatial locality – closer to the earth and therefore (according to their view that divine beings are less perfect the nearer the earth they come) secondary and inferior to God Himself.

The Stoics, on the other hand, did not postulate evil of the δαίμονες. For them the δαίμων was the divinely related element in man, equated with νοῦς. Like the authors of the LXX, the Stoics preferred to describe this reality in terms of πνεῦμα.[42] In the teachings of the Stoa there is an attempt to give some systematic understanding of the concept of πνεῦμα.

Although the Stoics sometimes speak of πνεῦμα as ἀήρ, one of the four elements,[43] usually they regarded it as having an οὐσία of its own, which was the source and divine principle of the elements. Therefore, it constituted a kind of quintessence.[44] For the philosophers of the Stoa, πνεῦμα was the universal reason (λόγος or νοῦς), which permeates, integrates and gives life to the cosmos. This universal principle was embodied in man himself. Hence it could also be equated with ψυχή.[45]

---

36 Cf. Plato, Phaedr. 246E. The LXX translators of Isaiah, far from using δαίμων of God, however, explicitly retain it as a contemptuous term for heathen gods. See Isa 13:21; 34:14; 65:3.
37 Menander, Fr.482, equates τύχη with πνεῦμα θεῖον.
38 Cf. Origen, C.Cels.6.8.
39 Cf. Plutarch, Def.Oracl.13.11.416E.
40 Origen, C.Cels.3.35.
41 Posidonius, Philostorg. E.H.8.10.
42 Cf. Posidonius, who described God as πνεῦμα, Stob.Ecl.1.1.
43 Chrysippus, Fr.440 (V.Arnim, II, 145.1–3).
44 Chrysippus, Fr.310 (V. Arnim, II, 112.33–35).
45 Zeno, Fr.135 (V. Arnim, I, 38.3–5).

It would therefore seem that only in Stoicism was πνεῦμα normally applied to God. It is evident that, in choosing the phrase πνεῦμα θεοῦ or πνεῦμα θεῖον, the LXX introduced a new dimension into the usual Greek usage. Apart from Stoicism, πνεῦμα had only secondary significance in Greek philosophical and religious writings. In faithfully translating the Hebrew term *ruach* as πνεῦμα, when it applied not only to wind, breath and life, but also to God, the LXX played a significant part in the development of its meaning in subsequent Greek literature.

3
ΠΝΕΥΜΑ AND THE NATURE OF GOD

Πνεῦμα and the Divine

Underlying the theological use of the term πνεῦμα is a reference to the divine. Thus, it is described by Hellenistic Jewish writers as πνεῦμα θεοῦ or πνεῦμα θεῖον. Therefore, any understanding of the concept of πνεῦμα can only be gained via an appreciation of the Jewish concept of God. Pneumatology is but an aspect of theology.

In pagan Greek thought there is a possible identification of πνεῦμα with the divine as early as Anaximenes (sixth century B.C.). He believed that ἀήρ and πνεῦμα compassed the world, and, according to Diogenes Laertius,[1] regarded ἀήρ as the first principle of the universe. Cicero tells us that Anaximenes made ἀήρ God.[2] If Anaximenes used ἀήρ and πνεῦμα synonymously, then he would be the first pagan Greek writer to use πνεῦμα as a predicate of the divine. However, since we are dependent upon later authors for these statements of Anaximenes's beliefs (and even these authors do not state that ἀήρ and πνεῦμα are synonymous) the evidence is far from conclusive. In the third century B.C. Menander referred to the πνεῦμα θεῖον which controlled man's destiny,[3] and the pseudo-Platonic dialogue, *Axiochus,* mentioned the πνεῦμα θεῖον which imparts intelligence and knowledge to the human soul.[4] However, it is not until the later pre-Christian Stoics that there is an explicit statement of πνεῦμα being predicated of the divine. This occurs in Posidonius.[5]

That God and πνεῦμα share the same nature would not be disputed — at least in the philosophy of the Stoa. Where Stoicism and Judaism did diverge was in their understanding of exactly what constituted that nature. There was nothing particularly distinctive in the fact that the Jews believed in a deity, or that they associated πνεῦμα with the deity. This they shared with Stoicism. What was unique was what the Jews believed about the nature of God. This is reflected in their concept of πνεῦμα.

---

1 Diog. Laert. 11.3.
2 Cicero, De nat. deor. I, 10, 26.
3 Men. 482.3.
4 *Axiochus,* 370C.
5 Stobaeus, Ecl. I, 1, 29 (Diels, p. 302).

Thus, since Judaism insisted upon the sanctity and moral perfection of God, equally spirit is spoken of as ἅγιον.[6] Stoicism did not use the epithet ἅγιον of spirit, since to do so would have been contrary to its immanentist theology. The Stoic philosophers endowed matter with the characteristics of spirit, or, viewed another way, they endowed spirit with the characteristics of matter. 'The strict immanentism of the Stoa can be taken to assert either the divine character of the cosmos or the strictly mundane character of the divine.'[7] Either way, Stoicism would allow no dualism between spirit and matter. Both were of the same essence and that essence was reason (λόγος); whereas in Jewish belief the gulf between God and man and an insistence upon the immaterial nature of the deity were central. These beliefs were conveyed by the word ἅγιον. For the Jews there could be no equation of God and the world, nor of the divine with matter. This is in contrast with Posidonius, who although using πνεῦμα as a predicate of God, still retained a materialistic view of both πνεῦμα and the deity.[8]

Against such views, Philo asserts that it is precisely because of the incorporeal and moral nature of the spirit, that it cannot remain a permanent possession of man, who is corporeal and sinful.[9] For Philo, πνεῦμα is that which is of God – both in that God is its author,[10] and in that it is the essence of the divinity. Hence, God and πνεῦμα can be described in the same terms. As God is invisible, so πνεῦμα is invisible.[11] As God is one and His nature is simple (φύσις ἁπλῆ)[12] so the spirit is indivisible, 'susceptible to neither severance nor division'.[13]

Thus the main tenet of Jewish theology, i.e. its belief in the One God who is holy, moral and powerful,[14] is reflected in the concept of πνεῦμα. We will have to consider later whether πνεῦμα was thought of as in any sense independent of God. Whatever conclusions we reach about that particular question, it is undeniable that, as in the O.T.,[15] there are passages in Hellenistic Jewish literature which closely identify πνεῦμα and God.

---

6 Sap Sol 1:5; 7:22; 9:17. Sib. Or. III, 701 also stresses the moral nature of πνεῦμα, which 'all over the world . . . cannot lie'.
7 P. Merlan, 'Greek Philosophy from Plato to Plotinus', *The Cambridge History of Later Greek and Early Medieval Philosophy*, ed. A.H. Armstrong (Cambridge, 1967), p. 125.
8 Cf. E. de Witt Burton, *Spirit, Soul and Flesh* (Chicago, 1918), p. 121.
9 Philo, Gig. 19; 28; 53; Immut. 2; Qu. Gen. I, 90.
10 Leg. Alleg. I, 37   11 Plant. 18.
12 Leg. Alleg. II, 2; Mut. 184; Immut. 56. However, unlike the Neo-Pythagoreans, Philo refuses to equate God with the One. He is above the One.
13 Gig. 26f.
14 Cf. Sap Sol 11:20 which retains the O.T. idea of the power of God's breath (πνεῦμα). Cf. Isa 11:4.
15 Cf. Isa 30:1; 40:13; 53:10 where *ruach* is used in the sense of the divine 'I'.

The author of the Wisdom of Solomon describes σοφία in terms of πνεῦμα and in some passages identifies the two.[16] Thus, in Sap Sol 1:6 he speaks of the πνεῦμα σοφία. In Sap Sol 9:17, 'Whoever learnt to know Thy purposes, unless Thou hadst given him wisdom (σοφία) and sent Thy Holy Spirit (τὸ ἅγιόν σου πνεῦμα) down from on high?', there is a clear identification of wisdom with the Holy Spirit.[17] Sap Sol 7:7 also parallels φρόνησις with πνεῦμα σοφίας. Grimm[18] sees in this verse a distinction between the wisdom of God (πνεῦμα σοφίας) and human wisdom (φρόνησις), which is communicated by God to man. The Aristotelian distinction between theoretical wisdom (σοφία) and practical wisdom (φρόνησις) could be cited in support of such an interpretation. However, not all Greek philosophers made such a rigid distinction and frequently σοφία and φρόνησις were used interchangeably.[19] Thus the Stoics defined wisdom as 'knowledge of things human and divine'.[20] By such a definition they gave σοφία both a theoretical and practical content. The Stoa attributed a high value to the study of the natural sciences precisely because they did not maintain a distinction between knowledge of God and knowledge of the world. Although the Stoics regarded God as the principal object of wisdom,[21] they believed all natural phenomena to be a manifestation of the divine; therefore its study had a deeply religious significance. Since the major Greek philosophical influences on the author of Sap Sol seem to have come via the Stoa, it would seem unlikely that he made any distinction between σοφία and φρόνησις. In the light of this, Grimm's interpretation of Sap Sol 7:7 would appear untenable.

The author of Sap Sol not only closely associates πνεῦμα with σοφία; he also uses terminology which stresses the affinity (and sometimes the identification) of πνεῦμα/σοφία with God. In 7:25 wisdom is described as the vapour or mist (ἀτμίς)[22] of God's power. Such an image suggests the intimate relationship between God and the vapour of His breath (πνεῦμα). This affinity between God and His wisdom/spirit is again stressed in 7:25f where the author seems

---

16 P. van Imshoot, 'Sagesse et Esprit dans l'A.T.', *Revue Biblique* (1938), pp. 23–49, believes that the author, in identifying πνεῦμα with σοφία, developed a tendency already begun in the O.T. Cf. p. 30 for the biblical antecedents which he cites. However, Imshoot maintains that it is not until Sap Sol that the identification becomes complete. Cf. p. 37, 'En outre la sagesse n'est seulement un effet de l'esprit divin, elle est son équivalent'.

17 The O.T. uses the phrase 'holy spirit' in Isa 63:10f and Ps 50(51):11.

18 C.L.W. Grimm, *Das Buch der Weisheit* (Leipzig, 1860).

19 Cf. C. Larcher, *Etudes sur le livre de la Sagesse* (Paris, 1969), p. 350, n. 8.

20 H. von Arnim, *Stoicorum Veterum Fragmenta* (Leipzig, 1903–1924), Vol. II, p. 15, fr. 35–36.

21 Hence, to deny the existence of the gods was to deny the principal object of wisdom. Cf. V. Arnim, op. cit. Vol. II, p. 304, fr. 1017.

22 Cf. Ecclus. 24:3.

to be using one image after another to convey the same idea – the inseparability of God and His wisdom/spirit. Thus she is His effluence (ἀπόρροια); the reflection (ἀπαύγασμα)[23] of the eternal light;[24] the flawless mirror of the active power of God;[25] the image (εἰκων) of His goodness.[26] She is above the light,[27] surpasses the stars and is more beautiful than the sun.

Thus, the πνεῦμα/σοφία is the effulgence of God Himself. The vocabulary (especially in Chapter 7) seems to have been chosen by the author to emphasize the point that wisdom shares the divine nature. Hence, like God, she is ἅγιον and μονογενές.[28] To her are ascribed the two major divine attributes: omnipotence (παντοδύναμον) and omniscience (πανεπίσκοπον).[29]

Larcher[30] regards this whole passage (Sap Sol 7:22–30) as inspired by the biblical notion of the δόξα of God. An examination of the text would seem to support this, for, like δόξα, in no sense is the πνεῦμα/σοφία independent of God. She is firmly attached to her luminous source, of which she is a pure reflection, image and mirror.[31] The author of Sap Sol is affirming that the πνεῦμα ἅγιον transcends the natural order, and like wisdom (with which it is identified) is situated in the sphere of the divine. Although not explicitly stated, Sap Sol is affirming the immaterial nature of πνεῦμα over against Stoic materialism.

Just as the vocabulary used stresses the affinity between God and the πνεῦμα/σοφία, so Sap Sol attributes the same activities to God and the πνεῦμα/σοφία. As wisdom is a spirit devoted to man's good (φιλάνθρωπον),[32] so God loves all that lives (φιλόψυχε).[33] As the πνεῦμα/σοφία knows all that is said,[34] so

23 Sap Sol is the earliest Jewish writing to use this term. It was later adopted by Philo. Cf. Spec. Leg. IV, 123.
24 Cf. Isa 60:19f. where the Lord is Israel's everlasting light. For the relationship of the divine light to the divine δόξα cf. S. Aalen, *Die Begriffe 'Licht' und 'Finsternis' im Alten Testament, im Spätjudentums und im Rabbinismus* (Oslo, 1951), p. 201.
25 Cf. Plato, Rep. VI, 510E for the image of the mirror.
26 Plato, Rep. VI, 509A where the sun is the image of the Good. For εἰκων in Philo, cf. Mut. 128; Som. II, 189; Prob. 43; Det. 161; V. Mos. I, 158 etc.
27 Cf. Philo, Leg.Alleg. III, 171, where the λόγος is described as unfading, and Som. I, 75, where God is the archetype of all light.
28 Sap Sol 7:22. It seems unnecessary to interpret μονογενές in the Stoic sense of a world soul which, although having many manifestations, is one. Rather the author, like Philo (e.g. Leg. Alleg. II, 2; Mut. 184; Immut. 56), is stressing Judaism's monotheism.
29 Sap Sol 7:23.
30 Larcher, op. cit., pp. 387–388.
31 Plotinus was later to stress that the image and its exemplar shared an identical substance and nature.
32 Sap Sol 1:6.
33 Sap Sol 11:24.
34 Sap Sol 1:6.

words cannot be hidden from God.[35] As wisdom is the mother of all good things,[36] so God is the source of all knowledge and skills.[37] As wisdom is the artificer (τεχνῖτις),[38] so God is the artificer.[39]

In three passages the author of Sap Sol explicitly associates πνεῦμα with God: in 12:1 τὸ γὰρ ἄφθαρτόν σου πνεῦμά ἔστιν ἐν πᾶσι; in 1:7 ὅτι πνεῦμα κυρίου πεπλήρωε τὴν οἰκουμένην καὶ τὸ συνέχον τὰ πάντα γνῶσιν ἔχει φωνῆς; and in 9:17 βουλὴν δὲ σου τίς ἔγνω, εἰ μὴ σὺ ἔδωκας σοφίαν, καὶ ἔπεμψας τὸ ἅγιόν σου πνεῦμα ἀπὸ ὑψίστων.

This last passage, in its parallelism, obviously identifies σοφία with ἅγιον πνεῦμα. Some authors have seen in the first two, i.e. 1:7 and 12:1, the influence of Stoic thought. They could be interpreted in the light of Stoic beliefs about the all-pervading nature of πνεῦμα, and the reference to the spirit which 'fills the whole world' and which 'holds all things together' could be seen as echoing Platonic/Stoic beliefs in the permeating, cohesive *anima mundi*.[40] Those who see here a reflection of Stoic philosophy interpret μονογενές[41] similarly as referring to the one world soul, with its countless manifestations.

Exactly how much weight should be given to Stoic parallels is a debatable point. How far the language reflects a conscious use of Stoic philosophy is not easy to determine. These questions cannot be answered without reference to the whole purpose of the author. If it is assumed that Sap Sol was written for a Gentile audience, it would be likely that its Stoic terminology and ideas were consciously employed. If, with Wolfson, we regard the book as 'a conscious effort to interpret scriptural teaching in Greek philosophical terms',[42] this would give even more weight to its Stoic terminology. However, there is little evidence to suggest that it was addressed to a non-Jewish audience. Simply because heathen kings are addressed in Sap Sol 6:1–11 is no reason to assume that the work was intended for Gentiles.[43] It could be a typical preacher's device of addressing (and usually attacking) those who are not present! Furthermore, the fact that O.T. worthies are not named but merely alluded to in chapter 10 need not point to a Gentile audience who were not particularly interested in their names. It is far more likely that the author did not provide the names because they were so well known to his audience.

---

35 Sap Sol 1:9, 11.   36 Sap Sol 7:12.   37 Sap Sol 7:16–20.
38 Sap Sol 7:22; 8:6   39 Sap Sol 13:1.
40 Cf. the Stoic idea of ἕξις.   41 Sap Sol 7:23f.
42 H.A. Wolfson, *Philo: Foundations of Religious Philosophy in Judaism, Christianity and Islam* (Cambridge [Mass.], 1947), Vol. I. p. 95.
43 Cf. W.L. Knox, *St Paul and the Church of the Gentiles* (Cambridge, 1939), p. 80, 'Wisdom is not a manual for kings but a book of devotion for the intellectual Jew of Alexandria'.

Far from trying to interpret Judaism in Greek terms, the author appears to be combating Epicurean tendencies,[44] and, as we have seen, in describing πνεῦμα as ἅγιον opposes Stoic immanentism. Certainly one can detect elements in the author's thought which echo those found in Plato. Thus, 11:17 can be regarded as a reference to the notion of creation from formless matter: 9:8 could be interpreted in the light of the Platonic theory of Ideas. Some scholars see in 8:19f a belief in the pre-existence of the soul, and others see further Platonic influence in the description of God as ὁ ὤν in 13:1. However, Sap Sol need not be viewed primarily in terms of Platonism. Many of the ideas which have been labelled 'Platonic' could equally have their source in the O.T. One can look to the LXX of Ex 3:14 for the designation of God as ὁ ὤν; and behind the description of Solomon's temple as 'a copy of the sacred tabernacle prepared ... from the beginning'[45] probably lies the influence of Ex 25:9, 40 and I Chron 28:11f, rather than any direct borrowing from Platonic philosophy. Unlike Platonism our author's transcendentalism does not take the form of a dualism between God and the world. God can and does make Himself known;[46] men can be His friends, open to His influence;[47] their very words and thoughts can be inspired by Him.[48]

Similarly, it can be maintained that, although Sap Sol contains Stoic terms, these are not interpreted according to the Stoa's philosophy. The immanentism of our author did not have its source in Stoicism, but in the O.T. conviction of the omnipresence of God.[49] The use of Stoic terminology should not blind us to the fact that there are major divergencies between the Stoa and Sap Sol. The former not only regarded πνεῦμα as material, but insisted on its presence in everything – including evil.[50] Against this Sap Sol affirms the immaterial nature of the spirit, which is ἅγιον and therefore cannot be present in those with whom she has no affinity.[51]

Undoubtedly the author of Sap Sol used terminology current in the Schools.[52] However, unlike Philo, his use of this language is inexact and unconscious.

44 Cf. especially Sap Sol 2 which, against Epicureanism, upholds a doctrine of life after death and asserts a belief in divine providence. Epicureanism can be seen reflected in Eccles 2:23; 5:17; 6:4f; 8:13; 9:17 etc.
45 Sap Sol 9:8.
46 Sap Sol 1:1f; 1:12; 15:1–3.
47 Sap Sol 7:27.
48 Sap Sol 7:15f.
49 Cf. Jer 23:24; Ps 138(139): 7.
50 E.g. Chrysippus. Cf. V. Arnim, op. cit. Vol. II, p. 307, fr. 1037–1040.
51 Sap Sol 7:24.
52 Cf. especially the description of life after death in terms of ἀθάνατος in Sap Sol 1:15; 3:1; 3:3f; 4:7; 5:15f; 8:13; 15:3.

It is indicative of no more than the fact that such philosophical terms were part of common parlance. Unlike Philo, Sap Sol does not appear to be an attempt either to reconcile Jews to Hellenistic culture, or to win Gentile adherents for Judaism. The book is intensely nationalistic, rather than conciliatory. The passages describing Israel's triumph over Egypt,[53] and of Jahweh arising for the onslaught,[54] would hardly be appropriate in a work whose main aim was apologetic. Although a universalistic note is struck in 11:23—26, where God's love and mercy for all men are eulogized, the predominant theme is a particularist one.[55] Judgement is between individual Jews — the good and the bad — rather than including the Gentiles.

Post-Exilic literature in general reflects the problems which arose from a doctrine of exact retribution.[56] How could God's justice be maintained in the teeth of evidence which pointed to the prosperity of the wicked and the sufferings of the faithful? Sap Sol partly gets over this problem by transferring the scene of retribution from this world to an unseen world. This is common in apocalyptic literature. That Sap Sol speaks of Wisdom as existing before the creation of the world[57] could be but another aspect of the author's tendency to project ultimate realities on to an invisible world, which is outside the time-span. It is interesting to note that the combination of wisdom and apocalyptic motifs is also to be found in the book of Daniel. If we are right in claiming that Sap Sol reflects a nationalistic eschatology, then it would follow that the book is an example of the more particularist reaction to Hellenism. That it also reveals elements of the terminology of Hellenistic philosophy, far from disproving this thesis, merely confirms what we have maintained, i.e. that even the most nationalistic and non-conciliatory literature was not immune from Hellenistic influence (albeit unconscious).

The writings of Philo provide an interesting contrast. His works were addressed, not only to Jews, but to the Gentile world. Although intensely proud of his people and their faith, he attempted to interpret Jewish beliefs in terms appropriate to the Hellenistic world in which the Jews of the Diaspora were living. Hence, his reaction to the Diaspora situation was different from that of the author of the Wisdom of Solomon. This is reflected in his eschatology, which is that of a man who was more at home in this world. In fact there is very little emphasis on eschatology in Philo. Rather he adopts the theocratic position of not awaiting a new revelation, but of stressing the necessity of understanding

---

53 Sap Sol 11:16—19; 18:15f.
54 Sap Sol 5:17—23. Cf. Isa 59:17; 66:15; Ezek 38:18—22.
55 E.g. Sap Sol 12:10f.
56 Cf. especially Job.
57 Sap Sol 7:22; 8:3; 9:4; 9:9.

what had already been given, i.e. the Law. What he does have to say about the future is essentially in terms of the consummation of God's purposes in this world rather than in some supra-terrestrial sphere. His eschatology stands in the prophetic[58] rather than the apocalyptic tradition. For Philo the ultimate vision of God is not so much attained in some future consummation, however, be it this or other worldly, but in the ecstatic, mystical experience which the righteous may achieve in the present.

However, in spite of these fundamental differences between Philo and the author of the Wisdom of Solomon, they are united in their basic view of God, and this is reflected in their pneumatology. We have already seen that Philo stresses the affinity of God and the spirit, and that God is one, holy and omnipotent. In some passages Philo equates πνεῦμα with God.[59] Thus in Gig. 26f he stresses that it is not Moses' own spirit, but God's – the wise, divine and excellent. The identification of spirit and God is made explicit in Spec. Leg. IV, 123: 'And clearly what was then breathed was ethereal spirit (αἰθέριον πνεῦμα) or something, if such there be, better than ethereal spirit, even an effulgence (ἀπαύγασμα) of the blessed, thrice blessed nature of the Godhead'.

A similar identification is possibly reflected in Josephus, Ant. VIII, 114. Here Josephus has interpreted Solomon's prayer, 'that Thine eyes may ever be upon this house',[60] to read 'send some portion of Thy Spirit to dwell in the temple, that Thou mayest seem to us to be on earth as well'. In view of the fact that elsewhere[61] Josephus speaks of God Himself dwelling in the temple, it could be maintained that πνεῦμα and God are here used synonymously. If this interpretation is correct, πνεῦμα is spoken of in much the same way as the *shekinah*, to indicate the immanence of God.[62] In Rabbinic literature the *shekinah*

---

58 Thus he looks forward to the reunion of the Exiles (Praem. 164f), a time of national prosperity (Praem. 168; V. Mos. II, 44) and the universal reign of peace for men and nature (Praem. 79–94). Then the unrepentant enemies of Israel will be punished (Praem. 169; 171) and the Mosaic Law will be universally accepted (V. Mos. II, 14, 144). Philo appears merely to be adopting these themes from the biblical prophets. However, they seem to be part of the biblical heritage which he does not really utilize or contribute to.

59 A. Laurentin, 'Le Pneuma dans la Doctrine de Philo', *Ephemerides Theologicae Lovansienses* XVII (1951), pp. 390–437, maintains that it is precisely because it is a reference to the divine that it becomes possible to regard πνεῦμα as one unified concept. Cf. especially p. 395.

60 3 Kgdms 8:29.

61 Ant. III, 100; 102; VIII, 102; 106; B.J. V, 459.

62 Thus, in the O.T. *shekinah* is synonymous for God Himself. Cf. Ex 25:8; 29:45f; Num 5:3; I Kgs 6:13; Ezek 43:9; Zech 2:14 for God 'dwelling' among Israel. Zech 8:3; Ps 85:21; I Chron 23:25 speak of God's dwelling in Jerusalem; and Ezek 43:7 of God dwelling in the Temple.

became personified, but even then it was not an intermediary or independent from God.[63] It is a circumlocution for God Himself. Similarly, in the literature of Hellenistic Judaism, πνεῦμα can be used to indicate the presence and activity of God.

Transcendence and immanence

Pagan religion in its popular forms seems to have presented little threat to Judaism of the Hellenistic period. Most Hellenistic Jewish works[64] delight in its denunciation and ridicule. In this respect they follow the example of Deutero-Isaiah.[65] Their authors thought that the Jewish belief in the One God was infinitely superior to the polytheism[66] which they saw reflected in the deification of the elements[67] and dead heroes.[68] Thus, the Jewish Sibyl jubilantly prophesied the triumph of God over Isis and Serapis.[69] Not only was Jewish monotheism superior; so too were the stories of Israel's past, for, unlike the man-made mythologies of popular Greek religion, they were based on historical truth.[70] Firmly convinced of the superiority of their faith, our authors were particularly scathing about idolatry[71] — especially that associated with the Egyptian worship of animals.[72] Sap Sol 14:23f reflects the view that idolatry is the precursor of all immorality.

Of course, Jewish authors were not alone in condemning these particular beliefs and practices. Many Greek philosophers also inveighed against them. Xenophanes declared that there was 'but one God, the greatest among gods and men',[73] and Aristotle had also sought to maintain that there was but one

---

63 For the *Shekinah* cf. J. Abelson, *The Immanence of God in Rabbinical Literature* (London, 1912), pp. 74–145, 174–277; L. Blau, 'Shekinah', the *Jewish Encyclopaedia* XI, pp. 258–260; G.F. Moore, *Judaism in the First Centuries of the Christian Era; the Age of the Tannaim* (1927–1930), Vol. I, pp. 435–438, and *idem* 'Intermediaries in Jewish Theology', *Harvard Theological Review*, 15 (1922), pp. 41–85.

64 See also Palestinian works, e.g. Judith 8:18; *Jubilees* 11:3ff; 12:3ff; 20:8; *Enoch* 19:1; 46:7.

65 Cf. Isa 40:18–20; 44:9–20 etc.

66 *Aristeas* 134.

67 Sap Sol 13:2; Philo, Decal. 53.

68 *Aristeas* 135–137. Philo, V. Contempl. 6; Congr. 15; Prob. 105. That idolatry had its origin in the deification of dead heroes was the view of Euhemerus.

69 Sib. Or. III, 606–618.

70 Philo, Aet. 56 etc.

71 Cf. Epistle of Jeremiah, Bel and the Dragon 1–22, Josephus, C.Ap. II, 33–35.

72 *Aristeas* 138; Sap Sol 11:15; 12:24; Sib. Or. III, 30; Philo, Post.C. 2, 165; Decal.76–79; Spec. Leg. I, 79; V. Mos. I, 23 etc.

73 Quoted in H. Diels, *Die Fragmente der Vorsokratiker* (5th ed. Berlin, 1934–1935), Vol. I, p. 62, fr. 23. Xenophanes also attacked the Homeric gods for being portrayed as immoral. Cf. Diels, Vol. I, p. 59, fr. 11.

God.[74] Philosophers such as Heraclitus had ridiculed idolatry.[75] It is evident that among many Greek philosophers there existed conceptions of God which were far nobler than those reflected in popular beliefs. The *Letter of Aristeas* seems to be aware of this fact, for its author goes so far as to state that the God worshipped by pagans is none other than the God of Israel. Thus he says,

> The God who gave them their law is the God who maintains your kingdom. They worship the same God – the Lord and Creator of the universe, as all other men, as we ourselves, O King, though we call him by different names, such as Zeus or Dis . . . He through whom all things are endowed with life and come into being.[76]

Like other Jewish writers,[77] Pseudo-Aristeas had adopted a pagan guise and attempted to commend Judaism via the device of pretending to be a Gentile. Even so, it is most unlikely that this statement which identifies Zeus with Jahweh was a mere smoke screen designed to hide the author's true opinions. Other Jewish writings which purported to have Gentile authorship were not afraid to condemn pagan beliefs; neither, in other respects, does the author of Pseudo-Aristeas demur at a blatant glorification of Judaism. It would seem more likely that these verses reflect the author's awareness of nobler conceptions of God held by some Greek thinkers. Since his purpose was apologetic, he would thus wish to emphasize the points of contact between Judaism and the Hellenistic world.

The real challenge for Hellenistic Judaism was not the refutation of grosser forms of pagan belief, but the more sophisticated thinking of Greek philosophy. All the Diaspora authors were united in their attitude to the former. Where they differ is in their approach to the latter. Although these differences are real, however, they should not obscure the fact that Hellenistic Jews were united in their adherence to certain fundamental tenets of faith and practice. This underlying unity springs from the fact that their thinking was biblically controlled. To speak of Hellenistic Jews as being 'biblically controlled' does not, of course, mean that as exegetes they all used the same method of exposition. For example, Philo adopted an allegorical method of interpretation,[78] already used by the Stoics in their exposition of Homeric epics. On the other hand, the author of Sap Sol adopts a haggadic method of exposition, by adding

---

74 Aristotle, Phys. VIII, 6, 259A, 8ff.
75 Diels, Vol. I, p. 78, fr. 5.
76 *Aristeas* 15f.
77 E.g. *Pseudo-Hecataeus, Pseudo-Phocylides,* Sib. Or III–V.
78 However, it would be wrong to suggest that the allegorical interpretation was the only one given by Philo to Mosaic Law. For him the Law has both body and soul. It not only has an interior, allegorical meaning; it has an exterior, literal meaning, to which one must also remain faithful. Cf. Migr. 89–93.

various legends to the biblical accounts.[79] In their respective ways, both authors were equally free in their exposition. This suggests that, in the Judaism of the period, there was not one, normative interpretation of scripture. One of the basic weaknesses of Leisegang's appraisal of Philo[80] is that it presupposes that there is only one way to interpret biblical faith. Because, in Leisegang's opinion, Philo does not adopt this one, correct interpretation, he denies Philo's fidelity to the faith of his fathers. Hence, Leisegang asserts that Philo adopted an allegorical method of interpretation merely as a device to enable him to wander into the realms of pagan, Hellenistic philosophy. However, Leisegang has failed to see that, in common with all other Jewish exegetes, Philo felt an obligation to the scriptures which he expounded. The O.T. was his criterion of truth and the norm by which he judged other philosophies. It is this fidelity to scripture which explains the basic similarities between such diverse writers as the author of Sap Sol and Philo.

On the other hand, their differences can be seen in the light of their respective positions with regard to the pagan world. As we have already seen, the author of Sap Sol was not concerned to placate the Gentiles, nor was he attempting to translate Judaism into the terms of current philosophy,[81] whereas Philo attempted a philosophical defence and presentation of Judaism. As an apologist he wished, wherever possible, to stress the points of contact between Judaism and Hellenistic philosophy.

One of the main philosophical difficulties which Philo attempted to overcome was that of maintaining that God was both transcendent and immanent. Platonic philosophy asserted the one and Stoic philosophy the other. Biblical Judaism maintained both. Posidonius had attempted the reconciliation of Platonic transcendentalism with Stoic immanentism, and Leisegang believes[82] that Philo merely adopted Posidonius' eclectic philosophy in his attempts to grapple with the problem.

Undoubtedly Philo was influenced by Platonism. This is particularly evident in his interpretation of the variant creation stories in Genesis 1 and 2. These he explains in terms of the Platonic theory of creation taking place in two phases: the creation of the incorporeal world of Ideas ($\nu o \eta \tau o s$ $\kappa \acute{o} \sigma \mu o s$) followed by the creation of the material world. However, in stressing the transcendentalism of Platonic theory, we must not overlook the fact that it implies a

---

79 Cf. Sap Sol 11:15; 16:1f, 9, 18, 21f; 17:6, 15–19; 18:12f, 17–19; 19:11f, 17, 21. Similar haggadic tendencies can be seen in 2 Maccabees.
80 H. Leisegang, *Der Heilige Geist* (Berlin, 1919).
81 The fact that he uses Platonic and Stoic terminology is quite incidental to his main purpose.
82 Leisegang, op. cit., pp. 67, 100.

correspondence between the immaterial and the material. The world of Ideas is the ἀρχέτυπον παράδειγμα of the created cosmos.[83] In adopting the Platonic theory of creation, Philo emphasizes this correspondence even more than does Platonism, by claiming that the Ideas are the very thoughts of God.[84] 'Philo is the earliest witness to the doctrine that the Ideas are the thoughts of God.'[85] Therefore, even in adopting Platonic theory, Philo stresses the link between the human and the divine, the transcendent creator and the material creation.[86] Leisegang has failed to see that this reflects the fact that Philo's transcendentalism is derived from biblical sources, and is no mere adoption of Platonism.

Similarly, it is unnecessary to attribute Philo's immanent theology to Stoicism.[87] A belief in the affinity between the divine and the human was certainly stressed by the Stoa. But in this respect Stoicism and biblical faith shared a common view. Since Philo was concerned to build bridges between the two cultures, he was not averse to using Stoic terminology, when speaking of the immanence of God. This is reflected in his pneumatology. As God is everywhere,[88] so the spirit is everywhere, 'diffused in all its fullness everywhere and through all things'.[89] God is the intelligence and soul of the universe,[90] the universal mind,[91] the ruling mind (ἡγεμων νοῦς).[92] To all these assertions a Stoic could assent.[93] Yet a belief in the immanence of God is also found in the O.T., and it is because Philo is faithful to his biblical sources that he opposes the Stoic equation of the human with the divine. He denies an immanentism which would make the soul and body co-essential. Such he regards as a doctrine of impiety and confusion.[94] Although he believes in the 'transcendent in the midst', for Philo πνεῦμα signifies the divine and therefore, like God Himself, must ultimately be transcendent and indefinable. Thus to convey God's immanence Philo draws not only upon the terminology of Stoicism, with its descriptions of the all-pervading universal mind or spirit, but also upon the personal imagery of the O.T. which speaks of God as Father and Creator. Alongside this, however, jostle the Platonic and biblical statements which assert that God is transcendent.

---

83 Philo, Spec. Leg I, 327.
84 Opif. 20; Conf. 63; Cher. 49; Spec. Leg. I, 47–48.
85 H. Chadwick, 'Philo', *The Cambridge History of Later Greek and Early Medieval Philosophy*, ed. A.H. Armstrong (1967), p. 142.
86 Thus he quotes Num 27:16 LXX ὁ θεὸς τῶν πνευμάτων καὶ πάσης σαρκὸς.
87 As does Leisegang, op. cit., pp. 57, 100.
88 Leg. Alleg. III, 4; Conf. 136.
89 Gig. 27. Cf. Sap Sol 1:7; 12:1.
90 Opif. 8; Abr. 192.
91 Leg. Alleg. III, 31.
92 Sacr. 54.
93 For Philo's dependence on Stoic thought cf. M. Pohlenz, *Die Stoa* (Göttingen, 1948), Vol. I, pp. 367–378.
94 Heres. 228.

Whereas biblical authors give no philosophical or rational explanation of these two elements of the divine nature and activity, Philo attempted to justify to the pagan the reasonableness of revealed religion. Like the author of the Pseudo-Aristotelian tract *De Mundo,* he believed that God is both above the world, and a vital, pervading force within it. This is reflected in Philo's concept of spirit; πνεῦμα is of the holy, transcendent God, and therefore cannot be equated with the material, transient world. On the other hand, as we shall see when we come to consider the relationship between πνεῦμα and the world, spirit is also an attribute of man; it is a component of his nature and the power of reason which guides him to the truth. Thus Philo can describe πνεῦμα as both permanent and transient; as in the world but not of it.

These apparently contradictory statements can be baffling to any student of Philo's concept of πνεῦμα. However, they become explicable in the light of his whole theology, for they reflect his attempts to assert both the transcendence and immanence of God. Although it is true to say that Philo's use of the term πνεῦμα is far from systematic, this does not mean that it is incomprehensible. It is unsystematic because ultimately Philo does not resolve the philosophical difficulties involved in his task. However, what he was attempting is clear, i.e. a philosophical, presentation of biblical Judaism, couched in terms of his Hellenistic environment.

Thus he seeks to uphold both the transcendence and immanence of God by asserting that, whilst God cannot be known in Himself, He can be known through the lower levels of His Being. Philo's favourite title for God is τὸ ὄν.[95] God is the cause of all good,[96] yet above the good.[97] In his determination not to limit God in any way, Philo also insists that He is without qualities (ἄποιος).[98] God in His Being is unknown and incomprehensible. What man does know is appearance, rather than reality.[99] Although He reveals Himself in His powers (δυνάμεις) God completely overtops them.[100] By the less enlightened these appearances are taken for God Himself, whereas they are only his image (εἰκών).[101] Even for these images we are dependent upon God's gracious self-revelation.[102] God has no name, yet He allows men to name Him.[103]

---

95 Mut. 27; Leg. Alleg. II, 86 etc.
96 Sacr. 54; Fug. 131.
97 Opif. 8 κρείττων ἢ αὐτὸ τὸ ἀγαθόν. This is opposed to Plato's equation of God with the good. Cf. Rep. VI, 504D; 508E.
98 Immut. 56; Leg. Alleg. II, 36.
99 Mut. 27.
100 Sacr. 60.
101 Mut. 128; Som. II, 189; Prob. 43; Det. 161; V. Mos. I, 158.
102 Leg. Alleg. III, 78; Leg. Alleg. I, 31–42.
103 Heres. 170; V. Mos. I, 176.

In this way, Philo safeguards the transcendence of God, by claiming that God in His Being is superior to the ways in which He reveals Himself. At the same time, he manages to retain a belief in the immanence of God, who (albeit imperfectly) can be known. This implies that there are levels in the Being of God, only the lower of which may be known. This idea was later adopted by Middle and Neo-Platonism. Its implications for Philo's pneumatology will be discussed when we come to consider whether he regarded πνεῦμα as an inter-mediary or not.

God's holy nature and the existence of evil

How was a belief in the creation of the world by a holy God to be reconciled with the existence of evil in His creation? Inevitably this would prove a prob-lem for Judaism, particularly once its theology was subjected to philosophical scrutiny. Furthermore the difficulties involved were by no means felt only by the Jews of the Diaspora. The most famous example of an author's attempt to retain a belief in the justice and goodness of God, in the teeth of his experi-ence of injustice and evil in the world, is to be seen in the book of Job – a Palestinian work.

An intense interest in the origin of evil is reflected in the development of demonology, which is particularly evident in the literature of Palestinian Judaism – especially in popular and magical writings. Here we find a belief in evil spirits[104] or demons, who inhabit man and the universe and to whom is attributed the impetus to sin. In rabbinic theology this was to take the form of the doctrine of the two *yeserim*;[105] the *yeser hara* or evil impulse,[106] and the *yeser hatov* or good impulse,[107] constantly at war in man. There seems to have been no general agreement as to who was responsible for the evil impulse. Sometimes man is held responsible; at other times God is spoken of as in control. It is true that rabbinic theology ultimately regarded the *yeserim* as dependent upon God.[108] However, the *yeser* doctrine did reflect a dualistic view of man and the world. The danger was that it also conveyed a dualism

---

104 For a list of references to evil spirits in Palestinian writings cf. D.S. Russell, *The Method and Message of Jewish Apocalyptic* (London, 1964), p. 404.
105 For the doctrine of the two *yeserim* cf. S. Schechter, *Some Aspects of Rabbinic Theology* (London, 1909), pp. 242–292; G.F. Moore, Judaism, Vol. I, pp. 479–486; H. Strack, P. Billerbeck, *Kommentur zum Neuen Testament aus Talmud und Midrasch*, Vol. IV, pp. 466–483 (Excurs: Der gute und der böse Trieb).
106 Cf. Gen 6:5; 8:21.
107 Cf. Test. Jud. 20; Test. Ash. 1.
108 Cf. Eccles 7:29; Gen 8:21.

which was not only moral, but ontological; that it not only alluded to a
conflict between good and evil in man himself, but projected such a conflict
into the life of the godhead, and, in so doing, made evil some kind of cosmic
reality.[109]

Hellenistic Judaism also had its dualism. This was usually expressed in terms
of the body versus the soul, or the mind over against the passions. Such
expressions conveyed the sense of conflict between good and evil which man
experienced in himself. However, the Jews of the Diaspora managed to avoid
any suggestion of a dualism which was ontological. Indeed, Jewish philosophers
such as Philo were aware of the dangers to monotheism inherent in such a
position. To put evil on a par with good was to impinge upon the sovereignty
of the One God. To attribute evil to God was to blaspheme His holy nature.
Philo tried to avoid the dilemma by postulating that God has different levels
of His Being. He speaks of the lower levels in the Being of God as agents. These
are variously described as reason or word (λόγος), mind (νοῦς), and angels
(ἄγγελοι). Philo interprets the 'Let us make' of Gen 1:26 as God talking to His
agents. To these he attributes all that is unworthy in creation.[110] However, in
so doing, Philo does not really solve the problem, for he postulates no dualism
between God and His agents. These agents are always subordinate to τὸ ὄν.
'But the primal existence is God and next to Him is the word of God, and all
other things subsist in word only.'[111] Frequently God is spoken of as acting
Himself, directly, and without any intermediaries. 'Now (God) with no counsellor to help Him – who is there beside Him?'[112] Thus there is no dualism
between good and evil deities in Philo. Neither in his views on cosmology nor
in those on human psychology do we find any reference to evil spirits at war
with the good. Never does Philo mention an 'evil spirit'. Πνεῦμα is always of
God and therefore good. Thus, in attributing evil to God's agents in creation,
Philo merely pushes the responsibility for its existence one stage further forward. Rather than compromise God's sovereignty, he makes God ultimately
responsible for evil.

H.A. Wolfson[113] has argued that there is evidence of the *yeser* doctrine in Philo.
He sees this reflected in a passage where the symbolism of Isaac being the father
of twins is explained: 'For the soul of every man from the first, as soon as he
is born, bears in its womb twins, namely good and evil, having the image of

---

109 Such an ontological dualism lies at the heart of Zoroastrianism – a religion which
    undoubtedly influenced Jewish thinking.
110 Opif. 74f. Cf. Leg. Alleg. III, 178.
111 Leg. Alleg. II, 86.
112 Opif. 1.
113 H.A. Wolfson, op. cit., Vol. II, pp. 288–290.

both of them.'[114] However, it would seem unnecessary to interpret this in the light of a *yeser* doctrine. Wolfson himself admits that Philo usually expresses moral conflict in terms of the irrational versus the rational soul, or as a struggle between reason and emotion.[115] Furthermore, unlike Palestinian writers, those of the Diaspora have no worked out doctrine of the two *yeserim*. *4 Maccabees* 2:22f speaks of God implanting both the passions and the νοῦς in man at creation, and *Aristeas* 197 reiterates this point that God is the author of both the good and the evil in man. *Aristeas* 277, however, goes further when it suggests that in man there is a bias towards evil: 'All men are by nature intemperate and inclined to pleasure'.[116] This point of view is unusual in the writings of Hellenistic Judaism, where the doctrine of the evil *yeser* is rare.

If the Diaspora Jews were reluctant to speak of an evil *yeser*, they were even more loth to describe πνεῦμα as evil. The only occurrence of 'evil spirit' in the literature of Hellenistic Judaism is in *2 Enoch* and Josephus.[117] *2 Enoch* 31, 4(A) does state clearly that 'the devil is the evil spirit of the lower places'. However, since this apocalyptic work is only extant in Slavonic, it is impossible to determine whether the Greek originally read πνεῦμα here.

Josephus uses δαίμων in its various Hellenistic meanings. As in pagan Greek writings it can be a synonym for God[118] or divine providence,[119] as well as referring to that which is evil. That Josephus uses δαιμόνια for evil spirits is clear from B.J. VII, 185, where he says that δαιμόνια are 'the evil spirits (πνεύματα) of wicked men (πονηροί ἄνθρωποι)' which enter the living and kill them unless aid is forthcoming. Josephus therefore seems to understand δαιμόνια as the spirits of the evil departed, who can possess the living.[120] This was a popular and widespread belief.[121] Furthermore, there is a clear equation of δαιμόνια with evil spirits in Ant. VI, 211, where the words ὅτε σοι τοῦ πονηροῦ πνεύματος καὶ τῶν δαιμονίων are introduced by Josephus into the text of 1 Kgdms 19:4. It is important to notice how Josephus handles this particular O.T. passage. Whereas 1 Kgdms 19:9 reads πνεῦμα θεοῦ πονηρὸν, Josephus

---

114 Praem. 63.
115 E.g. Spec. Leg. IV, 123–124; Opif. 134; Leg. Aileg. I, 31 etc.
116 Some Palestinian writers only mention an evil *yeser*, e.g. 2 Esdras 3:21ff. This suggestion that evil is ingrained, led to a fatalistic view of man. 2 Esdras has no reference to human free will or responsibility.
117 Some commentators have claimed that 'the seducer of the desert' in 4 Macc. 18:8 was a reference to an evil spirit who was thought to have inhabited the desert. However, such an interpretation is far from certain. It could equally be a reference to the serpent of Gen 3.
118 Ant. XIV, 291; B.J. I, 68.
119 Ant. XIII, 314; B.J. II, 457; III, 341; VII, 82.
120 Cf. Vit. 402 and B.J. I, 556, where δαίμων means evil genius.
121 Cf. also Ant. XIII, 317; 416; B.J.I, 521. Whilst demonology was peripheral to O.T. belief (cf. 1 Sam 28:13) it was prominent in popular pagan theology.

substitutes τὸ δαιμόνιον πνεῦμα – thus separating the evil spirit from God Himself. A similar tendency can be seen in Ant. VI, 166. Here Josephus alters the LXX reading considerably in order to excise any suggestion that the evil spirit came from God.[122]

It would therefore seem that Hellenistic Judaism was reluctant to describe πνεῦμα as evil. For the Jews of the Diaspora πνεῦμα was so closely identified with God that to have done so would have compromised their belief in the holy and pure nature of Jahweh. Amongst Palestinian Jews, however, connotations of power and strength seem uppermost in their concept of πνεῦμα. Hence, to convey the powerfulness of evil, Palestinian writers were not averse to describing it as an evil *ruach*. The Jews of the Diaspora, on the other hand, could not afford to provide their pagan opponents with such potential ammunition; neither could they jeopardize their monotheism by attributing the existence of evil to a power other than God.

---

122 1 Kgdms 16:14 reads: καὶ πνεῦμα Κυρίου ἀπέστη ἀπὸ Σαοὺλ, καὶ ἔπνιγεν αὐτὸν πνεῦμα πονηρὸν παρὰ Κυρίου, whereas Ant. VI, 166 has πάθη τινὰ καὶ δαιμόνια πνιγμούς.

4
ΠΝΕΥΜΑ AND THE NATURE OF MAN

Πνεῦμα is not only applied to God; it is used with reference to man. Thus a study of the pneumatology of Hellenistic Judaism reveals not only its theology, but also its anthropology. However, it would be misleading to suggest by this that Jewish beliefs about God and man were entirely distinct and separate. On the contrary, perhaps nowhere is the interrelatedness of these concepts more evident than in the various ways πνεῦμα is used.

Πνεῦμα – one of the components of man

Πνεῦμα is spoken of as one of the components of man.[1] Thus it can be said to be man's own spirit.[2] However, as we have already seen, πνεῦμα is always closely associated with the divine, even when thought of as belonging to man. As such it is a gift, rather than an unalienable right. It is precisely because it is of God and from God that it is not always possible to distinguish the spirit of God from the spirit of man. In terms of its origin and nature it could be said that πνεῦμα is always πνεῦμα θεῖον.

It was given to man at creation. 'He breathed into his face the breath of life (πνοή ζωῆς) and man became a living soul.'[3] It is interesting to note that when Philo discusses this passage he refers to πνεῦμα ζωῆς.[4] However, πνεῦμα ζωῆς is used in the LXX of Gen 6:18 – a passage which Philo quotes in Qu.Gen.II, 8, and could therefore have been altered by a process of assimilation. It is obvious that he is aware that Gen 2:7 reads πνοή rather than πνεῦμα, because his exposition of the difference between the heavenly man of Gen 1 and the earthly man of Gen 2 is largely based upon it. According to Philo, only the immaterial, heavenly man, who was the copy of the original seal (i.e. the λόγος) possessed πνεῦμα in all its power. Material man had only the less robust reasoning power of πνοή.[5] Thus, Philo uses the occurrence of πνοή in Gen 2:7 to expound his theology of the imperfection of earthly man. However, he does not sustain this distinction, for elsewhere Philo speaks of earthly man as being created ἔκ τε γεώδους οὐσίας καὶ πνεύματος θεῖου.[6]

---

1 2 *Enoch* 30:8 (A).
2 Sap Sol 15:16.
3 LXX Gen 2:7.
4 Det. 80.
5 Leg. Alleg. I, 42; Opif. 144.
6 Opif. 135. Cf. Qu. Gen. I, 4, 51. Josephus, Ant. I, 34 also speaks of the created man of Gen 2:7 as possessing πνεῦμα and ψυχή.

Underlying the assertion that πνεῦμα was a component of man lies the conviction that man is dependent upon God and always has been so since creation. In the light of this, the connection of πνεῦμα meaning breath with πνεῦμα in this anthropological usage is understandable. As respiration is essential for life and its continuation,[7] so it can be regarded as synonymous with the life principle itself.[8] Just as its presence is essential for life, so its absence means death or lifelessness. Thus, idols are those ἔν οἶς οὐκ ἐστι πνεῦμα.[9] As the giver and sustainer of life πνεῦμα may be described as ζωτικόν,[10] ζωτικώτατον[11] or ζωῆς.[12]

Πνεῦμα and soul

We have already seen when discussing the occurrence of πνεῦμα in the LXX, that the usual pagan Greek usage for the 'soul' of man was ψυχή rather than πνεῦμα. If man's emotions were being emphasized θυμός would probably be used, whereas ψυχή was normally reserved to indicate thought or determination.

In the writings of Hellenistic Judaism, however, as in the LXX, πνεῦμα is employed in contexts where pagan Greek would use θυμός or ψυχή. In Baruch 3:1, ψυχή ἔν στενοῖς καὶ πνεῦμα ἀκηδιῶν, ψυχή and πνεῦμα are obviously equated. A similar equation can be seen in the Song of the Three Holy Children 63 (LXX Dan 3:86).[13] Philo, in stressing the affinity between God and man, states that man's reasonable soul (λογικὴ ψυχή) was 'a genuine coinage of that dread spirit (πνεῦμα) the Divine and Invisible One'.[14] Since he is here asserting the connection between the two, it is unlikely that Philo is making a distinction between ψυχή and πνεῦμα.

Sometimes Philo speaks of πνεῦμα as having been given to the ψυχή,[15] whilst on other occasions he describes πνεῦμα as the essence of the ψυχή.[16] We have seen that although Philo sometimes equates ψυχή with πνεῦμα, he also distinguishes two elements in the soul: the blood or sense perception which we share with animals, and the rational πνεῦμα which is the soul's true essence. In earthly man these two elements are always mixed.[18] In making this distinction between

---

7 For πνεῦμα as breath cf. Appendix B, III, (a).
8 Cf. 3 Macc 6:24; Esther 16:12 (LXX 8:13); Ant.XI, 240.
9 Epistle of Jeremiah 25. 10 Sap Sol 15:11
11 Opif. 30. Cf. Qu.Gen. III, 3. 12 Det. 80. Cf. Qu.Gen. II, 8.
13 LXX Dan 3:86, 'O ye spirits (πνεύματα) and souls (ψυχαί) of the righteous bless ye the Lord.' Cf. also Sap Sol 15:11: 'Because he did not recognise by whom he himself was moulded or who it was that inspired him with an active soul (ψυχή) and breathed into him the breath of life (πνεῦμα ζωτίκον)', and Ant. XI, 240.
14 Plant. 18. 15 Opif. 67.
16 Spec.Leg.IV, 123; Heres.55; Det.80. 17 Spec.Leg.IV, 123. 18 Qu.Gen.II, 59.

the two elements in man Philo is recognizing that man is both good and evil. To neglect the latter would be contrary to experience; to overlook the former would be to destroy the very basis upon which an appeal for faith could be made. Philo saw that a belief in the spiritual or pneumatic element in man was essential if he wished to assert the possibility of contact between God and man. This is stressed in his adoption of the Platonic understanding of creation, since behind Idealism lies a theory of correspondence; a conviction that the heavenly world of Ideas is an exemplar of the material world. Thus πνεῦμα is the 'impression stamped by the divine power', 'the image of God',[19] and man is the copy of the divine archetype of rational existence.[20] It is the presence of the divine πνεῦμα in man which makes contact between God and man possible.

E. Best has examined the occurrence of πνεῦμα in Josephus and has come to the conclusion that, in the sense of a component of man, it virtually disappears.[21] He arrives at this conclusion after analysing the ways in which Josephus handles his biblical material. He cites examples of personal pronouns being substituted by Josephus in places where the LXX uses πνεῦμα.[22] He also points to instances of Josephus substituting ψυχή for πνεῦμα.[23] On the basis of this, Best claims that Josephus has modified his use of πνεῦμα to accord with normal pagan Greek usage.

We have already noted this tendency in the LXX. However, just as we saw that the LXX on occasion does use πνεῦμα of man's spirit, so we shall find the same to be true of Josephus. Best can claim no more than to have pointed out a general tendency, for there are instances of πνεῦμα being used in its anthropological sense. For example, B.J.II, 92 uses πνεῦμα of the Romans' martial frenzy. Furthermore, although the LXX of Gen 2:7 describes man as receiving πνοή, Josephus substitutes πνεῦμα and ψυχή.[24] He does not seem clearly to differentiate between the terms. In fact Ant.XI, 240 equates the human ψυχή with man's πνεῦμα,[25] as does Ant.II, 260 where Josephus explains the prohibition of blood in terms of the blood being regarded as ψυχή and πνεῦμα. Here he has added a reference to πνεῦμα to Lev 17:10f (where there is no mention of it). Thus there are occasions when Josephus not only retains the LXX usage of πνεῦμα for man's soul, but actually introduces it into the text. Knowing

19 Opif. 72–74.
20 Det.83. Cf. Plant. 18.
21 E. Best, 'The use and non use of πνεῦμα by Josephus', NT 3 (1959), pp. 218–225.
22 E.g. Ant.VI, 360 (1 Kgdms 30:12); Ant.VIII, 356 (3 Kgdms 20:5 = 1 Kgs 21:5).
23 E.g. Ant.II, 75 (Gen 41:8); Ant.V, 345 (1 Kgdms 1:5); Ant.XI, 3 (2 Chron 36:22).
24 Ant.I, 34.
25 Ant.XI, 240: εὐθὺς ὑπεχώρει μοὶ τὸ πνεῦμα καὶ κατελειπόμην ὑπὸ τῆς ψυχῆς.

that Josephus used Greek amanuenses,[26] the retention of πνεῦμα in its 'psychic' sense is more remarkable than its replacement by ψυχή.

No doubt behind this usage lies the Hebrew *ruach*. This could be used to include not only the principle of life, but also human consciousness. The literature of Palestinian Judaism abounds in examples of *ruach* being used of man's soul.[27] However, as a term used of an emotional state or disposition, πνεῦμα, unlike *ruach*, is rare.[28] The more usual word θυμός is employed.[29]

Πνεῦμα and mind

In the writings of Philo, rather than being associated with the emotions, πνεῦμα is closely allied with man's reason. Although he sometimes uses ψυχή, νοῦς and πνεῦμα interchangeably,[30] he regards the νοῦς as the dominant part of the soul. As God is incomprehensible[31] so the νοῦς is unable to see itself or know of what it is made.[32] However, in spite of this statement, Philo elsewhere says that νοῦς is made of πνεῦμα.[33] It is into the νοῦς alone that God breathes.[34] Νοῦς is the recipient of the πνεῦμα,[35] given at creation,[36] as the force which generates thought.[37] Philo thus identifies πνεῦμα with man's reasoning faculty. Λογισμός is the divine in-breathing;[38] the λογικόν πνεῦμα is the dominant part of man, the archetypal form of the divine image.[39]

The association of πνεῦμα with reason is particularly Philonic. Apart from 4 Macc.7:13 it is not found elsewhere. Certainly Hellenistic Judaism associated πνεῦμα with σοφία, but this wisdom was thought of as a transient inspiration, granted to the few. Philo also has a concept of inspiration (particularly that granted to the prophets) as spasmodic. However, this is not to be confused with the πνεῦμα which is a permanent gift, graciously granted to man at creation. This πνεῦμα is that which is 'of God' in man; its presence is what Philo understands by man being made in God's image.

---

26 Cf. C.Ap.I, 50 where Josephus acknowledges his Greek assistants. For a discussion of the evidence of their hand in his works cf. H.St.J. Thackeray, *Josephus the Man and the Historian* (N.Y. 2nd ed. 1967), pp. 100–124.
27 For a classification of the 'psychic' use of spirit in Palestinian literature cf. D.S. Russell, op. cit., pp.402–404.
28 For the few occasions when πνεῦμα is used to describe an emotional state cf. Appendix B, IV (b), p. 151.
29 Cf. e.g. Sib.Or.III, 738; V, 260.
30 Cf. Fug. 133 where νοῦς and πνεῦμα are equated.
31 Qu.Gen.IV, 26; Immut.62 etc. 32 Leg. Alleg. I, 91.
33 Heres. 55. 34 Leg. Alleg. I, 33.
35 Leg. Alleg. I, 37. 36 Leg. Alleg. I, 33.
37 Spec. Leg. I, 6. Cf. Fug. 182 ('the spirit of vision').
38 Heres. 57. 39 Spec.Leg.I, 171. Cf. Spec.Leg.I, 277.

Since he locates it in the noetic part of the soul, Philo affords a high place to man's reason. The mind is God's deputy, inspiring the senses.[40] It is the divinest part of man;[41] the godlike image;[42] the copy of the divine reason,[43] and God's instrument.[44] Philo states that God is visible only to the mind,[45] and he identifies the manna of the wilderness with the divine food of knowledge.[46]

Philo makes his appeal to the Gentiles on the grounds that reason is the common possession of all men. He believes that God has not left the Gentiles without knowledge of Himself, and by appealing to reason Philo is appealing to a God-given faculty. Furthermore, one of Philo's main motives was an apologetic one. He wished to vindicate the rationality of biblical faith. We know from the fragments of their works which survived that there were other Jews of the Diaspora who wished to defend the reasonableness of Judaism.[47] Aristobulus had claimed that Moses was the originator of all that was best in Greek philosophy and culture.[48] A similar claim had been made by Artapanus, who also asserted that Moses had instructed the Egyptian priests in the art of hieroglyphics.[49] Artapanus also stated that Abraham had been the father of astrology,[50] and Joseph had taught the Egyptians various agricultural skills.[51] These apologetic works were no doubt written in response to anti-semitic attacks made by such pagan authors as Apollonius Molon,[52] Manetho[53] and Apion.[54] Philo stands firmly in this apologetic tradition. For him Judaism was the source of all that was highest in pagan learning. Far from being irrational and superstitious, its laws were demonstrably sensible.[55]

Yet Philo was not content to rest on the assertion that reason is the inspired gift of God. Ultimately he refused to rely on the power of reason to obtain

---

40 Leg. Alleg. I, 31–42.
41 Det. 29.
42 Opif. 137.
43 Opif. 136.
44 Abr. 190.
45 Cher. 100–101.
46 Leg. Alleg. III, 86; 164. Cf. Fug. 137 and Leg. Alleg. III, 175 where the λόγος is said to be the manna.
47 Fragments of Jewish apologetic works, collected by Alexander Polyhistor, are quoted by Eusebius, Praep. Ev. IX, 17–34.
48 Aristobulus, Praep. Ev. VIII, 12; XIII, 12; Hist.Eccl. I, 26–31.
49 Artapanus, Praep. Ev. IX, 27.
50 Artapanus, Praep. Ev. IX, 19.
51 Artapanus, Praep. Ev. IX, 23.
52 Apollonius Molon, cf. Josephus, C.Ap. II, 36 and Müller, op. cit., III, 208ff.
53 Manetho, cf. C.Ap. I, 26–31 and Müller, op. cit., II, 511–616.
54 Cf. Josephus, C.Ap. I, 1–13.
55 This apologetic was also taken up by Josephus. Cf. especially C.Ap. which refuted anti-semitic attacks and Ant. in which the author sought to demonstrate both the antiquity of Jewish origins and the reasonableness of Jewish belief and practice.

the vision of God. He was only too aware of the fallibility of human reason. It could be deluded and seduced,[56] for earthly man has only the πνοή of less robust reasoning.[57] We can know nothing for certain.[58]

Just as we can see an apologetic motive behind Philo's high regard for human reason, so equally an apologetic motive can be detected in his scepticism. In commending the Pentateuch to pagans, Philo wished to claim for it an authority which was beyond that of their own philosophers and sages. For him the Mosaic Law had an infallibility which could not be claimed for human reason alone. It contained the very oracles of God. Therefore, for Philo, inspiration *par excellence* is prophetic inspiration.

A similar position, although not so carefully worked out, is taken by the author of 4 Maccabees. Like Philo, 4 Macc. is primarily a defence of Judaism; the author attempts to defend his faith from pagan attack. Hence he asserts that the Law is not contrary to reason;[59] neither is it a preposterous philosophy.[60] On the contrary, it is perfectly reasonable. In fact the whole treatise is concerned to extol Judaism as ὁ εὐσεβὴς λογισμός. Like Philo, the author believes that the best of Greek philosophical ideas are to be found in the O.T. Thus he asserts that the Mosaic Law teaches the four cardinal virtues of Platonism and Stoicism.[61]

In the light of the purpose of 4 Macc. it is not surprising that, like Philo, the author associates πνεῦμα with reason. In 4 Macc. 7:13 we find reference to Eleazar becoming a young man again in 'the spirit of his reason' (πνεῦμα τοῦ λογισμοῦ) and 'possessing Isaac-like reason' (Ἰσάκειος λογίσμος). This passage obviously echoes Philonic thought. Philo uses the figure of Isaac to represent σοφία,[62] or ἐπιστήμη.[63] He also discourses on the Isaac-soul as the type of knowledge which is intuitive or possessed by nature rather than by effort.[64]

However, both Philo and the author of 4 Macc. assert the supremacy of inspired wisdom. This is not to be confused with the πνεῦμα which is in every man. It is possessed only by the sages and prophets of Judaism, whom God has chosen to be the recipients of His prophetic spirit. Together with his fellow apologists of the Diaspora, the author of 4 Macc. is not only conciliatory, looking for the

56 Cher. 116–117.   57 Leg. Alleg. I, 42.
58 Cf. Ebr. 170–172 where Philo incorporates the tropes of the sceptic Aenesidemus.
59 4 Macc. 5:22.   60 4 Macc. 5:10.
61 4 Macc. 5:23f.   62 Post. C. 78; Immut. 4; Congr. 37.
63 Sobr.9; Som.I, 160. Cf. also Heres. 57.
64 Sacr.5–7; Sobr.38; Migr.125; Congr.34–38; Mut.12 etc.

points of contact between Judaism and pagan belief. He is also intensely nationalistic[65] and convinced of the superiority of his faith and culture. He claims that it is not philosophy but the Law which is the cause of all virtue.[66] Stoic ideals can only be realized by fulfilling the Law.[67]

For all that the author of 4 Macc. and Philo tackled some of the philosophical questions of their time, and were not averse to doing so in philosophical terms, we should not let this blind us to the fact that ultimately they asserted the supremacy of revelation over reason, of theology over philosophy. As C.C. Torrey has said of 4 Macc., 'The book is a fine example of the way a treatise in Hebrew theology can wear with ease and grace a dress made in the Greek Schools'.[68] A similar assessment of Philo's work has been made by W. Bousset – 'Der altestamentliche Gottesglaube durchbricht bei Ihm doch die Hütte der philosophischen Spekulation'.[69] It is because Philo is a theologian rather than a philosopher that he speaks of an inspiration which is superior to reason. It also explains why his view of man has as its corner stone a conviction that man is subservient to and dependent upon God. The πνεῦμα of man, equated with reason, may be the permanent possession of all men, but nonetheless it is not man's by right, but by grace.

Πνεῦμα and conscience

We have seen that Philo regarded πνεῦμα as the nobler aspect of man. As such it obviously plays a large part in his ethical theory. In this connection we should note that πνεῦμα is closely allied to his concept of conscience. Philo claims that no soul remains without an idea of God, otherwise there would be an excuse for failing to believe in Him.[70] The conscience (συνειδός) is 'this man dwelling in the soul of each of us'.[71] Its function is to make men aware and conscious of their own misdeeds;[72] to convict man from within.[73] Philo's favourite synonym for conscience is 'convictor' (ἔλεγχος),[74] since its nature is to hate evil and love virtue, and to inculcate the same values in man.[75] It acts as both accuser and judge, gently admonishing unintentional lapses, but threatening deliberate wrong-doing.[76] As the impartial scrutineer from whom the

---

65 See the reference to Jewish martyrs in 4 Macc. as examples of true nationalism. 4 Macc. 6:29; 7:21 introduces the idea of the expiatory powers of martyrdom.

66 4 Macc. 1:18.   67 4 Macc. 7:17–23.

68 C.C. Torrey, *The Apocryphal Literature* (Yale, 1945), p. 104.

69 W. Bousset, *Die Religion des Judentums im späthellenistischen Zeitalter* (3rd edn. Tübingen, 1926), p. 446.

70 Leg. Alleg. I, 35.   71 Det. 23. Cf. Det. 87.

72 Virt. 124; Spec. Leg. II, 49; Det. 146.   73 Det. 23f.

74 Spec. Leg. I, 235; IV, 6; Prob. 149; Det.24; Fug. 203f; Conf. 121 etc.

75 Decal. 87.   76 Opif. 128.

truth cannot be hidden,[77] it is the only judge not taken in by oratory.[78] Immut. 134 equates conscience with ὁ θεῖος λόγος – the pure ray of light, which shows up the nature of sin. Without it man would be guiltless, because he would be ignorant of transgression.

This function of enlightenment is also attributed to πνεῦμα. Spirit is the guide into truth.[79] Like conscience it is the permanent, universal gift of God. It creates knowledge of good in all,[80] and is the 'self-dictated instinct' of the heart;[81] typified by the Isaac-soul, the 'self-taught'.[82] Like συνειδός, πνεῦμα is equated with reason.[83] Thus Philo can refer to the rational spirit (πνεῦμα λογικόν) which produces the purity of motive necessary for a true sacrifice.[84] Similarly, a pure, untainted conscience is necessary,[85] because only those who have it can approach God.[86] As the conscience assists man, so wisdom's fierce wind (πνεῦμα) slackens the impetus of pleasure[87] and raises the mind to God.[88]

Thus there appears to be no clear differentiation between the moral function of spirit and conscience. The only distinction is that συνειδός carries with it a negative connotation; it is that which convicts and convinces men of the nature of sin; whereas πνεῦμα is used more frequently in a positive sense – showing the nature of the good and enabling man to attain it. Πνεῦμα and συνειδός would appear to be the opposite sides of the same coin.

Πνεῦμα, therefore has a moral connotation – even as God has a moral connotation. Philo seems to think that, as a guide to right values, it is like reason, the possession of all. As the prophetic spirit, however, it is the gift of only the few. This is not resolved in Philo, any more than he resolves his belief that God is to be found in the uniformity of nature[89] with an assertion that He works miracles. In his ethical theory he wishes to leave a place for free will, whilst maintaining a view of grace which is positively Augustinian. As we shall see, in his theory of inspiration, Philo wishes to assert the divinity of human reason, whilst reserving God's right to possess and usurp that reason, under the control of the prophetic spirit.

---

77 Post.C. 59.

78 Virt. 206.

79 V.Mos. II, 265.

80 Leg. Alleg. I, 37–38.

81 Conf. 59.

82 Mut.55; Som.II, 160; Abr.52; 54 etc.

83 In Cher. 30 συνειδός is equated with λόγος. Cf. Post.C. 59 and Qu.Ex. II, 13 where συνειδός is equated with νοῦς.

84 Cf. Spec.Leg. I, 277 where Philo stresses the inward nature of sacrifice. Yet in Qu.Ex. II, 33 he claims that the sacrificial laws re blood were enjoined so that men could be inspired by the 'Holy Spirit'. Since Qu.Ex. is not extant in Greek and this is the only place where spirit is described as 'holy' in Philo, it is probably a Christian interpolation made by the Armenian translator.

85 Praem. 163.

86 Heres. 6f.

87 Som.II, 13.

88 Plant. 23–24.

89 Mut. 135.

5
ΠΝΕΥΜΑ AND THE RELATIONSHIP
BETWEEN GOD AND THE WORLD

Πνεῦμα and the creation of the cosmos

The LXX translators of Gen 1:2 used the term πνεῦμα for the spirit of God in creation καὶ πνεῦμα θεοῦ ἐπεφέρετο ἐπάνω τοῦ ὕδατος. Therefore, in attributing a creative function to πνεῦμα[1] Philo was hardly introducing something new into the beliefs of Judaism. What is interesting is his interpretation of this verse. He seems to understand the πνεῦμα as bringing about order, rather than as a hurricane which is part of the chaos. This is borne out by the fact that he describes Noah's flood (Gen 7:4) as 'a symbol of spiritual dissolution',[2] i.e. as a reversal of the spiritual order which was brought about at creation. It is also the spirit which restores order by bringing about the cessation of the flood (Gen 8:1).[3]

Philo describes this principle of order in the life of the cosmos as πνεῦμα, just as we have seen that he describes the principle of order in the life of man (i.e. reason) by the same term. In so doing he draws upon the terminology of Stoicism. The Stoa also believed that there was a permanent, all-pervading power active in the universe, holding its various disparate elements together, and preventing the cosmos from falling into the chaos of dissolution.[4] This principle they called ἕξις, τόνος[5] or πνεῦμα ἑκτικόν, and they identified it with the divinity. Such Stoic thoughts are echoed in Philo. Thus in Immut. 35 he says: ἕξις ἡ δέ ἐστι πνεῦμα ἀναστρέφον ἐφ᾽ ἑαυτό.[6]

We have seen that Stoicism thought of πνεῦμα as one of the elements, ἀήρ, or more often as a quintessence which constituted the basis of the other four. Philo agrees with the Stoa in regarding πνεῦμα as one of the elements.
A. Laurentin has argued that Philo does not equate πνεῦμα with ἀήρ. He claims that there is a clear distinction between the two, since ἀήρ provides the material

---

1   Cf. Gig. 22; Leg. Alleg. I, 33; Qu. Gen. IV, 5.
2   Qu. Gen. II, 15, σύμβολον τῆς πνευματικῆς καταλύσεως.
3   Qu. Gen. II, 28.
4   Cf. M. Pohlenz, op. cit., Vol. I, p. 218, on this theory in Posidonius.
5   Cf. Chrysippus' theory of τόνος discussed in M. Pohlenz, op. cit., Vol. I, pp. 74–75.
6   Cf. also Aet. 86 (ἐξεως πνευματικῆς); Aet. 125 (πνεύματικος τόνος); Opif. 131.
    F.C. Colson, *Philo* (Loeb edition) also interprets Prob. 26 πνευματικος ἀθλητικοῦ in a semi-physical Stoic sense of ἕξις. However, Leisegang, op. cit. translates it as the good wind of an athlete.

upon which πνεῦμα works, determining its form.[7] However, it is difficult to see how Laurentin can maintain this position, since the equation of πνεῦμα with ἀήρ seems irrefutable in Cher. 111: γῆς μεν οὐρανός, οὐρανοῦ δε γῆ, ἀήρ δε ὕδατος, ὕδωρ δε πνεύματος.[8] Furthermore, in Gig. 22 the πνεῦμα of creation is described as a στοιχεῖον. It is a current of air,[9] which is sacred;[10] the spirit of the deity by which all things are made secure; the invisible power of God,[11] by which all creatures live.[12]

However, unlike the Stoics Philo will not accept that this elemental life principle is material. It is the divine πνεῦμα which is at work in the creation of the cosmos. What is more, creation is viewed by Philo, not only as an event in the past, but as a continuous activity. Πνεῦμα not only played a part in the event of creation; its presence is essential for the continuation of life. Just as man dies without breath, so the universe would fall into dissolution without the cohesive force of πνεῦμα.[13] Although πνεῦμα as air has a physical manifestation, it would be wrong to think that Philo understood it simply in a physical sense.[14] The πνεῦμα in man is not merely physical breath, but the life principle itself or the faculty of reason, of which physical breath is the sign. Similarly, the πνεῦμα in the cosmos is not merely one of the elements; it is the principle of order, of which the elements are an expression.

Just as it is the presence of the πνεῦμα in man which makes contact with God possible, so it is the presence of the πνεῦμα in the cosmos which brings the world within God's domain and makes it possible to speak of it as His creation. Πνεῦμα signifies the divine in the human, the immaterial in the material, the eternal in the temporal. We have already seen how, in his adoption of Platonic Idealism, Philo stressed the correspondence between God and the world in order to assert the possibility of such contact. Πνεῦμα may be described as that principle of correspondence.

It would be wrong to classify the statements which Philo makes with regard to the role of πνεῦμα as a cosmological principle as merely part of his scientific theory, rather than his theology. This is essentially what G. Verbeke has done

7 A. Laurentin, 'Le Pneuma dans la Doctrine de Philon', *Ephemerides Theologicae Lovansienses XXVII* (1951), pp. 395, 397, 403.
8 For further examples of πνεῦμα as ἀήρ cf. Sap Sol 5:11; Praem. 41; Ebr.106; Sacr.97.
9 Spec. Leg. II, 153. Cf. *Josephus*, B.J. IV, 477.
10 Virt. 135.
11 Qu. Gen. II, 28.
12 Gig. 10.
13 Opif. 131. Cf. Heres. 23f where God is spoken of as δεσμός. Also in Plant. 10; Det.187. This same cohesive force is attributed to the λόγος δεσμός.
14 The metaphor used in Praem. 48 clearly brings this out. Here Philo speaks of the current which paralyses passion, thus allowing the better part of the soul to dominate.

in arguing that, since Philo maintained a transcendentalism which was wholly in keeping with the O.T. he did not, like the Stoics, identify the πνεῦμα ἑκτικόν with the divinity. Verbeke maintains that the πνεῦμα ἑκτικόν should be understood as part of Philo's physical rather than metaphysical order.[15] However, Verbeke has failed to see that when spirit features in Philo's cosmology as the elemental life principle and cohesive force, it does not do so simply as a 'natural' phenomenon. Philo is making a theological affirmation[16] – that the world was created by God, whose continued activity in the natural order is essential for its preservation.

Πνεῦμα and revelation

Even Hellenistic Jews such as Philo, who wished to emphasize those elements which were common to Jew and Gentile, also stressed their differences. Only in so doing could Judaism have survived in the Diaspora. It was one thing for the apologists to imply that the divine πνεῦμα was not confined to Judaism. It would have been quite another not to have claimed some special sign of God's presence among his chosen people. Part of any definition of Judaism was a belief in the unique revelation granted to Israel; a conviction that God had revealed Himself in some special way to the Jews. Otherwise there would have been no basis for making unique claims for the Jewish faith; neither would there have been any doctrine of election.

In order to enable them to claim a superiority for Judaism, the authors of the Diaspora made a distinction between reason and wisdom. According to Philo, the former was also a divine gift, but he believed that of itself it could not enable a man to attain the vision of God. Philosophy could be a helpful preparation for theology,[17] but religious knowledge is far superior to all other forms of knowledge, which must be subservient to it.[18] Reason is not supreme. Only the wisdom granted by divine revelation can hold such a place. That wisdom is granted only to the few; and those chosen are to be found among the ranks of the fathers of the Jewish people.

Following the tradition of the O.T., our exegetes associated the spirit of God with the process of inspiration. The author of Sap Sol asserts man's need of such divine guidance: 'Who ever learnt to know thy purposes, unless thou hadst

---

15 G. Verbeke, *L'Evolution de la Doctrine du Pneuma du Stoicisme à S. Augustine* (Louvain, 1945), p. 242.

16 The same can be said of πνεῦμα as it features in Philo's anthropology. He is making an assertion of the possibility of contact between the human and the divine, on the basis of the divinity which God has given to man and thereby has in common with him.

17 Cong. 71–80.

18 Post. C. 78f.

given him wisdom (σοφία) and sent thy holy spirit down from heaven on high
(τὸ ἅγιόν σου πνεῦμα ἀπὸ ὑψίστων)?'[19] In answer to Solomon's prayer for
understanding (φρόνησις) the spirit of wisdom (πνεῦμα σοφίας) was sent.[20]
Solomon is used by the author of Sap Sol to typify Jewish inspiration. As a
gift from God it is superior to any insights which pagans may have. Far from
being the πνεῦμα which is the permanent possession of all men, it is an external
inspirational power,[21] which grants a wisdom far above that normally available
to reason. This is the πνεῦμα which inspired the prophets. Its possession is the
seal of their authority. Under the influence of this προφητικόν πνεῦμα[22] the
mind is inspired,[23] raised[24] and guided.[25] Yet this inspirational πνεῦμα is
transient[26] and sporadic because we are flesh.[27]

On the one hand possession of the divine πνεῦμα has a moral condition; it
requires singlemindedness[28] and a detachment from sensual preoccupations.[29]
Πνεῦμα being reserved for the wise and good,[30] the wicked cannot receive it.[31]
Yet, on the other hand, goodness does not automatically qualify a man for
the prophetic spirit. It is God's to dispose of as He will. The prophetic πνεῦμα
comes, not as a reward for merit, but as grace.[32] It is grace which is necessary
if man is to achieve virtue, and yet, at the same time, the gift which is dependent upon the prior goodness of its recipient. Such contradictions are evident
in Sap Sol 1:5, where the author speaks of the educative role of the spirit –
Ἅγιον . . . πνεῦμα παιδειάς – upon which men are dependent in order to achieve
true wisdom, whilst asserting that, because it is holy, πνεῦμα cannot abide
with the unholy. It 'will have nothing to do with falsehood', and 'cannot stay
in the presence of unreason and will throw up her case at the approach of
injustice'.

How are such contradictory statements to be understood? So far we have
maintained that the pneumatology of Hellenistic Judaism reflects the theological questions with which the Diaspora had to grapple. Thus, statements

---

19 Sap Sol 9:17.
20 For σοφία being the result of the divine πνεῦμα cf. Josephus, Ant. X, 239 (Dan 5:13f).
   Such an association of spirit with wisdom is unusual in Josephus. He tends to omit
   references to 'a spirit of wisdom'. Cf. Ant. II, 87 (Gen 41:38); Ant. III, 200 (Ex 28:3;
   31:3; 35:31). However the association is common in Philo. Cf. Gig. 24 which refers
   to the σοφία which resulted from the coming of the spirit upon the 70 Elders (Num
   11:17). He also quotes Ex 31:2f where σοφία and ἐπιστήμη are granted to Bezalel.
   Cf. also Susanna LXX 64.
21 Cf. Susanna LXX 42 (Th. 45).   22 Fug. 136.
23 Leg. Alleg. I, 36f.   24 Plant. 24.
25 V. Mos. II, 265.   26 Immut. 2; Gig. 19; Qu. Gen. I, 90.
27 Gig. 20; 28f.   28 Gig. 53.
29 Hence it is called 'the spirit of steadfastness' in Det. 17.
30 Immut. 3; Gig. 23.   31 Heres. 259.
32 Ebr. 145 where πνεῦμα is described as χάρις.

which assert both that πνεῦμα is the possession of all and that it is the gift of the few, should be viewed in the light of the dilemma which faced Judaism's apologists: how they were to find a common ground for discussion between their faith and that of their Gentile neighbours, whilst retaining a belief in the superiority of the revelation granted to their forefathers. Such contradictory statements about the nature and activity of πνεῦμα reveal the tensions inherent in the Diaspora situation. In them we can see the very real crisis of identity felt by Jews living in an alien land and culture. The questions 'Who is my neighbour?' and 'Who am I?' were inevitably asked of the traditional doctrine of election. Were Jews to regard themselves as the chosen people because they were worthy of such a calling, or as an act of divine grace? If by grace, then was there no need for human effort? 'Shall we continue in sin then that grace may abound?'[33] was a question raised by Philo as well as Saul of Tarsus. Of course, in Philo the question does not appear in this particular form, but it is inherent in his pneumatology — where divine grace and human effort are maintained, and yet where the philosophical difficulties of retaining a belief in both are not resolved.

What is evident is that a special place is claimed for prophetic inspiration. Philo states that it is the prophetic spirits whom we should emulate,[34] since their minds alone approach God.[35] The προφητικόν πνεῦμα[36] which they are granted brings with it a special inspiration. It was this πνεῦμα which came upon the 70 Elders,[37] enabled Jeremiah to prophesy,[38] and gave Abraham bodily beauty, a persuasive voice and a responsive audience.[39] However, the recipient *par excellence* of the divine spirit was Moses,[40] since it stayed with him longer than with other men.[41] Hence, Philo describes him as 'the purest of spirits'[42] upon whom the spirit came at decisive moments.[43]

The association of the divine πνεῦμα with prophetic inspiration is also apparent in the writings of Josephus. In a number of instances, where the LXX speaks of the πνεῦμα coming upon an O.T. character, he interprets this to mean that they prophesied.[44] There are also examples of Josephus adding references to πνεῦμα to the text of the O.T., where in the LXX they are absent. Thus, into Num 22 he introduces the idea of Balaam's ass being conscious of the divine

---

33 Rom 6:1.
34 Qu. Ex. I, 4.
35 Qu. Ex. II, 29.
36 Fug. 136.
37 Gig. 24 (LXX Num 11:17).
38 Conf. 44.
39 Virt. 217.
40 Fug. 132; V. Mos. I, 175.
41 Gig. 47.
42 V. Mos. II, 40.
43 Cf. the δαιμόνιον who inspired Socrates at decisive moments.
44 Thus Ant.IV, 165 (Num 27:18) re Joshua; Ant. V, 285 (Judg 13:25) re Samson; Ant. VIII, 295 (2 Chron 15:1) re Azariah; Ant.IX, 168 (2 Chron 24:20) re Zechariah.

spirit approaching.[45] We have previously noted that in Num 23:6 the LXX translators introduced the concept of the πνεῦμα θεοῦ coming upon Balaam before he prophesied. Josephus is therefore continuing a tendency already present in his text. Into Num 23 he introduces the notion of the compelling nature of the prophetic spirit.[46] A reference to the divine spirit coming upon David in 1 Kgdms 16 (1 Sam) is expanded to add that, as a result of the spirit's arrival, he prophesied.[47] Josephus' own understanding of prophecy is brought out in his rendering of 1 Kgdms 22:15, where, to 'but you shall know whether he is really a true prophet', he adds 'and has the power of the divine spirit'.[48] For Josephus, as for Philo, the prophet was one who had the gift of the spirit of God.

It is also evident that the prophets to whom these apologists for Judaism referred, were those of the biblical period. Since the common post-exilic tradition was that prophecy had ceased with the death of Haggai, Zechariah and Malachi, does this mean that Judaism confined inspiration to the past? Did they believe that the springs of inspiration had dried up or been turned off? Obviously not, for there is abundant evidence of a conviction that God continued His work of inspiration. Hence, Philo can speak of divine assistance which comes to him when his own literary inspiration dries up.[49] In considering the relationship between πνεῦμα and conscience, we have seen that Philo certainly believed in divine guidance. Furthermore, he not only speaks of the corybantic frenzy which inspired the prophets of the past; a similar frenzy drives the ascetics of his own day out into the wilderness.[50] For Philo, it is not only the prophets of the O.T. who were inspired; so were the translators of the LXX – καθάπερ ἐνθουσιῶντες.[51]

The ability to predict the future was thought to be part of the prophetic activity. Josephus claims that he himself could exercize this gift. Hence he foretold the accession of Vespasian,[52] and when this prophecy was fulfilled says that the Emperor referred to him as 'a minister of the voice of God' (διάκονος τῆς τοῦ θεοῦ φωνῆς).[53] This clearly echoes O.T. beliefs about the voice of God which spoke to the prophets.[54] Josephus not only claims prophetic gifts for himself; he also says that John Hyrcanus united in himself kingship, high-priesthood and 'the gift of prophecy' (καὶ προφητεία).[55] In the same passage he goes on to explain what he means by prophecy, i.e. foreknowledge or

---

45 Ant. IV, 108.   46 Ant. IV, 119f.
47 Ant. VI, 166.   48 Ant. VIII, 408.
49 Abr. 35. Cf. Migr. 34f; Cher. 27; Som. II, 252.
50 Mut. 39.   51 V. Mos. II, 37.
52 B.J. III, 399–408.   53 B.J. IV, 626.
54 Talmudic literature also speaks of predictive prophecy, inspired by the *bath.qol.*, i.e. the echo of the heavenly voice.
55 B.J. I, 69.

the power to predict the future.[56] For Simon the Essene, Josephus claims the ability to interpret dreams[57] – an ability normally associated with prophecy. Dreams were frequently thought of as a means of inspiration, and as such exercized a fascination for the ancient world. Philo devoted two treatises to the subject of dreams. He saw them as a means of foretelling the future.[58] Some dreams were clear in their meaning, whereas others needed interpretation.[59] Philo attributed Moses' ability to interpret the oracles of God to his possession of the divine spirit.[60]

It is therefore clear that both Philo and Josephus did not confine their belief in inspiration to the prophets of the O.T. In fact they cite evidence of certain prophetic activities, i.e. prediction and the power of dream interpretation, as continuing in their own time. However, they do not attribute this contemporary inspiration to the possession of the spirit. This they confine to the prophets of the biblical period. In so doing, they implicitly assert that the inspiration of the authors of scripture was qualitatively different from any subsequent insight.

It is also important to note Philo's understanding of the prophetic process itself. For him prophecy was synonymous with the oracular. He regarded the prophet as the passive vehicle of the divine in the same way that the Greeks thought of the Pythia as the human vehicle of Apollo's utterances. Like Plato,[61] he believed that inspiration comes only with the departure of human reason,[62] for the mind is evicted by the arrival of the πνεῦμα,[63] who becomes the new tenant and visitor.[64] H. Leisegang has maintained that Philo equates the Platonic νοῦς with the Stoic πνεῦμα, and, in so doing, has spiritualized the Stoic concept of πνεῦμα. He believes that this synthesis of Platonism and Stoicism had already been undertaken by Posidonius, upon whom Philo was dependent.[65] However, Leisegang has failed to notice a very important difference between Philo and Posidonius in their respective theories of inspiration. In Posidonius' view the immortal spirits need to get past the senses in order to ally themselves with the νοῦς. However, Philo is far more Platonic in his view, for it is the νοῦς and not the sense perception which is evicted.

In common with most of the Hellenistic world, Philo interpreted corybantic frenzy as a sign of true inspiration.[66] He therefore regards the prophet as an

---

56 Cf. also Ant. XIII, 299–300. 57 Ant. XVII, 346.
58 Abr. 190; Som. I, 2. 59 Som. II, 1–4.
60 Decal. 175. Cf. also Jos. 116 where Pharaoh recognized that it was the spirit which gave Joseph his ability to interpret dreams.
61 *Timaeus* 71D; *Ion* 533D; 534C. 62 Heres. 264.
63 Heres. 265. 64 Spec. Leg. IV, 49; Qu. Gen. III, 9.
65 H. Leisegang, op. cit., p. 100. 66 Heres. 69.

ecstatic,[67] totally possessed by God and His helpless instrument.[68] This is also Josephus' view, for he not only describes the prophetic experience in terms of possession,[69] but translates the πνεῦμα θεοῦ of 1 Kgdms 10:6 as γενόμενος ἔνθεος.[70] Similarly, ἐνθουσιασμός, ἐνθουσιῶν, and θεοφορητός are favourite Philonic synonyms for the coming of the prophetic spirit.[71] It is in the light of this that we should read Qu. Ex. II:105 – 'possessed by God and by the prophetic spirit'. There does not appear to be any distinction intended between God and the spirit. Since θεοφορητός is frequently employed by Philo to describe prophetic inspiration, it would seem that here we have an example of parallelism.

The ecstatic condition of the prophet is also described by Philo in terms of divine and sober intoxication – θεία καὶ νηφαλίος μέθη.[72] H. Lewy believes that this oxymoron is original to Philo, although he sees in it the influence of the Platonic concept of μανία, and the terminology of the Dionysiac mysteries.[73] For Philo, such ecstasy was essential for the achievement of the vision of God. When the prophetic mind is filled with God 'it becomes like the Monad, not being at all mixed with any of the things associated with duality . ... changed into the divine so that such men become akin to God and truly divine'.[74] This kind of knowledge which leads to the attainment of the beatific vision, is not the result of inferential reasoning. It is more akin to mystical experience.[75]

What we have seen then is that πνεῦμα was associated with the gift of prophecy. This was unusual in the Hellenistic world, for it is not until the accounts of the Delphic Oracle in the Roman period that we find πνεῦμα being associated with the prophetic process.[76] Here it is described as the vapour-like substance which was thought to have come from the fissure of the rock and to have entered the Pythia. Elsewhere πνεῦμα is not normally used of divine inspiration. In attributing the phenomenon to πνεῦμα Philo stands firmly in the biblical tradition.

---

67 Heres. 249.
68 Heres. 266.
69 Ant. VI, 222f; IV, 118.
70 Ant. VI, 56; 76.
71 V. Mos. II, 246.
72 Fug. 166; Leg. Alleg. III, 82; Opif. 71. Cf. Ebr. 145f where Hannah is filled with grace and enthusiasm, similar in its effect to drunkenness.
73 H. Lewy, *Sobria Ebrietas* (Giessen, 1929), especially pp. 64–66. Against Lewy, H. Chadwick, 'Philo', *The Cambridge History of Later Greek and Early Medieval Philosophy,* ed. A.H. Armstrong (1967), p. 150, n. 4, argues for a pre-Philonic origin for the oxymoron.
74 Qu. Ex. II, 29.
75 Cf. E.R. Goodenough, *By Light, Light* (New Haven, 1937) for a presentation of the mystical elements in Philo. However, W. Völker, *Fortschritt und Vollendung bei Philo von Alexandrien: eine Studie zur Geschichte der Frömmigkeit* (Leipzig, 1938), vehemently denies the presence of mysticism in Philo.
76 R.W. Parke and D.E.W. Wormell, *The Delphic Oracle* (Oxford, 1956), Vol. I, p. 23.

Biblical influence can also be seen underlying his understanding of prophecy as ecstatic and frenzied. It is usual to attribute this to Greek influence. Undoubtedly Philo's detailed description of the process, whereby the mind is evicted, owes much to Plato. However, we should not forget that parts of the O.T. also have an ecstatic view of prophecy.[77] This appears to have been the predominant type of prophecy in the early part of Israel's history. It is only with the major pre-exilic prophets such as Amos, Hosea, Micah and Isaiah, that such prophecy was eschewed.[78] Among these 'non-ecstatic' prophets there is very little reference to the spirit. They prefer to speak of the hand or word of Jahweh, rather than His spirit, as the source of their inspiration. It is only in the post-exilic period with the re-emergence of ecstatic prophecy[79] that spirit becomes once more associated with the process. Thus the attribution of prophecy to spirit invasion can be seen within Judaism itself.

What is also evident is that biblical prophecy was regarded by Philo and Josephus as qualitatively different from any other. Hence $\pi\nu\varepsilon\tilde{\nu}\mu\alpha$ is confined to prophecy in the biblical period. In this way they reflect the common view that prophecy had ceased. This does not mean that they believed that inspiration had stopped. By confining $\pi\nu\varepsilon\tilde{\nu}\mu\alpha$ to the biblical period, the apologists for Judaism were making a claim for the unique character of the revelation given by God and recorded in their scriptures. This obviously lies behind Philo's claim that Moses had more of the divine $\pi\nu\varepsilon\tilde{\nu}\mu\alpha$ than anyone else. What he is asserting is the supremacy of the Mosaic Torah. By emphasizing the ecstatic character of prophecy, he is once more claiming an inspiration which is superior to that of human reason for the experience which lies behind biblical inspiration. However much he may argue that the Jewish scriptures are reasonable, ultimately he maintains that their revelation is supernatural, ecstatic, and imparts a knowledge which is intuitive rather than inferential. On the basis of this he claims a supreme authority for the O.T. over all other oracles. The belief in the cessation of prophecy, evident in confining $\pi\nu\varepsilon\tilde{\nu}\mu\alpha$ to the biblical period, similarly places the O.T. in a unique position. It presupposes a belief in a canon of scripture which is authoritative, complete and to which no other inspiration can compare. Thus in its pneumatology can be seen the claims Hellenistic Judaism made for its scriptures.

---

77 Cf. 1 Sam 10:10–12.
78 Amos 7:14 can be interpreted as the prophet's refutation of ecstatic prophecy.
79 For e.g. Ezekiel.

Is πνεῦμα regarded as an intermediary between God and the world?

This question is really part of a much wider issue, i.e. whether post-exilic Judaism thought of God as needing the services of intermediaries to make contact between Himself and the world possible. Those scholars who have presumed this to be the case have largely assumed that the philosophical difficulties felt by Hellenistic Jews were the same as those which faced Plotinus. They believe that Jews such as Philo were equally concerned to explain how a diverse world could have emanated from a God who is one, simple and indivisible. The assumption of Plotinus was that one only could proceed from one.[80] Hence he postulated intermediaries between the One of the divine and the multiplicity of the world. Those who see intermediaries in the Jewish theology of the period,[81] tend to assume that Judaism's defenders felt an equal need to postulate their existence. In other words they believe that there was a philosophical necessity to bridge the gap between God and man, by some means other than God's own activity.

According to this view πνεῦμα is thought of as one of these intermediaries. What is more, to conceive of the spirit as an intermediary is also to pre-suppose that, in some sense, it was thought of as being separate from God, i.e. a hypostasis. Is there, however, any evidence in the literature of Hellenistic Judaism to suggest that πνεῦμα was thought of as an intermediary, through whose agency God was able to make contact with the world?

Some scholars have seen in the personification of wisdom in Sap Sol more than a literary device.[82] In chapters 6 to 8 wisdom/spirit is personified as a mother,[83] as a bride,[84] and as a counsellor.[85] She is described as an agent actively involved in creation.[86] Her educative role is also emphasized; she teaches all knowledge,[87] and all virtues;[88] communicates God's will to men[89]

80 Cf. *Enneads* V, 1.6.
81 E.g. E. Zeller, *Die Philosophie der Griechen* (5th ed. Leipzig, 1923), Vol.III, p. 407f, who asserts that Philo used the λόγος as an intermediary by which God was brought into contact with the world. A similar position has been adopted by P. Heinische, *Die griechische Philosophie im Buche der Weisheit* (Münster, 1908), pp. 122f, and J. Klausner, *From Jesus to Paul* (London, 1942), pp. 181–183 etc.
82 For a list of the major interpretations of this personification cf. C. Larcher, op. cit., pp. 393–403.
83 Sap Sol 7:12.   84 Sap Sol 8:2.   85 Sap Sol 8:9.
86 Although a role is assigned to wisdom in creation in Prov 8:23–31 and Ecclus 24:4–6, Larcher, op. cit., especially p.364, claims that Sap Sol is the first place where wisdom is given a genuinely active part to play. Cf. Sap Sol 7:22; 8:3; 9:4; 8:4; 9:9.
87 Sap Sol 7:21.
88 Sap Sol 8:7. Cf. Sap Sol 7:15 for God as the source of all knowledge.
89 Sap Sol 9:9.

and is the guide of action;[90] she leads men to keep the Law[91] and helps them to achieve immortality.[92] It is wisdom who makes holy souls friends of God and prophets.[93]

Furthermore, Sap Sol 7:22 could be interpreted also as evidence of the author understanding σοφία as a being separate from God, for it implies that wisdom has a spirit (ἐστι γὰρ ἐν αὐτῇ πνεῦμα). This would give a very different impression from those passages which speak of wisdom being a spirit.[94] The latter seem to assert the synonymous nature of σοφία and πνεῦμα, as well as emphasizing that the πνεῦμα/σοφία is one with the divine. However 7:22 could be taken to imply a distinction between wisdom and spirit, enhancing the idea that wisdom, like any other created being, required a πνεῦμα for its very existence. H. Leisegang does not accept that any such interpretation is necessary. He believes that in speaking of wisdom as 'having a spirit', the author is reflecting the ancient idea of the wind being the bearer of the spirit.[95]

None of these passages need be interpreted as evidence of the author's belief in wisdom as a hypostasis, however. The language which suggests that wisdom is an agent of God could be the natural outcome of the personification of σοφία. This would be the most natural interpretation of the figure of wisdom. It would account for the contradictory statements which the author makes about the nature and activities of wisdom.[96] Logical contradictions are often a feature of writing which employs the literary device of personification, because, as a technique, it is not primarily intended as a vehicle for philosophical logic and authors are not averse to sacrificing such logic in the interests of dramatic effect.

---

90 Sap Sol 9:11.
91 Sap Sol 6:17–20. Yet wisdom is not equated with the Law.
92 Sap Sol 8:13.
93 Sap Sol 7:27. Unlike πνεῦμα in Philo and Josephus, there is little about wisdom's connection with prophetic inspiration. However, various activities, normally associated with prophecy, are attributed to wisdom. Thus she knows the past and the future (Sap Sol 8:8), can interpret riddles and has foreknowledge of natural phenomena.
94 E.g. Sap Sol 1:7; 12:1.
95 H. Leisegang, op. cit., pp. 69–74.
96 These contradictions are discussed in H. Heinze, *Die Lehre vom Logos in der griechischen Philosophie* (Oldenburg, 1872), pp. 197–201, J. Drummond, *Philo Judaeus* (London, 1888), Vol. I, pp. 219–225, and R.H. Charles, *Apocrypha and Pseudepigrapha* (Oxford, 1913), Vol. I, p. 328. However, H.A. Wolfson, op. cit., Vol. I, 287–289 attempts to reconcile these contradictions by stating that they reflect three stages of the existence of wisdom, analogous to the three stages he sees in the Philonic λόγος. In the first stage wisdom is the property of God (Sap Sol 9:9; 11:24; 13:1; 15:1), in the second it is a being created by God prior to the world (Sap Sol 7:22; 8:3; 9:4 etc.), and in the final stage it is a being immanent in the world (7:24; 8:1; 7:27). Against Wolfson it can be argued that the author's thought is not so systematic.

The author of Sap Sol does not seem concerned with the production of systematic theology. Hence there are a number of occasions in the book in which wisdom is not personified, i.e. the device of personification is not consistently employed.[97] Far from such personification being used to overcome any difficulty which the author felt about the possibility of God making contact with the world without the services of an intermediary, God is, as we have already seen, frequently spoken of as acting Himself.[98] Were the author attempting to postulate any notion of intermediary agency, one would have thought that he would have been far more careful to make a clear distinction between God and wisdom. Therefore, it seems most unlikely that Sap Sol presents wisdom as an intermediary. As Larcher has pointed out, if this had been his intention, the author would have been over-successful in preserving the transcendence of God, for wisdom would have been given such a central place that there would be no need for God Himself.[99]

If intermediaries have no place in Sap Sol, do they not figure in the works of Philo? We have seen that Philo speaks of the lower levels of God's Being, i.e. λόγος, σοφία, δυνάμεις, ἄγγελοι, and in many respects πνεῦμα also can be classified as one of these levels. But are these regarded by Philo as intermediaries, as beings who in some sense have their own distinct identity?

As with wisdom in Sap Sol, language is used of these levels which would suggest that they were God's agents. From this Leisegang argues that πνεῦμα is a created being.[100] Yet just as we have seen that the author of Sap Sol does not sustain a distinction between God and wisdom, so we can see that Philo does not always speak of God acting through these lower levels of His Being. Thus, God is also described as acting Himself, without agents or intermediaries.[101] Philo warns his readers against giving any independent status to angels. He says that it is only because we cannot know τὸ ὄν that we take the aspects of God to be the sum. 'Angels are God's household servants and are deemed gods by those whose existence is still one of toil and bondage.'[102] They would seem, therefore, to be personifications of divine attributes, rather than separate beings. As H.A. Wolfson has pointed out, they are only intermediaries in the sense of patterns or plans in the divine architect's mind.[103]

---

97 Cf. pp.20–22.
98 Cf. Sap Sol 9:1; 9:17; 1:3; 14:6 etc.
99 C. Larcher, op. cit., p. 408.
100 H. Leisegang, op. cit., pp. 25, 121.
101 Cf. Opif. 74 where to God Himself is attributed the creation of everything in the world except the body and irrational soul of man.
102 Fug. 212. Cf. also Som. I, 238 where God is said to take the form of angels for the benefit of finite men.
103 H.A. Wolfson, op. cit., Vol. I, p. 286.

A. Laurentin has argued that from certain aspects πνεῦμα may be regarded as an intermediary in Philo. From the point of view of its origin πνεῦμα is God Himself; from the point of view of its effects it is like a created being, whereas from the point of view of its actions it becomes an intermediary and an instrument.[104] However, what Laurentin does not make clear is whether he means that this distinction is a linguistic one, or whether he is claiming some kind of ontological status for it. If he is maintaining the former then he is saying no more than we should expect, i.e. that Philo's language with reference to πνεῦμα is inexact and that this is due to the different roles which he sees the divine spirit playing. If Laurentin is claiming that the author himself made such theological distinctions believing them to be part of the nature of πνεῦμα, then it would presuppose a systematic approach, absent from Philo's work.[105]

We have already noticed that Philo does not maintain a systematic distinction between πνεῦμα and the other levels in the Being of God. If we follow Wolfson in thinking that the latter are not intermediaries, then we may assume this to be true of πνεῦμα. In fact, if πνεῦμα is compared with λόγος, it emerges that spirit has even less claim to the status of intermediary than the others, for whereas λόγος is spoken of in terms of agency, πνεῦμα is not.

Λόγος and πνεῦμα are frequently equated in the role which they play in Philo's theology.[106] Both are described as being involved in creation; the λόγος as the pattern and mediator of creation,[107] and πνεῦμα 'moving above the face of the water'.[108] Also both are active in the task of bringing enlightenment to men; the λόγος since he is the archetype of human reason,[109] and the πνεῦμα, since it is the invisible, secret tenant,[110] guiding the mind to truth.[111]

However, there is one important difference between them. Whereas λόγος is spoken of as both instrumental and also as that which is imparted, πνεῦμα is only described as the latter. Spirit is not so much the agency by which something is given; it is the content of what is imparted. Whereas λόγος is 'the man

---

104 A. Laurentin, op. cit., p. 431.
105 In saying that Philo's work is not systematic, we are not going so far as A.J.Festugière, *La Révélation d'Hermès Trismégiste*, II: *Dieu Cosmique* (Paris, 1949), who denies that Philo has any system at all. He argues that Philo's works are simply a hotchpotch of Hellenistic commonplaces. On the other hand Laurentin and Wolfson seem to endow Philo with complete coherence, which one suspects to be a reflection of their minds rather than that of Philo.
106 Both λόγος and πνεῦμα are referred to as angels. Cf. Cher. 3 ἀγγέλος ὅς ἐστι θεῖος λόγος. For the equation of angels with πνεύματα cf. Qu.Gen. II, 8; Abr. 113.
107 Conf. 63; Immut. 57; Leg. Alleg. III, 96; Cher. 127.
108 Gen 1:2. Cf. Gig. 22; Leg. Alleg. I, 33; Qu. Gen. IV, 5.
109 Heres. 230–232; Leg. Alleg. I, 31.
110 Som. II, 252.
111 V. Mos. II, 265; Plant. 24.

of God',[112] His agent in the creation of man,[113] πνεῦμα is what is given to man at creation. We have seen that in some passages Philo says that it was only given in its full strength to the archetypal, incorporeal man of Gen 1.[114] However, elsewhere he speaks of it as the possession of the earthly man of Gen 2.[115] Πνεῦμα is the οὐσία of the soul,[116] the archetypal form of the divine image,[117] impressèd by the seal of God (σφραγίς θεοῦ), who is Himself the 'dread spirit, the Divine and Invisible One'.[118] Πνεῦμα, rather than blood, is the essence of life.[119] Thus, for Philo, πνεῦμα is one of the constituents of man. Unlike λόγος it is never referred to as one of the craftsmen employed in man's making.

The same can be said if one looks beyond man to the cosmos. Whereas the λόγος is the agent in the creation of the universe, πνεῦμα is the life-principle itself.[120] We have seen that Philo adopts the Stoic terminology of the ἐκτικόν πνεῦμα to describe this life which pulsates throughout the cosmos. Although he disagrees with the Stoa's understanding of πνεῦμα as matter, like the Stoics he does not envisage πνεῦμα as an agent of the divine.

In the work of revelation, once more we see that πνεῦμα is not so much an agent as enlightenment itself. G. Verbeke claims, however, that the prophetic spirit is not identified with the divine, but is an intermediary between God and man. He states, 'Le pneuma prophétique de Philon, au contraire, ne peut être identifié avec Dieu: il apparaît plutôt comme un être intermédiaire entre la divinité transcendante et les hommes'.[121] Max Pulver, adopting the view originally put forward by H. Leisegang,[122] goes even further and states that God Himself moves out of the way in order to allow the heavenly beings to meet the soul. 'Gott selbst zieht sich zurück und gibt dadurch den in der Luftregion Seelen, den Logoi, Engeln und Dämonen die Möglichkeit auf die weilenden Menschenseele einzuwirken.'[123]

It is difficult to see the grounds on which these scholars base their conclusions, for the literature itself would suggest that Philo did not regard πνεῦμα as an intermediary agent of God who imparts wisdom, understanding, mind, reason and soul. For spirit itself is wisdom,[124] spiritual light[125] and understanding.[126]

---

112 Conf. 41; 62; 146.
113 Immut. 57 etc.
114 Leg. Alleg. I, 42; Opif. 144.
115 Opif. 135; Qu. Gen. I, 4: 51.
116 Spec. Leg. IV, 171.
117 Spec. Leg. I, 171.
118 Plant. 18.
119 Det. 80.
120 Cf. Opif. 30; Spec. Leg. IV, 217; Qu. Gen. III, 3 etc.
121 G. Verbeke, *L'Evolution de la Doctrine du Pneuma du Stoicisme à S. Augustin* (Louvain, 1945), p. 256.
122 H. Leisegang, op. cit., pp. 211–212.
123 M. Pulver, 'Das Erlebnis des Pneuma bei Philon', *Eranos Jahrbuch* 13 (1945), p. 130.
124 Σοφία cf. Qu. Gen. I, 90; Gig. 23.   125 Qu. Ex. II, 7.
126 Ἐπιστήμη Qu. Ex. II, 7. For πνεῦμα as pure knowledge (ἀκήρατος ἐπιστήμη) cf. Gig. 22.

It is νοῦς;[127] it is equated with λογισμός[128] – the divine inbreathing; and is described as ψυχή.[129] 'That which inbreathes is God . . . that which is inbreathed is spirit.[130]

In the light of this, both Verbeke's contention that the spirit is an intermediary, and Leisegang and Pulver's claim that it is an independent being, are untenable. On no occasion does Philo speak of πνεῦμα as if it were separate from God. In fact it could be maintained that, although Philo does not confine God, even by such a definition as 'God is spirit', πνεῦμα is the nearest he gets to defining τὸ ὄν. Whereas he sometimes uses language which could suggest that the λόγος is an agent with some independent existence, Philo refrains from this when using the concept of spirit. Therefore, in terms of Philo's thought, πνεῦμα can be said to be closer to God in His Being than is λόγος.

There would therefore appear to be no substantial evidence to suggest a doctrine of intermediaries in Hellenistic Judaism. Certainly it would not be true to say that πνεῦμα is portrayed as such. In fact as a number of scholars have pointed out there is no evidence to suggest that such a doctrine was ever part of Jewish thinking.[131] H.A. Wolfson, in a sub-heading in his book on Philo, sums up his opinion in the words 'The Fiction of Intermediaries'.[132] He points out that Jewish thinkers saw no necessity for postulating intermediary agents, because they did not feel any need to justify God's involvement in the world. When angels are spoken of as acting for God, they do so entirely at the command of God, who can equally do without them. Although we have seen that Philo postulates various levels in the Being of God, this is not so much in order to make contact between God and the world possible, as to be able to assert the biblical notion of the incomprehensibility of God, together with the conviction that God reveals Himself. Plotinus may have developed this Philonic notion of levels in God's Being, but he does so for different philosophical

---

127 A. Laurentin, op. cit., p. 415, in an attempt to maintain that Philo's use of πνεῦμα is wholly consistent, denies that he ever equates πνεῦμα with νοῦς. However, see Heres. 55; Fug. 133 and Qu. Gen. I, 90 where the two are obviously synonymous.
128 Heres. 57.
129 Cf. Leg. Alleg. I, 36 where 'breathe' is said to be the same as 'besoul'.
130 Leg. Alleg. I, 37. Τὸ μὲν οὖν ἔμπνεόν ὁ θεός . . . τὸ δὲ ἐμπνεόμενον τὸ πνεῦμα. This hardly suggests, as Laurentin (op. cit., p. 414) maintains, that πνεῦμα is instrumental.
131 E.g. G.F. Moore, Judaism, Vol. I, p. 417 and idem. 'Intermediaries in Jewish Theology', *Harvard Theological Review* 15 (1922), pp. 41–85, Strack-Billerbeck, op. cit., Vol. III, pp. 302–333, J. Abelson, *The Immanence of God in Rabbinical Literature* (London, 1912), pp. 146–173 etc.
132 H.A. Wolfson, op. cit., Vol. I, p. 282.

reasons. Certainly the Neo-Platonists developed a whole theology of intermediaries. In Philo, however, these levels in God's Being would seem to remain
divine attributes rather than take on a life of their own as independent beings.
Hence they essentially remain part of the process of personification, similar
to that found in Sap Sol.

6
IS ΠΝΕΥΜΑ ONE CONCEPT?

The problem

How meaningful is it to speak of πνεῦμα as one concept? We have examined how the word is used in the literature of Hellenistic Judaism, and we have seen that it is employed in a variety of contexts and with diverse meanings. Yet to call πνεῦμα a *single* concept implies that there is some kind of unity underlying the word's various usages. Is this in fact true or have we superimposed our own conceptual framework on a patchwork of references? This is the kind of criticism which James Barr makes of Kittel's *Theological Dictionary*,[1] when he accuses its authors of employing 'illegitimate totality transfer'.[2] By this he means the adding up of all the various meanings which can be deduced from a word's usage in different contexts, and the assumption that wherever the word occurs it contains within it all its other meanings.

This is certainly not a criticism which could have been levelled at such scholars as Leisegang and Verbeke. For them the meaning of πνεῦμα, as it occurs in Philo, falls into separate and distinct categories. Thus it is possible to consider πνεῦμα as wind, air, cohesion, the human soul, or as an inspirational force – usages in which the word has radically different senses.

However, Laurentin has argued against this approach, insisting that it is possible to see in the use of πνεῦμα by Philo a unified, coherent concept.[3] He claims that what gives πνεῦμα its unity is that, behind each occurrence of the word, lies a reference to its divine origin. It is always the divine, active power, all pervading and yet external to all it pervades. Laurentin maintains that whenever the word is used it conveys the idea of movement between God and man and is that which extends God's presence, allowing it to reach its object – man and the world.

Here we have two opposing points of view; the former regarding πνεῦμα as the linguistic symbol employed to convey a whole series of incompatible and radically different meanings, and the latter maintaining that wherever the term

---

1   Ed. G. Kittel and G. Friedrich, *Theologisches Wörterbuch zum neuen Testament* (Stuttgart, 1933–1973).

2   James Barr, *The Semantics of Biblical Language* (Oxford, 1961), p. 218.

3   A. Laurentin, 'Le Pneuma dans la Doctrine de Philon', *Ephemerides Theologicae Lovanienses* XXVII (1951), pp.390–447.

is employed it has a common referent. In the first case πνεῦμα would be seen as representing a number of concepts, whereas in the second it would be regarded as one concept.

Is πνεῦμα always πνεῦμα θεοῦ?

The strength of Leisegang's view is that it takes the contextual situation in which the word occurs seriously.[4] This cannot always be said for Laurentin. For example, in the interests of maintaining that πνεῦμα is one concept, he sometimes seems to ignore the straightforward interpretation of a passage. We have already noted that this has led him to deny that πνεῦμα and ἀήρ are ever equated, in spite of instances where they clearly are. Similarly, he refuses to allow the equation of πνεῦμα with νοῦς. These conclusions would seem to reflect his own theological perspective. For Laurentin πνεῦμα is always πνεῦμα θεοῦ. Hence, he refuses to allow that it could be spoken of as one of the elements, or even as one of the constituents of man. Rather he asserts that Philo means to indicate that πνεῦμα is the instrumental power which acts upon the mind of man and the elements of the cosmos. One suspects, however, that Laurentin has allowed his own theological presuppositions about the immaterial, abstract nature of the Spirit, to obscure his reading of the actual texts. This is particularly apparent in his refusal to treat the occurrence of πνεῦμα meaning 'wind' as different from its usages with reference to the divine.[5] Undoubtedly ancient peoples did regard the wind as incomprehensible and mysterious. The Greeks thought of the winds as controlled by the gods.[6] However, it is extremely unlikely that wherever πνεῦμα as 'wind' occurs in Greek literature (and we have seen that this was the most common usage) there is a conscious or unconscious reference to the divine. Although Philo's writings are theological in *genre*, it would seem equally unlikely that his use of the term πνεῦμα always carries with it explicit theological overtones. Whatever the original connection between πνεῦμα as 'wind' and πνεῦμα as a signification of the divine, by the Hellenistic period the two uses of the word have become so divergent as to suggest that they are two different concepts.

---

4 The importance of context for determining the meaning of a word has also been emphasized in modern linguistic studies. These have revealed that the unit of language is not the word, since words fall into habitual patterns. Therefore, the meaning of a word can only be understood in the context of these larger units. For an admirable discussion of modern trends in semantics cf. R.A. Waldron, *Sense and Sense Development* (London, 1970).
5 Cf. A. Laurentin, op. cit., pp. 399–401.
6 Cf. the place of Aeolius, the ruler of the winds in Graeco-Roman mythology. Cf. Homer, Od. 10, 2ff; Virgil, Aen. I, 51ff.

As we have seen in our examination of πνεῦμα in the LXX, an emphasis on the divine referent of πνεῦμα was one of the major contributions made by the translators of the O.T. Apart from Stoicism, πνεῦμα, other than in the sense of 'wind' or 'breath', played little part in pagan Greek usage. It was in retaining the same term – as does the Hebrew – for the spirit of God as well as wind, that Hellenistic Judaism emphasized and extended ways in which πνεῦμα was used and understood. However, the fact that a theological dimension was emphasized by Hellenistic Jews in the ways in which they used the term πνεῦμα, does not necessarily imply that they understood it to have an exclusively theological meaning. In spite of Laurentin's attempt to ignore the fact, it is evident that πνεῦμα continued to be used to signify wind. Furthermore, there is no evidence to suggest that when used in this sense it inevitably carried with it theological overtones. To assume otherwise is indeed to commit the 'illegitimate totality transfer' condemned by Barr.

On the other hand, does this mean that Leisegang is right in understanding the various occurrences of the term as unrelated? We have seen that πνεῦμα occurs in three major contexts: as a term used of the life principle in the cosmos; as the animating force in man; and as a signification of the divine. Leisegang has treated these as separate categories, whereas Laurentin has insisted upon their relatedness. Even if we have taken issue with Laurentin for treating 'wind' in the same category and for over simplifying and over systematizing his data, basically we believe that πνεῦμα in all other senses except that of 'wind', can be said to be one concept. Wherever the term appears it has a theological reference. In denying this, Leisegang has been influenced by his desire to see Greek philosophy as the major influence on Philo's thinking, and hence to neglect the role of the LXX in determining Philo's usage of the term πνεῦμα.

The main bulk of Philo's work consists of exposition of the Pentateuch, and hence, it is to his elucidation of those scriptural passages in which the word occurs that we must look if we are to gather how he understood the term. He found the word in the creation story of Gen 1, where it was associated with the creation of the cosmos. It also features in Gen 2:7 in the account of the creation of man. Πνεῦμα is also said to be given to the 70 Elders in Num 11:17. It is evident that these scriptural contexts determine the way Philo understands πνεῦμα, since for him πνεῦμα is connected with the creation of the cosmos, the creation of man, and prophetic inspiration. Thus the LXX provides the major categories in which Philo uses the term πνεῦμα. In fact Philo does not use the word in any way which cannot be paralleled in the LXX. This is not to deny the influence of Stoic terminology on his works, but to assert that their usage is biblically controlled. Whereas the Stoic πνεῦμα carried with it material overtones, πνεῦμα for Hellenistic Judaism was always immaterial, since it referred to a God whom they refused to equate with matter.

Just as Hellenistic Jewish writers mostly drew upon the Greek bible for their vocabulary for God,[7] so it is to the LXX that we must look for their understanding of πνεῦμα. Since the predominant and distinctive use of the term in the LXX was as a theological term, i.e. 'spirit of God', so it is this theological reference which is the unifying factor which makes it possible to speak of πνεῦμα as one concept.

In claiming that πνεῦμα has a common referent, we are not implying any theory of language which would give a word a false fixity of meaning or independence. We are not attempting to give πνεῦμα a 'definition' which holds good in every context in which it occurs. But as R.A. Waldron has pointed out about language in general, the meaning of a word is already fixed by custom and usage before it is employed in any context, otherwise we would not consciously notice, as we do, when a word occurs in a novel context. It is, of course, fallacious to assume that a word has a central, root meaning. However, it is equally mistaken to assume that it means something different in every context in which it occurs.[8] If this were true, language, understood as the commonly accepted use of symbols or signs, would be non-existent. As T.S. Eliot observed 'the particular has no language'.[9] What we are claiming is that it is not so much the Stoa as the LXX which has provided Hellenistic Jewish writers with the commonly accepted use and meaning of πνεῦμα. To say this does not preclude the authors of the Diaspora from using πνεῦμα in new contexts and, in so doing, from introducing new ideas about the spirit. However, it is to claim that it is meaningful to regard πνεῦμα as one concept, which has been biblically controlled.

If πνεῦμα can be regarded as having the same reference, how are we to explain the fact that Philo makes contradictory statements about its nature and activity? He describes it as human and divine; permanent and transient; the possession of all and the gift of a few. These statements could be interpreted as referring to something different and therefore not necessarily contradictory in nature. However, we have maintained that, although Philo is not systematic in his treatment of πνεῦμα, there is a discernible coherence in his use of the term. This is not to deny the contradictions, but to understand how they arise.

We have seen that they can be explained in terms of the author's *Sitz im Leben*. To understand Philo's pneumatology one must appreciate the questions he, as an apologist for Judaism, was attempting to answer. An analysis of Philo's pneumatology reveals that he was attempting to reconcile Hellenistic and

---

7 Cf. R. Marcus, 'Divine Names and Attributes in Hellenistic Jewish Literature', *Proceedings of the American Academy for Jewish Research* (1931–1932), pp. 43–120.
8 R.A. Waldron, op. cit., pp. 207, 233.
9 R.A. Waldron, op. cit., p. 84 quotes this observation.

biblical thought. The purpose of his work was not only to show the reasonableness of Mosaic faith, but also to assert its supremacy. In this attempt he employed the current terminology of Hellenistic philosophy, not only for the benefit of the Greeks to whom he was commending Judaism, but also for the Jews of the Diaspora, who were living in a Hellenistic *milieu* and wanted, as far as possible, to come to terms with its culture.

In order to understand Philo's concept of πνεῦμα it is essential to realize that this apologetic motive was paramount in his works. In the light of this, it is not therefore surprising that some of the tenets and terminology of Hellenistic philosophy (especially Stoicism) loom large in his writings. However, it is equally important to note that these are used as handmaids in his exposition and commendation of the Pentateuch. Although he adopts the language of Stoic pneumatology, particularly to stress the immanence of the divine, he does not do so uncritically. Since, for Philo, πνεῦμα signifies the divine, and since his understanding of God is basically biblical, he vigorously opposes the Stoic equation of πνεῦμα with matter.

Similarly, Philo not only adopts Platonic ideas, he adapts them. The Platonic theory of creation presents him with a reasonable way of accounting for the variant creation stories of Gen 1 and 2. Also Platonic transcendentalism accords with his understanding of biblical theology. However, he modifies Platonism to stress the principle of correspondence between the world of Ideas and the created cosmos. In this way he avoids the dualism inherent in Platonism and retains the biblical assertion that man was made in God's image.

We have seen that in understanding prophecy in terms of the oracular, Philo was adopting a point of view common to certain parts of the bible and to most Hellenistic thinking. However, it is important to note that an ecstatic interpretation of prophecy accorded with Philo's apologetic motive, for it enabled him to claim a supremacy for the Mosaic oracles, to affirm the superiority of Jewish beliefs over against any reasoned philosophy.

To claim that the key to Philo's pneumatology is the appreciation of his apologetic motives, and that these motives explain the mixture of biblical and Hellenistic ideas, does not necessarily imply that Philo was a systematic theologian. Indeed Philo's use of the term πνεῦμα is far from systematic. Whilst using it to assert both the immanence and transcendence of God, he does not resolve the philosophical difficulties which arise from trying to maintain both. Thus πνεῦμα is seen as the principle of order and cohesion in the life of man and the cosmos. As such it is permanent and all-pervading. It is the principle of reason, which is the link between God and His creation. As conscience, it is the possession of all, necessary for the apprehension and attainment of the truth. However, since Philo rejects Stoic pantheism, for him the πνεῦμα in man must also be spasmodic and transient, not man's by his unalienable right, but the gift of God possessed by only the few. In asserting the universality of the divine πνεῦμα in all men, Philo is able to claim the possibility of faith for all men – Greek and Jewish. In emphasizing that the προφητικόν πνεῦμα is wholly attributable to divine grace, he is also able to assert the supremacy of Judaism and the unique inspiration of her scriptures. Thus the very contradictions which may be found in Philo's use of the term πνεῦμα, far from indicating that they reflect totally different categories of usage, are an indication of his attempt to hold all these different ideas together. In other words, it is only if one recognizes that πνεῦμα has one referent, that one can appreciate Philo's philosophical problems or his attempted answers.

Conclusions

Apart from its usage as 'wind' it would therefore appear that, since it has a common reference to the divine, πνεῦμα may be considered as one concept. We have noted the importance of the LXX in determining later Hellenistic Jewish authors' understanding of πνεῦμα as πνεῦμα θεοῦ or πνεῦμα θεῖον. Continuing the tendency of the LXX we have also noted that the term πνεῦμα, unlike ψυχή, is not so commonly employed to designate human personality. Assimilating to more common pagan Greek usage Hellenistic Judaism is inclined to use the word ψυχή instead. (However, we should stress that this is only a tendency, and there are instances in which πνεῦμα is used of the human ψυχή.) This inevitably emphasized the divine nature of πνεῦμα. It could be maintained that it was Judaism which introduced a theological content into the word πνεῦμα, which in its pagan usage (apart from in the Stoa) was rarely so used.

There is no evidence to suggest that πνεῦμα was developed in Hellenistic Judaism to describe an intermediary being, employed by a transcendent God as His agent in the world. Some scholars have seen this in the figure of wisdom in Sap Sol. However we have argued that the language of agency is to be understood as arising out of the use of personification, rather than indicating any theological perspective. Similarly, we have asserted that πνεῦμα in Philo's writings cannot bear a hypostatic interpretation.

Thus we have seen that the Judaism of the Diaspora, starting from the translators of the LXX, introduced a new dimension into the normal Greek understanding of πνεῦμα. On the other hand, as we can see in the works of Philo, the Gentile world posed a number of theological questions to Judaism, which are reflected in its pneumatology.

PART TWO

Spirit in the New Testament

7

INTRODUCTION

The New Testament — a Greek work

Henry Chadwick begins his book on *The Early Church* with the following
words: 'The first Christians were Jews differentiated from their fellow country-
men by their faith that in Jesus of Nazareth the Messiah of the nation's expec-
tation had now come.'[1] No one would seriously question this statement since
Christianity's Jewish parentage has long been conclusively established. However,
in his T.W. Manson Memorial Lecture Chadwick has also reminded us of the
fact that the language in which early Christian beliefs have come down to us is
Greek. 'We cannot take too seriously the basic fact that the New Testament is
entirely in Greek.'[2]

Such a combination of Jewish theology and the Greek language is to be found
in the Diaspora in the centuries immediately prior to and contemporary with
the Christian era. It was the Jews of the Dispersion who originally adopted and
adapted Greek concepts of $\pi\nu\epsilon\hat{\upsilon}\mu\alpha$ to accord with their own beliefs. In part one
of this study we have examined what Hellenistic Jews meant when they spoke
of $\pi\nu\epsilon\hat{\upsilon}\mu\alpha$. Now we are to look at the N.T. to see whether Hellenistic Judaism's
previous use of the term throws any light on the ways in which it occurs in the
writings of the early church.

In discussing the definition of 'Hellenistic Judaism' we found it necessary to
point out that by 'Hellenistic' we meant Greek-speaking rather than 'pagan' or
'unorthodox'.[3] Similarly in describing the N.T. as a 'Greek' work we are making
a statement about language rather than origins. It is no longer necessary to
assume that the use of the Greek language is a sign of either a non-Palestinian
origin or a late (i.e. post A.D. 70) date. The caves at Qumran have furnished
evidence of Greek fragments, some of which may date from the first century
A.D.[4] From his investigation into knowledge of Greek among Palestinians in
the first century of the Christian era, J.N. Sevenster concludes that even

---

1 H. Chadwick, *The Early Church* (Harmondsworth, 1967), p. 1.
2 H. Chadwick, 'St. Paul and Philo of Alexandria', BJRL 48 (1966), p. 287.
3 See pp. 1–5.
4 See J.T. Milik, *Ten Years of Discovery in the Wilderness of Judea* (London, 1959),
   pp. 31–35, and J.N. Sevenster, *Do You Know Greek?* (Leiden, 1968), pp. 149–173.

members of the general populace would have had a smattering of the language.[5]
He goes so far as to suggest that Jesus himself may have known some Greek.[6]
As James Barr has pointed out, 'Even if we deny that Jesus taught in Greek,
we should not minimize the importance of Greek in the earliest stages of the
transmission of his teaching and even in the original teaching situation itself.'[7]

Furthermore we should not minimize the importance of the work of Hellenistic
Jews in providing the early Christian writers with the language in which they
were to express their faith. It was this debt which Kirsopp Lake acknowledged
when he wrote, 'It is to be remembered that to the student of the New Testament it is πνεῦμα in the LXX, not *ruach* in the Hebrew which is important.'[8]
It is customary to speak of Christianity as the heir of Hellenistic Judaism, but
nowhere is the inheritance more evident than in the use of the Greek language
itself. It would therefore seem wholly appropriate that we should look to
Hellenistic Judaism for the elucidation of the N.T. concept of πνεῦμα.

Literary dependence or common *milieu*?

In our examination of πνεῦμα in the N.T. we shall attempt to see whether its
previous usages in Hellenistic Judaism have any bearing on the way in which
early Christian writers use the term. First of all, however, it is necessary to
establish what we mean by 'bearing on'. Are we seeking to prove direct literary
dependence of the N.T. authors upon their Hellenistic Jewish predecessors, or
are we claiming a less direct kinship, which rests upon the assumption of their
being part of the same intellectual, cultural and linguistic *milieu*?

Of recent years the discoveries at Qumran have particularly absorbed the
attention of scholars interested in the early origins of the church. As a result
of this, emphasis upon and interest in the Hellenistic Jewish strand in the
Christian tradition has waned. The focus has shifted from the Alexandrian
metropolis to the Judean desert. Thus the Epistle to the Hebrews, previously
thought to be the most Alexandrian of all N.T. works, has been given a
Palestinian setting by Y. Yadin, who argues that it was addressed to Christian

---

5   J.N. Sevenster, op. cit., pp. 176–191. Cf. also S. Liebermann, *Greek in Jewish Palestine*
    (New York, 1942), who points out not only that a number of the rabbis were conver-
    sant with Greek, but that 'Greek language was known to the Jewish masses'. However,
    since Liebermann was writing before the Qumran discoveries most of his evidence is
    taken from the second century A.D. or later.
6   J.N. Sevenster, op. cit., p. 25.
7   J. Barr, 'Which language did Jesus speak? Remarks of a semitist', BJRL 53 (1970),
    p. 10.
8   F.J.F. Jackson and K. Lake, *The Beginnings of Christianity* (London, 1933), Vol. V,
    p. 96.

converts who had been former members of the Qumran sect.[9] Millar Burrows also looks to wholly Palestinian sources for the background to John's Gospel. 'The scrolls show that we do not need to look outside Palestinian Judaism for the soil on which the Johannine Theology grew.'[10] Furthermore in Pauline studies there has been a major tendency no longer to view the apostle against his Diaspora background,[11] but to see him in the light of rabbinic thought.[12]

In spite of this change of emphasis in N.T. scholarship it would be difficult to maintain that Hellenistic Judaism has no bearing on some parts of the N.T., however. Since the authors of the N.T. used the Greek version of the O.T., this is one important area of direct literary dependence upon Hellenistic Judaism which cannot be disputed; neither should it be underestimated, since the LXX had considerable influence upon the formation of Christian concepts.

However, apart from those occasions when N.T. writers quote directly from the LXX, it is extremely difficult to prove the literary dependence of any N.T. book upon the writings of Dispersion Judaism. Perhaps the most worthy attempt was made by C. Spicq, who tried to demonstrate that the author of the Epistle to the Hebrews, prior to his conversion to Christianity, had been a disciple of Philo and had actually sat at the Alexandrian's feet.[13] R.Williamson,[14] however, has questioned Spicq's evidence of literary dependence. He asserts that there are no irrefutable signs of direct borrowing,[15] and that the existence of common themes and ideas merely demonstrate that the respective authors moved within a similar intellectual orbit.[16]

---

9 Y. Yadin, 'The Dead Sea Scrolls and the Epistle to the Hebrews', *Scripta Hierosolymitana* IV (1958), pp. 36–55. *Contra* see A.J.B. Higgins, 'The Priestly Messiah', NTS 13 (1966–1967), pp. 211–239, F.F. Bruce, ' "To the Hebrews" or "To the Essenes"?', NTS 9 (1963), pp. 217–232, and J. Coppens, 'Les Affinités qumraniennes de l'épître aux Hébreux', *Novelle Revue Théologique* 84 (1962), pp. 270f.

10 M. Burrows, *More Light on the Dead Sea Scrolls* (London, 1958), pp. 339f. Cf. also W.F. Albright, 'Recent Discoveries in Palestine and the Gospel of St. John', in *The Background of the New Testament and its Eschatology,* ed. W.D. Davies and D. Daube (Essays in Honour of C.H. Dodd, Cambridge, 1954), pp. 153–171 and especially p.169.

11 W.C. van Unnik, *Tarsus or Jerusalem?* (London, 1962) argues that Paul may have been born in Tarsus but he was brought up in Jerusalem and to all intents and purposes should be regarded as a Palestinian.

12 See W.D. Davies, *Paul and Rabbinic Judaism* (2nd ed. London, 1955).

13 C. Spicq, *L'Epître aux Hébreux* (Paris, 1952), Vol. 1, pp.39–91. As early as 1750 J.B. Carpzov, *Sacrae exercitationes in S. Paulii epistolam ad Hebraeos ex Philoae Alexandrine* (Helmstadii) had attempted to collect parallels from Philo for almost every verse of Hebrews.

14 R. Williamson, *Philo and the Epistle to the Hebrews* (Leiden, 1970).

15 R. Williamson, op. cit., pp. 11–136.

16 R. Williamson, op. cit., pp. 137–495.

Williamson claims that

> It is one thing to concede, as the evidence compels us to, that the writer of Hebrews drew upon the same wealth of literary vocabulary and moved in the same circles of educated thought as a man like Philo, and quite another to speak, as Spicq does, of 'une coloration philonienne uniforme', of the presence in the Epistle of 'Philonisms', and of its writer as a Philonist converted to Christianity who brought into his exposition of Christian truth many of the terms and ideas of the Alexandrian philosopher.[17]

He also accuses Spicq of falling into the trap of seeing only the similarities between the two authors.

> It is my considered judgement that Spicq, among other things, isolates the linguistic aspect of the problem to the point where he loses sight of basic differences of outlook and attitude between the two authors.[18]

H. Montefiore, whilst conceding the differences between Philo and the author of Hebrews,[19] nonetheless thinks the latter may have known Philo. Certainly it is reasonable to assume that the writer of Hebrews knew the Philonic logos doctrine,[20] and it is possible that he was familiar with the writings of the Alexandrian Diaspora.[21] But to place the Epistle to the Hebrews within the general *milieu* of Alexandrian Judaism[22] is one thing; to prove literary dependence is another, as Williamson has rightly reminded us.

The same can be said of the Fourth Gospel. Parallels between Philo and John can be established,[23] but whether A.W. Argyle's suggestion of direct borrowing[24] can be proved is doubtful. Similarly E.M. Sidebottom's thesis that the Wisdom Literature of Hellenistic Judaism was 'an actual source from which he (John) borrowed'[25] is untrue, if Sidebottom is suggesting that John contains direct quotations from this source. Possible allusions and common themes do not constitute irrefutable evidence of literary borrowing. The most that can be said is that John 'belongs to the Jewish Hellenistic strain which was probably

17 R. Williamson, op. cit., pp. 296f.
18. R. Williamson, op. cit., p. 9.
19 H. Montefiore, *The Epistle to the Hebrews* (BNTC London, 1964), pp. 9–11, where he also argues that the author of Hebrews was probably Apollos.
20 See S.G. Sower, *The Hermeneutics of Philo and Hebrews* (Zürich, 1965), p. 69.
21 So T.H. Robinson, *The Epistle to the Hebrews* (MNTC London, 1933), p. xvi.
22 Cf. also A. Nairne, *The Epistle to the Hebrews* (Cambridge, 1922), p. cxxxii; idem, *The Epistle of Priesthood* (2nd ed. Edinburgh, 1915), p. 31 and B.F. Westcott, *The Epistle to the Hebrews* (London, 1889), p. lxi.
23 See W.L. Knox, *Some Hellenistic Elements in Primitive Christianity* (London, 1944), pp. 55–90, C.H. Dodd, *The Interpretation of the Fourth Gospel* (Cambridge, 1953), pp. 54–73.
24 A.W. Argyle, 'Philo and the Fourth Gospel', Exp.T.63 (1952), pp.385–386. See *contra* R. Mc.L. Wilson, 'The Fourth Gospel and Hellenistic Thought', NT 1 (1956), pp. 225–227, and J.H. Bernard, *The Gospel According to St. John* (ICC Edinburgh, 1928), Vol. I, pp. xcii–xciv.
25 E.M. Sidebottom, *The Christ of the Fourth Gospel* (London, 1961), p. 207.

in Christianity almost from the beginning'.[26] What is true of Hebrews and John in this respect also applies to the rest of the N.T., i.e. that there is insufficient evidence to warrant claims of any direct borrowing from any of the works of Dispersion Judaism, with the notable exception of the LXX.

Having discussed some of the similarities between Philo and Paul, H. Chadwick does not attempt to claim more than that they reflect a common *milieu*.[27] However, he does regard the study of that *milieu* of Hellenistic Judaism as instructive for the student of the N.T.

> I believe that the theology of the Hellenistic synagogue, as recorded in the long printed and familar texts of Greek-speaking Judaism, still throws more light on the world of St. Paul, St. John and the Epistle to the Hebrews, than any other single non-Christian source.[28]

The value of these same sources has also been acknowledged by Samuel Sandmel – an eminent Jewish scholar.

> In my judgement, if we distinguish between the Gospels, which are Greek documents, and the Judean scene that they depict, more light is thrown on the Gospels by Hellenistic Judaism than by Rabbinic sources.[29]

It is no part of the purpose of this study, however, to enter into the debate as to which of Christianity's sources was the most influential. The strands which contributed to early Christian thought were many; in concentrating on one we are not intending to make exclusive claims for the influence of Hellenistic Judaism. We are maintaining, however, that there is sufficient kinship between the linguistic and cultural *milieu* of the Diaspora and that of the writers of the N.T. to warrant a comparative study of their respective literatures. Judgements as to the exact nature and extent of that kinship must be left open to emerge as we look at the evidence.

---

26 C.H. Dodd, Interpretation, p. 5.
27 H. Chadwick, 'St. Paul and Philo of Alexandria', BJRL 48 (1966), pp. 286–307.
   For a list of parallels cf. also H.St.J. Thackeray, *The Relation of St. Paul to Contemporary Jewish Thought* (London, 1900), pp.233–240.
28 H. Chadwick, op. cit., p. 287.
29 S. Sandmel, *The First Christian Century in Judaism and Christianity: Certainties and Uncertainties* (Oxford, 1969), p. 46, n. 25.

8
ΠΝΕΥΜΑ AND ANTHROPOLOGY

Πνεῦμα – an anthropological or a theological term?

The debate as to whether πνεῦμα can be regarded as an anthropological term or whether it is to be confined to statements about the divine has centred upon Pauline usage. Some commentators have denied that πνεῦμα is ever used by Paul as a description of the nature of man. G.S. Duncan has claimed that, 'In every reference to the Spirit it is the divine Spirit that is thought of'.[1] To accord with this he interprets the πνεῦμα ὑμῶν in Gal 6:18[2] as part of the divine spirit bestowed upon the believer. Similarly E. von Dobschütz[3] identified πνεῦμα ὑμῶν in I Thess 5:23 with the spirit of God permanently dwelling in the individual Christian. If this interpretation is accepted then πνεῦμα can only be regarded as a term applicable to the Christian and not to man in general. It would therefore be part of a specifically Christian 'anthropology', better considered rather as a statement about God than about man.

W.G. Kümmel, on the other hand, argues that πνεῦμα is used in the Pauline Epistles of man in general, and that the spirit of man is not particularly related to the divine. 'The context shows that this human πνεῦμα stands in no way particularly close to God but rather belongs entirely to the side of σάρξ.'[4] He concludes, 'From the examination of these terms used to denote the inner man it is clear that Paul knows no inner life related to God, but only the complete man, who is σάρξ, σῶμα, ψυχή etc.[5] and wholly stands over against God.[6]

We shall now have to examine the evidence of N.T. usage before we can decide which of these two positions is the more likely.

Πνεῦμα as a designation of man

Undoubtedly there are instances in the N.T. where πνεῦμα is used in place of the personal pronoun, 'himself' or 'myself'. To the Romans Paul writes, 'God

---

1 G.S. Duncan, *The Epistle to the Galatians* (MNTC London, 1934), p. 166.
2 Cf. Philem 25; 2 Tim 4:22.
3 E. von Dobschütz, *Die Thessalonischerbriefe* (Leipzig, 1909), p. 229.
4 W.G. Kümmel, *Man in the New Testament* (London, 1963), p. 44.
5 W.G. Kümmel has already stated that πνεῦμα is one of the terms used by Paul of the inner man (op. cit. pp. 43–44) and therefore we may assume that it is included in the 'etc'.
6 W.G. Kümmel, op. cit., p. 47.

is my witness, the God to whom I offer the humble service of my spirit.'[7]
Πνεῦμα is here a designation of the apostle himself. This is by no means an
isolated instance of πνεῦμα being used by Paul as a signification of selfhood.[8]
Examples of this type of usage, although infrequent, can also be found in the
Gospels. In the Marcan account of the healing of the paralytic, ἐπιγνοὺς . . .
τῷ πνεύματι αὐτῷ in Mk 2:8 is no different in meaning from ἐπιγνοὺς ἐν
ἑαυτῷ which is used elsewhere.[9] In the quotation from Ps 30:5 (MT 31:5)
which Luke puts into the mouth of the dying Jesus – Πάτερ, εἰς χεῖράς σου
παρατίθεμαι τὸ πνευμά μοῦ[10] – πνεῦμα obviously indicates the self.

We have noted that in Hellenistic Jewish writing πνεῦμα is occasionally used
to indicate mood, disposition or inclination, i.e. in the sense of ψυχή or
θυμός.[11] N.T. writers also use πνεῦμα in this way. Paul can speak of a numbness
of spirit (πνεῦμα κατανύξεως)[12] coming upon men; he exhorts his converts to
be fervent in spirit[13] and encourages them to exhibit a spirit of meekness
(πνεῦμα πραΰτητος).[14] A similar use of πνεῦμα is to be found in the Matthean
version of the beatitude, 'Μακάριοι οἱ πτωχοὶ τῷ πνεύματι ὅτι αὐτων ἐστιν ἡ
βασιλεία τῶν οὐρανῶν'.[15] The Lucan version omits πνεῦμα and simply reads
οἱ πτωχοί[16] and some scholars[17] regard this as the more original form of the
pericope. However, it seems likely that Matthew has the more authentic form,[18]

---

7 Rom 1:9, μάρτυς γάρ μού ἐστιν ὁ θεός, ᾧ λατρεύω ἐν πνεύματί μου.

8 For other instances of πνεῦμα used as a personal pronoun see 1 Cor 5:4; 14:14; 16:18;
   2 Cor 2:13; 7:13; Gal 6:18; 1 Thes 5:23; 2 Thes 2:2; 2 Tim 4:22.

9 Mk 5:30.

10 Lk 23:46. This follows the LXX except in the substitution of the present παρατίθεμαι
   for the future παραθήσομαι. Cf. Stephen's dying prayer in Acts 7:59. See also Lk 1:47
   where τὸ πνεῦμα μοῦ is parallel to ψυχή in the preceding verse.

11 See pp. 11f, 15.

12 Rom 11:8 which is quoting the LXX of Isa 29:10.

13 Rom 12:11. C.K. Barrett, The Epistle to the Romans (BNTC London, 1957), takes
   this as a reference to the holy spirit. However, with F.J. Leenhardt, The Epistle to the
   Romans (London, 1961), we take this to refer to the human disposition of enthusiasm.
   Cf. Acts 18:25 where Apollos is described as one who was fervent in spirit (ζεων τῷ
   πνεύματι), i.e. full of enthusiasm.

14 Gal 6:1. In the light of Gal 5 where gentleness is one of the fruits of the spirit, G.S.
   Duncan, The Epistle of Paul to the Galatians (MNTC London, 1934), takes this to be
   the holy spirit. However, it would be more natural to take this as a genitive of characteristic, i.e. the human spirit characterized by gentleness. Cf. 1 Cor 4:2; 1 Pet 3:4;
   Mt 11:29.

15 Mt 5:3.

16 Lk 6:20.

17 E.g. F.F. Filson, A Commentary on the Gospel According to St. Matthew (BNTC
   London, 1960), p. 77, A.H. McNeile, The Gospel According to St Matthew (London,
   1915), p. 50, T.W. Manson, The Sayings of Jesus (London, 1949), p. 47.

18 So P.A. Micklem, St. Matthew (WC London, 1917), p. 37, W.C. Allen, The Gospel
   According to St. Matthew (ICC 3rd ed. Edinburgh, 1912), p. 39, T.H. Robinson,
   The Gospel of Matthew (MNTC London, 1928), p. 28.

expressing the humility of those who need God. Contrition was a favourite theme of O.T. writers and the LXX translators of Ps 33:18 (MT 34:18) express this as ταπεινούς τῷ πνεύματι.[19] Furthermore, in the *Psalms of Solomon*[20] the term 'the poor' designates 'those who are pious':

> And the pious shall give thanks to the assembly
> of the people:
> And on the poor shall God have mercy in the gladness
> of Israel.[21]

Matthew seems to reflect a similar idea and his use of πνεῦμα to indicate a disposition would accord with what we know of Septuagintal usage.

There is also evidence of πνεῦμα being used for the seat of the emotions, i.e. in the sense of θυμός. Mark mentions Jesus's spirit (πνεῦμα) being deeply moved[22] and John similarly mentions his πνεῦμα being disturbed at the news of the death of Lazarus.[23] Paul's exasperation at the idolatry practised in Athens is described by Luke in terms of his spirit being vexed.[24]

There are also instances in the N.T. where πνεῦμα is used of the breath or life principle upon which man's existence depends. This is aptly illustrated by the author of the Epistle of James when he uses the simile of a corpse to describe faith apart from works: ὥσπερ γὰρ τὸ σῶμα χωρὶς πνεύματος νεκρόν ἐστιν, οὕτως καὶ ἡ πιστις χωρὶς ἔργων νεκρά ἐστιν.[25] Here πνεῦμα is employed for the *Lebensgeist;*[26] that by which man is animated. Hence death is depicted as the departure of this breath or life force. Cf. Mt 27:50, ὁ δὲ Ἰησοῦς πάλιν κράξας φωνῇ μεγάλῃ ἀφῆκεν τὸ πνεῦμα.[27] Life, on the other hand, is signified by the presence of πνεῦμα.[28] The LXX translators could also use πνεῦμα in this sense,[29] although they preferred the more usual Greek word ψυχή.[30]

---

19 See Isa 11:4 ταπεινούς τῆς γῆς.
20 The *Psalms of Solomon* is generally accepted as a Palestinian work, originally written in Hebrew and to be dated 80–40 B.C. See A-M. Denis, Introduction, pp. 60–69.
21 Ps. Sol. 10:7. Cf. Isa 61:1 where the poor and the contrite are addressed.
   For a discussion of the *anawin* see A. Gelin, *The Poor of Jahweh* (Collegeville, Minnesota, 1964).
22 Mk 8:12, καὶ ἀναστενάξας τῷ πνεύματι αὐτοῦ.
23 Jn 11:33, ἐνεβριμήσατο τῷ πνεύματι καὶ ἐτάραξεν ἑαυτόν. Cf. Jn 13:21, Ἰησοῦς ἐταράχθη τῷ πνεύματι.
24 Acts 17:16, παρωξύνετο τὸ πνεῦμα αὐτοῦ ἐν αὐτῷ. Cf. LXX of Isa 63:10 where it is God's anger which is provoked.
25 Jas 2:26. Cf. Ecclus 38:23; Sap Sol 16:14 for the departure of the πνεῦμα/ψυχή at death.
26 So F. Mussner, *Der Jakobusbrief* (Freiburg, 1964), p. 151. Cf. Gen 2:7; 6:17; Ps 104:30.
27 Cf Mk 15:37 and Lk 23:46 where ἐκπνέω is used instead.
28 See Lk 8:55 where the raising of Jairus's daughter is expressed as ἐπέστρεψεν τὸ πνεῦμα αὐτῆς.
29 E.g. Ecclus 38:23.   30 Cf. Gen 35:18; Sap Sol 16:14.

We have already noted the tendency in Hellenistic Judaism to assimilate to pagan Greek usage and to use ψυχή or θυμός as a designation for man. The same trend can be seen in the N.T. where the examples cited above are few and exceptional.[31] Apart from the Pauline writings πνεῦμα is rarely used for the human soul. This can be seen in the Third Gospel, where of the three anthropological uses of πνεῦμα, two have been influenced by the LXX. One of these two is a direct quotation from Ps 30:5 (MT 31:5)[32] and the other is obviously intended to echo biblical usage.[33] Elsewhere Luke omits references to the spirit of man which he finds in his sources.[34]

When we come to Paul, however, πνεῦμα is used far more frequently, not only as a designation of the divine but as a term for man. Along with ψυχή, νοῦς, καρδία, and συνείδησις it is one of a number of words used, as Kümmel puts it, 'promiscuously'[35] by the apostle when he wishes to describe the inner man. In spite of R. Jewett's assertion that πνεῦμα and ψυχή are never used interchangeably by Paul,[36] it is possible to regard Phil 1:27 – ἐν ἑνὶ πνεύματι, μιᾷ ψυχῇ – as an example of synonymous parallelism, employed for the purposes of rhetoric.[37] J.B. Lightfoot's attempt to see here a distinction between a principle of higher life (πνεῦμα) and the seat of the affections (ψυχή)[38] is an over-systematization of Paul's anthropology. In 1 Thes 5:23 Paul uses language which could suggest that πνεῦμα is one of three components in man, who consists of spirit, soul and body. However, this also is probably no more than a reflection of popular terminology. Far from adopting some rigid trichotomy the apostle seems to be emphasizing man in his entirety. Elsewhere he can refer to only two elements in man, πνεῦμα and σῶμα.[39] It therefore seems that in his anthropology Paul did not make a rigid distinction between πνεῦμα and ψυχή.

It is also unlikely that the author of the Epistle to the Hebrews intends any distinction between πνεῦμα and ψυχή when he writes: 'For the word (λόγος) of God is alive and active.[40] It cuts more keenly than any two edged sword,[41]

---

31 See Appendix D, pp. 154–156.   32 Lk 23:46.
33 Lk 1:47. Cf. 1 Kgdms 2:1–10.
34 Thus he omits Mk 2:8; 8:12; 14:38; 15:37. In Lk 6:20 he substitutes οἱ πτωχοί for οἱ πτωχοὶ τῷ πνεύματι.
35 W.G. Kümmel, *Man in the New Testament* (London, 1963), p. 148.
36 R. Jewett, *Paul's Anthropological Terms* (Leiden, 1971) p. 195.
37 So J. Gnilka, *Der Philipperbrief* (Freiburg, 1968). Cf. Lk 1:46f; Jn 11:33.
38 J.B. Lightfoot, *St. Paul's Epistle to the Philippians* (London, 1903).
39 E.g. 1 Cor 7:34.
40 For the idea of the power of God's word see Jn 6:63; Isa 55:11; Ps 32:9 (MT 33:9); Jer 23:29. See O. Michel, *Der Brief an die Hebräer* (Göttingen, 1960), p. 117, 'Die Attribute ζῶν und ἐνεργής sind typische Gottessagen'.
41 For the image of the sword see Rev 1:16; 19:15; Eph 6:17; Judg 3:16; Prov 5:4; Isa 49:2; Sap Sol 18:15–17.

piercing as far as the place where life (ψυχή) and spirit (πνεῦμα), joints and marrow divide.'[42] The language here is reminiscent of that used by Philo, as even Williamson has to concede,[43] although he concludes that Philo and Hebrews represent 'different strands in the intricate pattern of Jewish-Christian logos speculation.'[44] In Philo the λογος τομεύς is discussed in Heres. 130—148 and is described as that which divides the soul into rational and irrational.[45] He cites Heraclitus as the author of the theory of a principle which divides things into opposites and equals,[46] although Philo asserts that it is 'God alone who is exact in judgement and alone able to divide in the middle.'[47] The question we have to ask is whether the author of Hebrews here intends any Philonic distinction between πνεῦμα[48] — the rational part of the soul — and ψυχή, which represents the lower nature of man. From the context it would seem unlikely that any such distinction was intended by the author of Hebrews. He appears to be employing metaphorical language upon which it would be dangerous to build any theory of a systematic anthropology. Far from indicating a distinction between πνεῦμα and ψυχή the author is stressing their closeness. Hence he employs a rhetorical parallelism, using both terms to signify the same life principle present in man.

To return to Paul is to find that he has a more developed concept of man's inner nature. See for example his use of the phrase ὁ ἔσω ἄνθρωπος in Rom 7:22 and 2 Cor 4:16.[49] Furthermore he uses πνεῦμα more often than ψυχή as a designation of that inner nature.[50] As W.D. Stacey has expressed it, 'Πνεῦμα is central and ψυχή has a lesser function . . . Spirit has made a dramatic advance and soul a dramatic retreat'.[51] We have seen that Hellenistic Judaism sometimes equated this inner nature (πνεῦμα) with νοῦς.[52] Does Paul also identify the highest part of man with reason? Stacey has claimed that he does not.[53] However Paul is not averse to quoting Isa 40:13[54] from the LXX, where the

---

42 Heb 4:12.
43 R. Williamson, *Philo and the Epistle to the Hebrews* (Leiden, 1970), pp. 390—394.
44 Williamson, op. cit., p. 430.
45 Heres. 132. Cf. Cher. 28, 30 where the sword is the symbol of reason (λόγος).
46 Heres. 214.
47 Heres. 143.
48 See Leg. Alleg. I, 31—41 where the dominant part of man is πνεῦμα rather than ψυχή.
49 Cf. also Eph. 3:16, 'that He may grant you strength and power through His spirit in your inward being (ἔσω ἄνθρωπος).' Here the spirit of God and the inner man, although closely related, are not identified. Cf. I Pet 3:4 ὁ κρυπτὸς τῆς καρδιάς ἄνθρωπος.
50 In contrast to the O.T. where *nephesh* is used more often than *ruach*.
51 W.D. Stacey, *The Pauline View of Man* (London, 1956), p. 126.
52 See pp. 38—41.
53 W.D. Stacey, op. cit., p. 204.
54 1 Cor 2:16; Rom 11:34.

translators have already made the equation by using νοῦς to translate *ruach*.[55] Furthermore Paul's assertion in Rom 2:14–16 that Gentiles possess knowledge of God's law 'by the light of nature'[56] to which conscience (συνείδησις) bears witness,[57] is very close to the idea of reason as man's guide.

However, in Pauline thought there is less emphasis upon πνεῦμα as man's rational aspect than we find in Philo and *4 Maccabees*. This may be because the apostle was not primarily concerned to employ πνεῦμα as a term which would open up the possibilities of dialogue with the pagan world. Jews such as Philo sometimes equated πνεῦμα with νοῦς in order to assert the reasonableness of Judaism and in an attempt to find common ground with Hellenistic thought. In addressing the Corinthian church Paul is also concerned that their worship should not give rise to ridicule among any pagans who witnessed it. Hence in discussing the phenomenon of glossolalia[58] he insists that it should always be controlled by reason, taking the form of an interpretation for the benefit of the congregation. The ecstatic condition of the man who speaks in tongues is described in typical Hellenistic terms of divine possession and the eviction of reason. 'If I use such language in my prayer, the spirit (πνεῦμα) in me prays, but my intellect (νοῦς) lies fallow.'[59] In asserting that the divine spirit which inspires glossolalia should be under the control of the human νοῦς, the apostle is speaking to a particular situation in which the ecstatic element was in danger of disrupting the life of the Christian community. He is not claiming the superiority of human reason over divine inspiration.

So far it is evident that Paul uses πνεῦμα as an anthropological term. Is it also true that he postulates an anthropological dualism, in which man is portrayed as consisting of antithetical elements? In his writings we can certainly find language which could suggest such dualism. In 1 Cor 5:3 he speaks of being absent in the body (σῶμα) but present in spirit (πνεῦμα). A similar mode of expression occurs in Col 2:5 where the apostle is absent in the flesh (σάρξ)[60] but present in the spirit (πνεῦμα). Discussing the remedial purposes of punishment for sin Paul writes of the destruction of the flesh (σάρξ) so that the

---

55 In Eph 4:23 (probably Deutero-Pauline) πνεῦμα τοῦ νοὸς ὑμῶν could be a genitive of apposition, in which case πνεῦμα and νοῦς would be synonymous. J.M. O'Connor, 'Truth: Paul and Qumran', RB 72 (1965), pp.29–76, cites examples of a similar use of synonymous terms in the Dead Sea Scrolls, where they are employed for the purposes of emphasis.
56 Rom 2:14.
57 Rom 2:15. Conscience is also connected with πνεῦμα in Rom 8:16 where it is the divine spirit which attests the Christian's sonship. In Rom 9:1 συνείδησις bears witness ἐν πνεύματι ἁγίῳ to the truth of what the apostle says.
58 1 Cor 14.   59 1 Cor 14:14.
60 In this sense there is no distinction between σῶμα and σάρξ.

spirit (πνεῦμα) might be saved.[61] These instances would suggest that he believes that man is divided into body (σῶμα or σάρξ) and spirit (πνεῦμα or ψυχή).[62]

Such an antithesis was common in pagan Greek thought. Plato had used the σῶμα/ψυχή distinction to assert the supremacy of reason over passion.[63] Philo adopted this position, describing reason and emotion as the twin parts of human personality, whose antithetical nature expresses itself in moral conflict.[64] It is because man's nature is mixed, i.e. he is also σάρξ,[65] that the spirit of God cannot permanently reside with him.[66] Furthermore, it is not only Diaspora Judaism which had adopted the popular Hellenistic distinction between body and soul.[67] The writings of Palestinian Judaism also furnish evidence of such a belief.[68] What needs to be borne in mind, however, is that the authors of Dispersion Judaism, in adopting the σῶμα/ψυχή distinction of the Hellenistic world did so in order to express an ethical rather than an ontological dualism.

The same can be said of Paul. In his writings the body is usually spoken of as σάρξ and associated with sin. However it is not equated with evil. Therefore he can say, 'Let us cleanse ourselves from all defilements σαρκὸς καὶ πνεύματος.'[69] He sees the aim of celibacy as the sanctification of σῶμα and πνεῦμα.[70] Although he uses it normally when thinking of man's moral frailty,[71] for Paul σάρξ is not always a term of moral opprobrium,[72] as it would be if he were a thorough-going dualist. Πνεῦμα, on the other hand, as in the anthropology of Hellenistic Judaism, in Pauline thought always carries with it moral and religious approval. Sanday and Headlam have described it as 'essentially that part of man which holds communion with God.'[73] Yet πνεῦμα is not so much the highest 'part' of man as man in his divine aspect.

---

61 1 Cor 5:5.
63 Rep. IV, 439E–441B.
65 Gig. 19; 28; 53.
66 *Aristeas* 277 goes further than postulating a moral ambiguity in man. It claims that man has a bias toward evil.
67 See also Sap Sol 9:5.
69 2 Cor 7:1.
62 See also 1 Thes 5:23; 1 Cor 7:34.
64 Praem. 63.

68 E.g. 2 Esdr 7:7f; Apoc. Mos. 32:4.
70 1 Cor 7:34.
71 This is not the same as Mk 14:38; Mt 26:41, τὸ μὲν πνεῦμα πρόθυμον, ἡ δὲ σὰρξ ἀσθενής, where physical rather than moral weakness is meant. W.L. Knox, *Some Hellenistic Elements in Primitive Christianity* (London, 1944), p. 3, sees the Synoptic usage as a reflection of Hellenistic psychology. However it is doubtful whether the borrowing is more than linguistic.
72 See also Rom 15:27 where there is no particular moral connotation in the use of the πνευματικός/σαρκικός antithesis. Paul is talking of the collection and argues that since they have received spiritual gifts they should give material (σαρκικός) gifts. For a similar use of σαρκικός see 1 Cor 9:11.
73 W. Sanday and A.C. Headlam, *The Epistle to the Romans* (ICC 5th ed. Edinburgh, 1902), p. 196.

The injunction to walk by the spirit and not to fulfil the lusts of the flesh in Gal 5:16 is a theological rather than an anthropological statement. Here Paul is not so much contrasting man's πνεῦμα with his σάρξ as describing the antithesis between the divine and human spheres. Similarly living κατὰ σάρκα which Paul says in Rom 8:13 leads to death is the opposite of living κατὰ πνεῦμα by which 'the base pursuits of the body (σῶμα)[74] are put to death.'[75] Πνεῦμα and σάρξ are used to categorize two spheres of existence rather than to describe two different constituents of man's nature. As F.J. Leenhardt has said of this use of the κατὰ σάρκα/πνεῦμα contrast, 'These formulae do not denote, as will be understood, a physiological locus of being, but a certain mode of living according to contrary realities to which are assigned a deterministic function for man's acts and thoughts.'[76] It certainly cannot be used as evidence of an anthropological dualism in Paul's thought, for where the apostle contrasts πνεῦμα with σῶμα/σάρξ, as in Hellenistic Jewish writings, it is to emphasize the gulf between God and the world or to express the moral conflict which is part of being human.

We have seen that Paul sometimes uses πνεῦμα and ψυχή co-terminously. Yet what of the occasions when he contrasts πνευματικός and ψυχικός? Do they reflect some kind of anthropological dualism? Writing to the Corinthians he says: 'Κἀγώ, ἀδελφοί, οὐκ ἠδυνήθην λαλῆσαι ὑμῖν ὡς πνευματικοῖς ἀλλ᾽ ὡς σαρκίνοις, ὡς νηπίοις ἐν Χριστῷ.'[77] The context of this statement is the presence of a group who were claiming superior knowledge and a greater share of the divine πνεῦμα.[78] Far from being πνευματικοί the apostle says that they are merely σαρκινοί or ψυχικοί.[79] Clearly Paul is referring to the gift of the divine πνεῦμα which is for the Christian alone. This is therefore not a statement about man in general but about the eschatological endowment of the divine spirit which is given to the elect. The same can be said of 1 Cor 15:44–46, where Paul is discussing the resurrection, not of humanity in general, but of man incorporated in Christ. The σῶμα ψυχικόν is raised as σῶμα πνευματικόν. It is unlikely that Paul means a body made of heavenly as opposed to earthly πνεῦμα. Such an interpretation of πνεῦμα as substantial would accord with Stoic beliefs, but not with what we know of Hellenistic Judaism's insistence upon the

---

74 The interchangeability of σῶμα and σάρξ in Pauline writing is reflected in the various textual variants of this verse.

75 *Contra* Sanday and Headlam, Romans, who interpret πνεῦμα here as referring to the human spirit.

76 F.J. Leenhardt, *The Epistle to the Romans* (London, 1961), p. 205.

77 1 Cor 3:1.

78 See Jude 19 where the author is condeming a similar 'gnostic' tendency. Far from being πνευματικοί, superior to the ψυχικοί, Jude says that they themselves have not got πνεῦμα. The divine spirit is clearly meant.

79 Ψυχικοί and σαρκινοί are synonymous here. See 1 Cor 3:3 where σαρκινοί is used.

immaterial nature of πνεῦμα. Rather, in keeping with his general usage, the apostle is emphasizing the life-giving element of the divine πνεῦμα. Hence he characterizes the existence of the first Adam as ψυχικός, but that of Christ, the last Adam, as πνευματικός:[80]

> οὕτως καὶ γέγραπται, Ἐγένετο ὁ πρῶτος ἄνθρωπος Ἀδαμ εἰς ψυχὴν
> ζῶσαν.[81] ὁ ἔσχατος Ἀδαμ εἰς πνεῦμα ζωοποιοῦν.[82]

Philo had also drawn the distinction between the πνοή given to man in Gen 2:7 and the πνεῦμα of creation in Gen 1:2. In accordance with Platonic theory he interpreted the latter as the creation of the heavenly man who had the full life-force of πνεῦμα, as opposed to the earthly man who had πνοή, a weakened form of it.[83] Although the Pauline antithesis is between ψυχή and πνεῦμα, the apostle may have been aware of a tradition, also to be found in Philo, which interpreted the variant accounts of creation in Genesis in Platonic terms. This would account for Paul emphasizing that it is not the first but the second which is πνευματικός, i.e. he denies the usual Platonic order of the archetype being the highest.[84] It is not the first creation which had the full divine πνεῦμα, but the second creation, located in Christ. If this exegesis is correct then this passage reflects Paul's views on the supremacy of Christ and his followers, over against the claims made by Judaism. It cannot, therefore, be used as evidence of his views on the nature of man apart from Christ.

The relationship between anthropology and theology

J.B. Lightfoot has said of Gal 5:5, 'It is almost always difficult and sometimes as here impossible to say when πνεῦμα refers directly to the Holy Spirit and when not.'[85] An analysis of Paul's use of πνεῦμα confirms the truth of this statement. It is frequently difficult to determine whether 'spirit' is being used in an anthropological or a theological sense, and this is because the two are closely related in the apostle's thinking.

R. Jewett has argued that for Paul πνεῦμα is always the divine πνεῦμα which is given to the individual Christian in such a way that he can identify it as his own. Only in 1 Cor 2:11 does the apostle distinguish between the human and the divine πνεῦμα, and that is because he wished to refute the gnostics' claim to possess the spirit of God.[86] Against such a thesis, which would deny that Paul uses πνεῦμα as an anthropological term, we have maintained that there are

---

80 For further use of the Adam-Christ typology see Rom 5:12–19.
81 Gen 2:7 LXX.
82 1 Cor 15:45. Cf. Rom 8:2, 10, where the πνεῦμα τῆς ζωῆς is also located in Christ.
83 See p. 35.   84 1 Cor 15:46.
85 J.B. Lightfoot, *Saint Paul's Epistle to the Galatians* (7th ed. London, 1881), p. 204.
86 R. Jewett, *Paul's Anthropological Terms* (Leiden, 1971), especially pp 167–200, 451–453.

instances where πνεῦμα refers to the spirit of man. However, we cannot agree with Kümmel when he asserts that πνεῦμα when used of man stands over against God.[87] Even in its anthropological usages, πνεῦμα is always holy; it is man in his divine aspect. Here Paul stands firmly in the tradition of Hellenistic Judaism. In the whole of the N.T. the only possible exception to spirit in man carrying connotations of the holy is Jas 4:5: πρὸς φθόνον ἐπιποθεῖ τὸ πνεῦμα ὃ κατῴκισεν ἐν ἡμῖν. This is a notoriously difficult verse, since it is amenable to more than one interpretation. If πνεῦμα is taken as the object of ἐπιποθεῖ then it is God who yearns over the spirit which He has implanted in man.[88] J.B. Mayor, however, regards πνεῦμα as the subject of the verb[89] and translates the sentence as 'the spirit which He made to dwell in us jealously yearns for the entire devotion of the heart'.[90] Alternatively, it is possible to interpret this verse in the light of the doctrine of the two *yeserim* and to see here a reference to the divinely implanted evil *yeser* which turns away from God towards envious desires. In spite of which 'the grace which He gives (i.e. the good *yeser*) is stronger'.[91] If such an interpretation is correct it is an unusual use of πνεῦμα in the New Testament, where, as in Hellenistic Judaism, 'spirit' is not normally associated with evil.

Certainly in Paul we find that πνεῦμα – even when it refers to the spirit of man – is always that of the transcendent, holy and divine.[92] Stoic belief in πνεῦμα as that which makes knowledge of God possible, since it constitutes the link between man and God, had been adopted by Philo and utilized by him in commending Judaism to his pagan contemporaries. For Paul also πνεῦμα is a term of kinship between God and man, and this explains why he does not clearly distinguish between its anthropological and theological usage. Πνεῦμα stresses man's affinity with God, just as σάρξ emphasizes his dissimilarity. The

---

87 W.G. Kümmel, *Man in the New Testament* (London, 1963), p. 44.
88 So F. Mussner, *Der Jacobusbrief* (Freiburg, 1964), p. 183, J. Moffatt, *The General Epistles* (MNTC London, 1938), pp. 60f, M. Dibelius, *Der Brief des Jacobus* (11th ed. Göttingen, 1964), pp.264–268, E. Schweizer, *Spirit of God* (London, 1960), p. 101, B. Reicke, *The Epistles of James, Peter and Jude* (New York, 1964), p. 46. This would take ἐπιποθεῖ in the sense of 'long for' rather than 'be jealous of'. Cf. Phil 1:8, 1 Pet 2:2.
89 So too the NEB.
90 J.B. Mayor, *The Epistle of St. James* (2nd ed. London, 1897), p. 137.
91 Jas 4:5.
92 So W.D. Davies, *Paul and Rabbinic Judaism* (2nd ed. London, 1955), p. 186. See also Heb 9:14 where Christ's passion is described, ὃς διὰ πνεύματος αἰωνίου ἑαυτὸν προσήνεγκεν ἄμωμον τῷ θεῷ. T.H. Robinson, *The Epistle to the Hebrews* (MNTC London, 1933), takes αἰωνίου as masculine nominative, i.e. as God or the holy spirit. Cf. textual variant ἁγίου in ℵ[c] p.35, 88, 206 etc. The NEB relates the phrase to the sacrifice rather than to Jesus and translates 'spiritual and eternal sacrifice'. However, we probably have here a reference to Christ's personality or eternal nature. So H. Montefiore, *The Epistle to the Hebrews* (BNTC London, 1954), pp. 154f.

former is that by which man is open to the transcendent life of God.[93]
B.E. Gärtner has shown how in 1 Cor 2:6–16 the apostle uses the Greek
principle of 'like by like'[94] in asserting that $\pi\nu\epsilon\tilde{\upsilon}\mu\alpha$ is the link between God
and man, given to man by God to enable knowledge of Himself: 'Among men
who knows what man is but the man's own spirit ($\pi\nu\epsilon\tilde{\upsilon}\mu\alpha$) within him? In
the same way, only the spirit of God knows what God is.'[95] This illustrates
how, in stressing the difference between the spirit of man and the spirit of
God, Paul does not identify the two; and yet, at the same time, his very
analogy is dependent upon their relatedness.

This is what R. Bultmann was attempting to point out when he made his now
famous statement about Pauline theology: 'Every assertion about God is simultaneously an assertion about man and *vice versa*. For this reason, and in this
sense, Paul's theology is at the same time, anthropology.'[96] One does not need
to accept Bultmann's interpretation of Pauline anthropological terms as an
expression of Existentialism, to acknowledge the truth of his insistence upon
the relatedness of the doctrines of God and man in the apostle's thought. This
is borne out by a study of the concept of $\pi\nu\epsilon\tilde{\upsilon}\mu\alpha$, where every assertion about
the spirit of God can be said to be simultaneously an assertion about the spirit
of man and *vice versa*.

In our examination of $\pi\nu\epsilon\tilde{\upsilon}\mu\alpha$ in Philo we have found two apparently contradictory statements about man's spirit; that as the divine aspect and link
between God and man it is the possession of all, and yet as the special $\pi\nu\epsilon\tilde{\upsilon}\mu\alpha$
given to the prophets it resides only within Judaism. The same two types of
statement are to be found in Paul. He too speaks of $\pi\nu\epsilon\tilde{\upsilon}\mu\alpha$ as man's spirit and
seems to assume that it is present in all men, whether Jew or Gentile, pagan or
Christian. However, Paul's predominant use of $\pi\nu\epsilon\tilde{\upsilon}\mu\alpha$ is of the eschatological
gift which he believed to be the prerogative of those who are 'in Christ'. Like
Philo Paul's main understanding of 'spirit' is a theological one. Both writers
are dominated in their thinking about $\pi\nu\epsilon\tilde{\upsilon}\mu\alpha$ by ideas about the spirit of God,
especially as it has been given to the elect. Where they differ is in the identifica-
tion of the chosen; for Philo it is Judaism which has been the recipient of this

---

93 See J.A.T. Robinson, *The Body* (London, 1952), pp. 19–20.
94 B.E. Gärtner, 'The Pauline and Johannine Idea of "to know God" against the
   Hellenistic Background', JTS 14 (1968), pp. 200–231.
95 1 Cor 2:11.
96 R. Bultmann, *The Theology of the New Testament* (London, 1952), Vol. I, p. 191.
   Bultmann has frequently been accused of reducing theology to anthropology on the
   basis of his statement, ibid., 'Therefore, Paul's theology can best be treated as his
   doctrine of man'. However, this needs to be read in context, for Bultmann goes on to
   say, 'He (Paul) sees man always in his relation to God'.

unique revelation, whereas for Paul it is the Christian community. But in both Paul and Philo, πνεῦμα, even when referring to the spirit of man, is never free from its divine signification. In this respect, we can see a theological orientation even in their anthropologies, since both writers are faithful to their Jewish heritage, according to which man is made in the image of God.

9
ΠΝΕΥΜΑ AND ESCHATOLOGY

Πνεῦμα as an eschatological category in contemporary Judaism

We have seen that, with the possible exception of the Wisdom of Solomon, Diaspora writers were not primarily orientated towards eschatological thinking. It is not, therefore, surprising that πνεῦμα is not used in an eschatological context in the literature of Hellenistic Judaism.[1] Here it is most often associated with the past rather than the future activity of God, and is predicated of the unique revelation granted to Israel's prophets (especially Moses). Since this revelation is regarded as unique and final, no special stress is placed upon any future inspiration. This does not mean that Hellenistic Jews ceased to believe that πνεῦμα was active. For Philo it is very much a permanent principle at work in the present, both in man and the universe. As such it is the power for everyday living; the divine in the midst; that which makes possible the beatific vision. However, such power is conceived of in terms related to the need for help in living out the revelation already given, rather than in those of bringing fundamentally new insights.

The conviction that God had already granted to Moses knowledge of His ultimate will and purposes was by no means confined to the Jews of the Dispersion. The ultimacy of the Torah was axiomatic for all Jews. Even those writers who wished to add to or elucidate Mosaic teaching felt obliged to publish their works under the name of one or other of the founding fathers. Hence the spate of pseudepigraphical literature in the inter-testamental period. However, the pseudepigraphical writers, by and large, represent theologies which look to the future rather than to the past and who therefore couch their thoughts in the form of Apocalyptic. It is to this literature of Palestine rather than to that produced by the Diaspora that we must look for the re-emergence of eschatology in the inter-testamental period. However, we must beware of assuming that these Apocalyptic writers were necessarily representative of Palestinian thinking. Certainly among ruling Sadducean circles in Jerusalem a theocratic attitude still reigned.

---

1 The only eschatological context in which πνεῦμα occurs in the literature of Hellenistic Judaism is Sib. Or. IV 46, 189, where it is the eschatological gift of a further period of life on earth imparted to the righteous dead at judgement.

Both Palestinian and Diaspora Judaism had, however, inherited a prophetic tradition in which the eschatological theme of the consummation of God's purposes was never completely submerged. What is more, a number of O.T. prophets had associated *ruach* with this final consummation. By translating *ruach* even when it occurred in these eschatological contexts in terms of πνεῦμα, the LXX translators had once more introduced Jewish theological ideas into the pagan Greek concept of πνεῦμα, baptizing it, as it were, in the waters of Jewish eschatology.

Thus πνεῦμα became associated with God's judgement. The LXX of Isa 4:4 reads ἐν πνεύματι κρίσεως καὶ πνεύματι καύσεως. In Isa 11:4 it is the breath (πνεῦμα) of God's lips which will slay the wicked.[2] Πνεῦμα also becomes associated with eschatological renewal. It is part of the prophetic hope for Israel that, as the elect of God, she will be renewed by the outpouring of His spirit: 'I will pour out my spirit on your offspring and my blessing on your children',[3] and 'I will give them a different heart and will put a new spirit into them'[4] (πνεῦμα καινὸν δώσω ἐν αὐτοῖς).[5] In Ezekiel's vision of a renewed, revivified Israel,[6] it is Jahweh's πνεῦμα which is to be breathed into the corpse of the present nation. Until the coming of πνεῦμα ἀφ' ὑψηλοῦ,[7] Israel only experiences the devastation of judgement. Then she will be given the spirit of grace and pity (πνεῦμα χάριτος καὶ οἰκτιρμοῦ).[8]

The O.T. regards the exceptional abilities of outstanding men to be due to their endowment with the spirit. This is particularly true of the prophet:[9]

> The spirit of the Lord is upon me
> because the Lord has anointed me;
> he has sent me to bring good news to the humble,
> to bind up the broken hearted,
> to proclaim liberty to the captives,
> and to release those in prison.[10]

Joel 2:28f looks forward to a universalizing of this prophetic experience, this endowment with the spirit. Just as Isa 11:2 looks to a pneumatic king: καὶ ἀναπαύσεται ἐπ' αὐτὸν πνεῦμα τοῦ θεοῦ; and Isa 42:1 to a spirit-filled servant, Israel: ἔδωκα τὸ πνεῦμά μου ἐπ' αὐτὸν, so Joel looks forward to the time when this will not be the spasmodic experience of the exceptional few, but the norm of the whole people of God.

---

2   See also Sap Sol 11:20 for the crushing might of God's πνεῦμα.
3   Isa 44:3.   4   Ezek 11:19.
5   See also Ezek 36:26.   6   Ezek 37.
7   Isa 32:15.   8   Zech 12:10.
9   Just as true prophecy is attributed to the activity of the spirit of God, so false prophecy can be described in terms of an evil spirit. So Zech 13:2 can look forward to the time when the unclean spirit, i.e. false prophecy, will be finally driven out.
10 Isa 61:1.

However, in spite of this inheritance from the O.T. where πνεῦμα is associated
with the eschaton, it is noticeable that πνεῦμα plays very little part in the eschatological thinking of the period. In the writings of the Diaspora this is hardly
surprising, since Hellenistic Judaism was not eschatologically orientated. What
is striking, however, is the minor role played by *ruach* in the eschatological
thinking of Palestinian Judaism. 'In the apocryphal and pseudepigraphical
writings there are only a few instances of the link between eschatological renewal
and endowment with the Spirit.'[11] *The Psalms of Solomon* 17:37 connects
some Messianic figure with pneumatic endowment:

> And (relying) upon God, throughout his days
> > he will not stumble;
> For God will make him mighty by means of (His)
> > holy spirit;
> And wise by means of the spirit of understanding,
> > with strength and righteousness.

Here the author has obviously drawn upon the figure of the ideal king in Isa 11.

Apart from this the only evidence we have of the spirit being part of the eschatological hope of our period is in the writings of the Qumran sect.[12] Here its
importance within an eschatological setting is all the more striking in view of
its paucity elsewhere. As F. Nötscher has pointed out, in the Qumran literature
ruach is a wide-ranging concept whose meanings are not always clear.[13] However,
there are a number of passages in which spirit clearly has an eschatological reference. Indeed it could be argued that this is the primary use to which the terms
'spirit of God' or 'holy spirit' are put in the Dead Sea Scrolls. We would agree
with W. Förster that, 'Die Sendung des Heiligen Geistes ist für Qumran . . . ein
eschatologisches Ereignis.'[14]

It is true that the *Dead Sea Scrolls* do not speak only of the spirit which is to
come. In the *Thanksgiving Hymns* God's holy spirit is depicted as a present
experience for which the author is grateful:

> I, the Master, know Thee O my God,
> > by the Spirit which Thou hast given to men,
> and by Thy Holy Spirit I have faithfully
> > hearkened to Thy marvellous counsel.[15]

---

11 E. Sjöberg, 'Πνεῦμα', TWNTE, Vol. VI (Grand Rapids, 1968), p. 384f.
12 For discussions of 'spirit' in the Dead Sea Scrolls see F. Nötscher, 'Geist und Geister in
den Texten von Qumran', *L'Evangile de Jean* (Recherches Bibliques, Louvain, 1958),
pp. 305–315; J. Coppens, 'Le Don de l'Esprit d'Après les Textes de Qumran et le
Quatrième Evangile', *Mélanges Bibliques rédigés en l'Honneur de André Robert* (Paris,
1957), pp. 209–223; W. Förster, 'Der Heilige Geist im Spätjudentum', NTS, 8
(1961–62), pp. 117–134.
13 F. Nötscher, op. cit., p. 305.
14 W. Förster, op. cit., p. 134, although we would disagree with him when he adds 'wie
überhaupt für die Gesamte Spätjudentums'.
15 1QH XII, 19.

Without God's spirit man can achieve nothing:

> The way of man is not established
>> except by the Spirit of God created for him
> to make perfect a way for the children of men,
>> that all His creatures might know the might of His power,
> and the abundance of His mercies
>> towards all the sons of His grace.[16]

However, it is mainly within the context of an eschatological conflict that the idea of spirit occurs at Qumran. The Covenanters were convinced that they were living in a time of crisis in which the spirit of God was locked in mortal combat with the spirit of evil. This is one of the major themes of the *War Rule*. Here the spirits of Beliar, the company of darkness, are described as fighting God and His hosts, the company of light.[17] The author looks forward to the imminent arrival of the archangel Michael who will overthrow the powers of evil and establish the reign of God.[18] Until that day the Covenanters believed that they were living 'during the domain of Satan'.[19]

In the *Community Rule*[20] the battle between the two spirits is seen as raging within man himself.[21] The opposing powers are variously contrasted; truth against falsehood, light against darkness, etc. The respective virtues and vices which they engender are also listed. Although the evil spirit is described as the enemy, nonetheless its ultimate origin in God himself is still affirmed. 1QS III, 25 explicitly states that God created both spirits.[22] No doubt this was an attempt to safeguard Judaism's monotheism. Certainly it avoids the ontological dualism of Zoroastrian belief.

The struggle between good and evil is described, on the one hand from a psychological point of view – as going on within man himself; and, on the other, from a cosmological point of view – as the opposition of the forces of good and evil in and beyond man and the universe. In Millar Burrows's opinion, 'The dualism of the Qumran theology is thus primarily ethical but with a cosmic dimension.'[23]

---

16 1QH IV 30–32.
17 1QM XIII, 10. Cf. CD. V, 18; VII, 19.
18 1QM XVII, 6–8.
19 1QS I, 18, 23.
20 1QS III, 18 – IV, 26.
21 Here there are obvious affinities with the later rabbinic doctrine of the two *yeserim*.
22 The description of the evil spirit as an angel (e.g. 1QS 111, 20 f.) is perhaps another way of asserting the ultimate sovereignty of God – even over evil.
23 M. Burrows, *More Light on the Dead Sea Scrolls* (London, 1958), p. 281.

The Qumran sect apparently regarded themselves as an eschatological community living in the 'meanwhile' of the crisis period.[24] For its members the
spirit was both a present possession and a future gift. J. Coppens has pointed
out the similarity of this view of the spirit with the Pauline notion of 'first
fruits'. 'Nous sommes donc bien autorisés, semble-t-il, à affirmer que la secte
de Qumran n'a pas cru la grande effusion eschatologique de l'Esprit Saint déjà
realisée, mais nous devons accorder à ses membres la croyance en une certaine
anticipation du don de l'esprit.'[25]

It is evident that the beliefs of the Qumran Covenanters offer the nearest
parallels to those of the N.T. authors for whom $\pi\nu\epsilon\hat{\upsilon}\mu\alpha$ is an eschatological
concept. Even so $\pi\nu\epsilon\hat{\upsilon}\mu\alpha$ plays a far greater part in the thinking of the Christian
community than in that of the sect. Although it would be dangerous to assume
that the importance of a concept like $\pi\nu\epsilon\hat{\upsilon}\mu\alpha$ can be judged merely by a word
count, the very frequency of the term is an indication of its centrality. $\Pi\nu\epsilon\hat{\upsilon}\mu\alpha$
and its cognates occur 409 times[26] and are used in every book of the N.T. with
the exception of 2 and 3 John.[27] It occurs most frequently in the Pauline
Epistles[28] and Luke–Acts. As we shall see, unlike the authors of the Diaspora,
those of the N.T. use the term predominantly in an eschatological context.

$\Pi\nu\epsilon\hat{\upsilon}\mu\alpha$ and the eschatological community

The concept of $\pi\nu\epsilon\hat{\upsilon}\mu\alpha$ as the power of God at work in the life of the church
is one which dominates the thinking of most N.T. writers. Whatever discre-
pancies may be found in the picture of the earliest Christian communities given
in the Pauline Epistles compared with that presented by Luke in Acts, both
ascribe a large place to the activity of the spirit within those communities.
Both are convinced that the presence of the spirit is evidence of the fact that
the Messianic Age has dawned.[29]

For Paul $\pi\nu\epsilon\hat{\upsilon}\mu\alpha$ is essentially an eschatological gift;[30] the power of the future
operative in the present. That is why he regards it as an anticipation, pledge or

24 See W. Förster, op. cit., p. 132.
25 J. Coppens, op. cit., p. 217.
26 See appendix C, p. 153. The number is 417 if we include the attitions of Codex
Bezae. See appendix E, p. 157.
27 See appendix C, p. 153 for the distribution of $\pi\nu\epsilon\hat{\upsilon}\mu\alpha$ throughout the N.T.
28 Paul has been called 'le théologien du $\pi\nu\epsilon\hat{\upsilon}\mu\alpha$ ἅγιον' by C. Spicq, *L'Epître aux Hébreux*
(2nd ed., Paris, 1952–53), p. 217.
29 Cf. Heb 2:4 where God has confirmed this fact 'by signs, by miracles, by manifold
works of power and by distributing the gifts of the holy spirit (καὶ πνεύματος ἁγίου
μερισμοῦ)'. Cf. Jn 3:34, οὐ γὰρ ἐκ μέτρου δίδωσιν τὸ πνεῦμα.
30 N.Q. Hamilton, *The Holy Spirit and Eschatology in Paul* (Edinburgh, 1957), stresses
the eschatological basis of Pauline pneumatology. He believes that for Paul the spirit
is primarily concerned with the future, albeit the power and life of the future at work
in the present.

down-payment – the ἀρραβών[31] of the final eschaton. Eph 1:13 describes the spirit as the ἀρραβών which had been promised to Israel and which the Christian community has now inherited.[32] Paul also uses the idea of first fruits (ἀπαρχή) to express his understanding of the church's reception of πνεῦμα. 'We to whom the spirit is given are first fruits of the harvest to come (αὐτοὶ τὴν ἀπαρχὴν τοῦ πνεύματος ἔχοντες ἡμεῖς).'[33] For the apostle, therefore, the existence of the church is a demonstration of the presence of the holy spirit and a sign of the imminent consummation of God's purposes. That consummation may lie in the future, but its 'earnest', the spirit, is the church's possession in the meantime. 'Διδόντα τὸ πνεῦμα αὐτοῦ τὸ ἅγιον εἰς ὑμᾶς.'[34]

Paul begins 1 Cor 12 with the phrase περὶ δὲ τῶν πνευματικῶν, i.e. concerning gifts bestowed by the spirit.[35] He goes on to enumerate some of these diverse gifts (wisdom, faith, healing, prophecy, glossolalia) in order to emphasize the unity of their source. 'There are varieties of gifts but the same spirit.'[36] 'All these gifts are the work of one and the same spirit.'[37] They are all but manifestations of the same power at work. God is one and therefore His spirit is one.

God is holy and therefore His holy spirit is closely involved in the work of sanctification,[38] the process of making men holy. The ethical nature of the spirit's activity is one of the most prominent features of Pauline pneumatology. 'Love,[39] joy,[40] peace,[41] kindness, goodness, fidelity, gentleness and self control'[42] are the fruits of the spirit. It is righteousness and peace rather than eating and drinking which are of the kingdom of God.[43] Eph 5:18 enjoins Christians

---

31 2 Cor 1:22; 5:5. In Eph 1:13; 4:30 the 'earnest of the spirit' is also linked with 'sealing'. Therefore, G.W.H. Lampe, *The Seal of the Spirit* (2nd ed., London, 1967), p.4, takes 2 Cor 1:22 as a reference to baptism, in which the holy spirit is bestowed. However, J.K. Parratt, 'The Holy Spirit and Baptism', Exp. T. 82 (1971), pp. 266–271, claims that there is no evidence of 'sealing' as a reference to baptism prior to 2 Clem. and the *Shepherd of Hermas*.

32 Cf. also Gal 3:14.   33 Rom 8:23, cf. Rom 9:16; 16:5.

34 1 Thes 4:8. The unusual construction εἰς ὑμας may be due to the influence of Ezek 37:14 LXX. Διδόντα emphasizes the timeless present.

35 Reading with J. Héring, *The First Epistle of Saint Paul to the Corinthians* (London, 1962), and H. Conzelmann, *Der erste Brief an die Korinther* (Göttingen, 1969), πνευματικῶς as neuter rather than masculine, i.e. spiritual gifts rather than spiritual men. For gifts of the spirit see also 1 Cor 14:1; 14:12.

36 1 Cor 12:4.   37 1 Cor 12:11.

38 Cf. Rom 15:16; 2 Thes 2:13. In 1 Pet 1:2, ἐν ἁγιασμῷ πνεύματος is another reference to sanctification. Here, like Mt 28:19; 2 Thes 2:13f and 2 Cor 13:14 it is part of a trinitarian formula. E.G. Selwyn, *The First Epistle of St. Peter* (2nd ed., London, 1947), p. 247, believes that 1 Pet 1:2 may have been influenced by the baptismal formula of Mt 28:19.

39 Of all the moral gifts bestowed by the spirit, Paul regards love as the most important. Cf. 1 Cor 4:21; Rom 5:5; Col 1:8; cf. also 2 Tim 1:7.

40 Joy is also associated with the spirit in Lucan theology. See for instance Lk 10:21.

41 For the association of peace with the spirit see 1 Thes 1:6.

42 Gal 5:22.   43 Rom 14:17.

not to be drunk with wine but to be filled with the spirit.[44] The theme of sober intoxication is also present in the Pentecost story of Acts 2, where Luke states that the spirit-filled disciples were at first thought by the crowd to be drunk.[45]

Πληρόω is a favourite verb used by the author of Luke–Acts to point to the spirit possession of the early church.[46] In Luke's Gospel such possession gives rise to prophecy.[47] Indeed it is largely in terms of the prophetic spirit that Luke views πνεῦμα.[48] He appears to equate the coming of the spirit with the prophetic power promised by Joel 2:28–32. In fact Luke explicitly states that the Pentecost experience was the fulfilment of this prophecy.[49]

'For the promise is to you, and to your children, and to all who are far away, everyone whom the Lord our God may call.'[50] Unlike Israel's major prophets, however, Luke stands firmly within the tradition which regards prophecy as essentially an ecstatic condition. Hence the use of πληρόω. Luke's understanding of the spirit is not only of its invasive nature, but also of its power. It is the δύναμις of the holy spirit with which Jesus himself was anointed,[51] which is promised by him to his disciples.[52] The various miracles and mighty works performed by the apostles in the Book of Acts, although not explicitly attributed to the spirit, are obviously portrayed as the outcome of their reception of pneumatic power. Thus Simon coveted the ἐξουσία of the spirit.[53] The violence of any such spirit possession is indicated in Acts 8:39, where, just as Elijah was bodily removed from one place to another,[54] so the spirit snatches Philip away.[55]

---

44 Cf. Philo's use of the oxymoron, behind which may lie a refutation of Dionysiac rites.
45 Acts 2:13, 15.
46 Acts 2:4; 4:8; 4:31; 13:9. See also Luke 4:1 where πληρόω is substituted for Mk 1:12 ἐκβάλλω.
47 E.g. Lk 1:41, 67.   48 Cf. Lk 1:80; 2:25, 26, 27, Acts 11:28; 13:2; 21:11; 28:25.
49 It is interesting to note that in the Pentecost story the reception of the spirit is associated with prayer. It was whilst they were praying that the spirit filled the room. Cf. Lk 11:13 where, according to Luke, it is πνεῦμα ἅγιον which will be granted in answer to prayer. The Matthean version (Mt 7:11) has ἀγαθά instead. T.W. Manson, *The Sayings of Jesus* (London, 1949), p. 82, regards the Lucan version as probably more original.
50 Acts 2:39.
51 In the account of the sermon at Nazareth (Lk 4:16–30) Luke implies that Jesus was anointed with the spirit at least from the outset of his ministry. Hence, Jesus applies the prophecy of Isa 61:1f to himself, 'The Spirit of the Lord is upon me, because he has anointed me'. Cf. Acts 10:38. This accords with the synoptic tradition about Christ's baptism. However, Acts 2:23 states that the spirit was given at his exaltation.
52 Acts 1:8.   53 Acts 8:19.
54 Cf 2 Kgs 2:16–18.
55 Revelation also has this ecstatic view of prophecy. Cf. Rev 1:10; 4:2; 21:10; 17:3.

The impersonal nature of such descriptions of the spirit in Acts has often been commented upon.[56] However, this is by no means the whole picture; Luke also uses very personal language of the spirit. It can be lied to,[57] fought against[58] or put to the test.[59] As the medium through which the risen Christ instructs his apostles,[60] the spirit is represented as personally directing the missionary strategy of the church. It directs Philip and Peter,[61] instigates the mission of Paul and Barnabas[62] and, throughout Paul's subsequent journeys, determines their route.[63] What is more, the momentous decision of the Council of Jerusalem to admit Gentiles to full membership of the church is attributed to the spirit.[64] In fact this approval is seen as merely confirmatory, for the gift of the spirit had been granted to the Gentiles prior to any decision of the Jerusalem church and this already constituted God's approval. The personal guidance of the holy spirit is not confined to the apostles, neither does it end with the establishment of the Gentile mission. Church leaders are still under its sway and receive their authority from the spirit.[65]

Primarily in Acts the miraculous power of the holy spirit is the power of preaching. This, rather than healing miracles, dominates the book, especially from the moment that Paul and Barnabas set out on their mission to the Gentiles. This particular understanding is not confined to the second half of Acts; it can be found at the very outset. Peter's preaching immediately follows the reception of the holy spirit at Pentecost.[66] It is because they were filled with the spirit that the disciples 'spoke the word of God with boldness',[67] and it is to Jesus that both they and the spirit witness.[68] Just as Acts opens with powerful prophetic testimonies to Jesus as Messiah, so Luke's Gospel begins with a series of prophecies which bear witness to the birth of Christ.[69] The author sees this re-emergence of prophecy as due to the outpouring of the spirit.[70] It is above all else as the power granted for the church's preaching that the gift is portrayed in Lucan theology. Hence, the spirit is primarily the prophetic spirit which we find so prominent in the writings of Hellenistic Judaism.

---

56 E.g. G.W.H. Lampe, 'The Holy Spirit in the Writings of St. Luke', *Studies in the Gospels* (Essays in memory of R.H. Lightfoot), ed. D.E. Nineham (Oxford, 1955), p. 163, and A.R.C. Leaney, *The Gospel According to St. Luke* (BNTC, 2nd ed., London, 1966), p.40.

57 Acts 5:3.   58 Acts 7:51

59 Acts 5:9.   60 Acts 1:2.

61 Cf. 'Εἶπεν δὲ τὸ πνεῦμα' in Acts 8:29; 10:19; 11:2. In Acts 10:19 the spirit who speaks to Peter is not differentiated from the angel (10:3) who directs Cornelius.

62 Acts 13:2, 4.

63 Acts 16:6f; 19:21; 20:22f; 21:4. See also Lk 4:14 where Jesus is motivated by the spirit to return to Galilee. For the spirit motivating a change of place in Lucan theology see K.L. Schmidt, *Der Rahmen der Geschichte Jesus* (Berlin, 1919), p. 37.

64 Acts 15:28.   65 Acts 20:28. Cf. 2 Tim 1:7.

66 Acts 2:14–39.   67 Acts 4:31.

68 Acts 5:32.   69 Lk 1:47–55; 1:68–79; 2:29–32.

70 Lk 1:41; 1:67; 2:26f.

Although, unlike Luke, Paul attributes a major place to the inner, ethical workings of the spirit, he too occasionally associates its gift with the church's mission to preach the gospel. To the Thessalonians he writes that the gospel which he proclaimed to them did not come merely in words but 'ἐν δυνάμει καὶ ἐν πνεύματι ἁγίῳ'.[71] A similar contrast between mere words and the power of Christian preaching is made in 1 Cor 2:4:

> The word I spoke, the gospel I proclaimed, did not sway you with subtle arguments; it carried conviction by spiritual power (ἐν ἀποδείξει πνεύματος καὶ δυνάμεως).[72]

Also, in Rom 15:19 Paul describes bringing the gospel to the Gentiles 'by word and deed, by the force of miraculous signs[73] and by the power of the holy spirit[74] (ἐν δυνάμει σημείων καὶ τεράτων ἐν δυνάμει πνεύματος)'.

However, unlike Luke, Paul seems very reluctant to associate πνεῦμα with prophecy. It is not that he finds no place for the Christian prophet. On the contrary, he writes to the Thessalonians, 'Do not stifle inspiration and do not despise prophetic utterances.'[76] It is rather that, unlike Acts, the Pauline Epistles display a certain wariness of any ecstatic phenomena. Far from becoming possessed of any ecstasy, it is for the prophet himself to control his own inspiration. In Ephesians (probably a Deutero-Pauline work) prophecy is also non-ecstatic in character. Prophets, along with apostles, are now part of the institutional leadership of the church and through them God has revealed His will for the Gentiles to be fellow heirs.[78] The sword which the spirit gives is not that of ecstatic utterance, but the word of God.[79]

---

71 1 Thes 1:5.
72 J. Héring, *The First Epistle of Saint Paul to the Corinthians* (London, 1962), reads this as a subjective genitive, i.e. proof coming from the spirit and power. A. Schlatter, *Die Korintherbriefe* (Stuttgart, 1962), takes it to be an objective genitive, i.e. proof consisting in spirit and power. The NEB translation leaves the matter open. Cf. 1 Cor 4:20 'The kingdom of God is not a matter of talk but of power.'
73 Gal 3:5 also connects the possession of the spirit with the working of miracles.
74 J.K. Parratt, Exp.T. 79 (1967–68), suggests that the subject of the sentence, the one who supplies the spirit, is not God but the gifted individual (possibly Paul himself). It is true that Paul regarded the power to work miracles as a mark of true apostleship (2 Cor 12:13), and in Rom 1:11 wants to bring some χάρισμα πνευματικόν to make the community strong. Yet here the more natural meaning is that it is God who is the bestower of the spirit.
75 This reading is attested by A C D F G. Cf. Rom 15:13. P46 D G add αὐτοῦ. P46 ℵ L P Orig. Chrys. add θεοῦ. B alone has πνεύματος without addition.
76 1 Thes 5:19 τὸ πνεῦμα μὴ σβέννυτε, προφητείας μὴ ἐξουθενεῖτε. Cf. 1 Cor 14:37 where προφήτης is synonymous with πνευματικός.
77 1 Cor 14:32 καὶ πνεύματα προφητῶν προφήταις ὑποτάσσεται.
78 Eph 3:5.
79 Eph 6:17 τὴν μάχαιραν τοῦ πνεύματος, ὅ ἐστιν ῥῆμα θεοῦ. Cf. Hos 6:6 (MT 6:5); Isa 49:2; 2 Cor 6:7.

For Paul, the church is composed of those who have received the gift of the spirit. 'For all who are moved by the spirit of God are the sons of God.'[80] Just as the possession of the spirit was regarded by Israel as the authentication of her claims to revelation, so the church's possession of the spirit constitutes her claim to be the true Israel. 'We are the circumcision who worship by the spirit of God.'[81] The Christian community is now the true and only heir to God's revelation.

In Acts the church and the spirit are inextricably connected by the link made by the author between the bestowal of the spirit and initiation into the eschatological community.[82] Acts is not consistent as to the exact moment of the spirit's bestowal. Sometimes, as in the case of the Gentiles at Antioch, the gift of the spirit precedes any initiation rite.[83] More usually it is depicted as following repentance and baptism.[84] However, on other occasions it is associated with the laying on of hands.[85] We are told that the former disciples of John had been baptized but had not received the spirit on the occasion of their baptism. They did so only after hands had been laid upon them.[86] Thus it is not baptism as such which is shown to be the characteristic of the Christian community. 'John, as you know, baptized with water.'[87] It is baptism with the spirit which constitutes the eschatological community. J.D.G. Dunn[88] has shown that $\beta\alpha\pi\tau\acute{\iota}\zeta\epsilon\iota\nu$ was used as a metaphor for entry into union with Christ, i.e. for conversion.[89] It is sometimes used as a metaphor for the coming of the spirit.

J.K. Parratt has shown that in the Pauline Epistles as well as in Acts, baptism itself is not necessarily regarded as the medium or occasion of the bestowal of the spirit. The coming of the spirit is associated with the whole process of initiation.[90] It is in terms of faith[91] rather than any rite that Paul primarily

---

80 Rom 8:14. Cf. 1 Cor 3:1.   81 Phil 3:3. Cf. Jn 4:21–24.

82 See also baptism $\epsilon\grave{\iota}s$ $\tau\grave{o}$ $\check{o}\nu o\mu\alpha$ $\tau o\hat{\upsilon}$ $\pi\alpha\tau\rho\grave{o}s$ $\kappa\alpha\grave{\iota}$ $\tau o\hat{\upsilon}$ $\upsilon\grave{\iota}o\hat{\upsilon}$ $\kappa\alpha\grave{\iota}$ $\tau o\hat{\upsilon}$ $\grave{\alpha}\gamma\acute{\iota}o\upsilon$ $\pi\nu\epsilon\acute{\upsilon}\mu\alpha\tau os$ in Mt 28:19. Even if the trinitarian formula is comparatively late the association of the spirit with baptism is clearly not.

83 Acts 10:45, 47.   84 Acts 2:38.

85 Acts 8:15, 17, 18.   86 Acts 19:2.

87 Acts 1:5; cf. Acts 11:16.

88 J.D.G. Dunn, *Baptism in the Holy Spirit* (London, 1970) *passim*.

89 In Heb 6:4 such conversion is described in terms of enlightenment, of tasting the gifts of heaven, of sharing the holy spirit and of experiencing spiritual energies of the world to come. Since $\phi\omega\tau\acute{\iota}\zeta\omega$ is used of baptism in later ecclesiastical writers, H.Montefiore, *The Epistle to the Hebrews* (BNTC London, 1964), p. 109 thinks that here it may be a reference to baptism. However, as A. Nairne, *The Epistle to the Hebrews* (Cambridge, 1922), p.67, pointed out, Heb may have influenced later writers to use $\phi\omega\tau\acute{\iota}\zeta\omega$ of baptism. J. Héring, *L'Epître aux Hébreux* (Neuchâtel, 1954), p.59, also thinks that in Heb it does not refer to baptism and is merely an extension of a common metaphor, light (cf Jn 8:12; Mt 5:15; 2 Cor 4:6; Eph 1:18; 3:9).

90 J.K. Parratt, 'The Holy Spirit and Baptism: Part II the Pauline Evidence', Exp.T.82 (1971), pp. 266–271.

91 Acts also stresses the importance of faith and obedience for the reception of the spirit. See Acts 5:32; 6:5; 7:55; 9:17; 10:44; 11:24; 13:52.

describes the possession of the spirit. The reception of the spirit through faith rather than by the works of the Jewish law is one of the major themes of Galatians. 'Did you receive the spirit by the keeping of the law or by believing the gospel message?' (ἐξ ἔργων νόμου τὸ πνεῦμα ἐλάβετε ἢ ἐξ ἀκοῆς πίστεως).'[92]

To have faith is to live and walk by the spirit rather than by the law,[93] for it is that spirit working through faith which achieves the Christian's righteousness.[94] Paul can speak of faith as the necessary prerequisite for the reception of the spirit.[95] On the other hand he can also describe the possession of the spirit as a necessary prerequisite for faith. 'No one can say, "Jesus is Lord" except under the influence of the holy spirit.'[96] Obviously, for Paul to say that a Christian is one who has received the spirit, is the same as saying that he has faith and *vice versa*.

Above all, for both Luke and Paul, the place of faith and the home of the spirit is the church. As G.S. Duncan has said, 'In the New Testament the sphere of the spirit's working is thought primarily as the Christian fellowship and not the Christian individual.'[97] E. Best has pointed out the same corporate emphasis in the Pauline use of ἐν χριστῳ. 'The formula describes the relationship of Christ to the believer.' It is 'not individualistic but social in its implications'.[98] It was A. Deissmann who originally stressed the importance of ἐν χριστῳ in Pauline theology. He went so far as to say that it was the characteristic expression of Paul's Christianity.[99] Furthermore, Deissmann saw a close connection between ἐν χριστῳ and ἐν πνεύματι, pointing out their parallel uses.[100] The formula 'in the spirit' occurs in Paul's writings only 19 times compared with 164 instances of 'in Christ'. However, as Deissmann has seen, in all these places it is connected with the same specifically Pauline ideas which elsewhere are associated with the formula 'in Christ'.[101]

---

92 Gal 3:2 ἀκοῆς πίστεως, i.e. a hearing which leads to faith. Cf. Acts 1:4; Eph 2:14–18; Gal 4:5.

93 Gal 5:25.   94 Gal 5:5.

95 Gal 3:14 ἵνα τὴν ἐπαγγελίαν τοῦ πνεύματος λάβωμεν διὰ τῆς πίστεως. E. Burton, *The Epistle to the Galatians* (ICC Edinburgh, 1921), takes πνεύματος . . . τῆς πίστεως as a metonymic phrase – 'the promised spirit'. However it could be a genitive of characteristic, i.e. characterized by faith, as in 2 Cor 4:13. Cf. Gal 6:1 'spirit of meekness'.

96 1 Cor 12:3.

97 G.S. Duncan, *The Epistle of Paul to the Galatians* (MNTC London, 1934), p.178.

98 E. Best, *One Body in Christ* (London, 1955), p. 3.

99 A. Deissmann, *Paul: a Study in Social and Religious History* (2nd ed. New York, 1927), p.140.

100 See A. Deissmann, op. cit., pp. 139–140, where these are listed.

101 Deissmann, op. cit., p. 138.

A similar parallel can be drawn between Paul's references to the spirit and to Christ in the believer. On some occasions he mentions Christ who is in the Christian;[102] on others it is the spirit in the Christian.[103] There does not appear to be any appreciable difference in meaning. In 1 Cor 6:17 being joined to the Lord is being joined to the one spirit. To follow Best in regarding ἐν χριστῷ as a formula of incorporation into the Christian community[104] makes these parallels even more illuminating.

Thus the image of the church as the temple in whom the spirit dwells is only another example of the corporate nature of Pauline pneumatology. Writing to the Corinthians Paul says, 'Surely you know that you are God's temple where the spirit of God dwells?'[105] To the Romans he can also speak of the church as the dwelling place of God's spirit.[106] Ephesians uses another corporate image, that of the church as the body of Christ, with which to associate the spirit. 'There is one body and one spirit.'[107] The author appeals to the spirit as the principle of unity (ἡ ἑνότης τοῦ πνεύματος) which ought to be at work in the church.[108]

One of the most explicit statements of the church's claim to possess the holy spirit is to be found in the Johannine writings. The author of the Fourth Gospel boldly asserts that it is not the Jerusalem temple but the church which is the sphere of true worship.[109] It is not to the manna of Moses that one must look for true sustenance,[110] but to Christ the bread of life, mediated through the church's sacraments.[111] These are life-giving because the spirit works through them. 'Τὸ πνεῦμά ἐστιν ζωοποιοῦν, ἡ σὰρξ οὐκ ὠφελεῖ οὐδέν.'[112] Unlike the water of the Feast of Tabernacles it is the living waters of the spirit[113] which are promised to Jesus's disciples after his glorification.[114] These images are designed to show the superiority of the Christian cult over that of Judaism.

---

102 Gal 2:20; Rom 8:10; Col 1:27.
103 Rom 8:9f; 1 Cor 3:16; 6:19.
104 *Contra* A. Deissmann, op. cit., pp. 138, 140 who interprets ἐν χριστῷ as an expression of Hellenistic mysticism.
105 1 Cor 3:16. Cf. 1 Cor 6:19 where the church as the recipient of the spirit is seen as united to Christ just as surely as in intercourse one's body is joined to a harlot. For further uses of the image of the church as a temple see 2 Cor 6:16 and 1 Pet 2:2.
106 Rom 8:11. Cf. 2 Tim 1:14.
107 Eph 4:4. Cf. 1 Cor 12:13 'For indeed we were all brought into one body by baptism, in the one spirit.'
108 Eph 4:3. Cf. 1 Cor 12:4, 11. In 2 Cor 12:18 to walk by the same spirit means being of the same mind; having a united course. Cf. Phil 2:5.
109 Jn 4:23f.   110 Jn 6:31f.
111 Jn 6:48–58.   112 Jn 6:63.
113 For living water as a symbol of the holy spirit in late Judaism see Strack-Billerbeck, Vol. II, pp. 434f.
114 Jn 7:39.

Like Paul, the author of the Fourth Gospel characterizes the latter by σάρξ.
Only the worship of the Christian community possesses πνεῦμα.

Similarly it is only Jesus's followers who are given the holy spirit. 'Καὶ τοῦτο
εἰπὼν ἐνεφύσησεν καὶ λέγει αὐτοῖς, Λάβετε πνεῦμα ἅγιον.'[115] The spirit-paraclete
will be sent to the disciples, for they alone will be able to receive him since 'the
world neither sees nor knows him.'[116] Unlike πνεῦμα in Judaism which has been
transient and partial, the spirit promised to the new Israel is to be a permanent
possession. John's frequent use of the verb μένω conveys this permanent, abiding
nature of the spirit. Sometimes μένω is used with reference to the mutual
indwelling of God and Christ;[117] at others it describes the mutual indwelling of
the believer with Christ[118] or God.[119] In Jn 14:17 it is the paraclete who will
remain forever with the church.[120] In the spirit the church claims to possess a
constant guide to all truth.[121]

In Johannine thought the nature of that truth is quite specific; it is located in
the person of Jesus. The spirit-paraclete acts as a constant reminder of and
witness to Christ. 'Ὁ δὲ Παράκλητος, τὸ πνεῦμα τὸ ἅγιον . . . ἐκεῖνος ὑμᾶς
διδάξει πάντα καὶ ὑπομνήσει ὑμᾶς πάντα ἃ εἶπον ὑμῖν ἐγώ.'[122] One of the main
functions of the paraclete is to bear witness to Jesus. He will convince the world
of Christ's ultimate vindication by God.[123] Just as the paraclete's function is to
witness to Jesus, so it is the disciples' task also to bear witness to him. 'And
you also are my witnesses, because you have been with me from the first.'[124]
Because of this stress upon the witnessing function of the paraclete in John's
Gospel, C.K. Barrett connects παράκλητος with παράκλησις, i.e. the exhorta-
tion of Christian preaching.[125] O. Betz, however, regards παράκλητος as a
derivative of παρακαλεῖν in its passive sense of an advocate or witness called
to bear testimony in a court of law.[126] He also connects the roles of advocate

---

115 Jn 20:22.
116 Jn 14:17.
117 Jn 14:10.
118 Jn 8:56; 15:4–7; 14:17; 1 Jn 2:6, 24, 27.
119 1 Jn 4:16.
120 Cf. 1 Jn 3:24; 4:13 where mutual indwelling is authenticated by the spirit.
121 Jn 16:13 τὸ πνεῦμα τῆς ἀληθείας, ὁδηγήσει ὑμας εἰς τὴν ἀλήθειαν πᾶσαν as in A B pc.
    The variant ἐν τῇ ἀληθείᾳ πάσῃ 'in the whole sphere of truth' (in ℵ D W 33) is
    accepted by Barrett, John, p. 407.
122 Jn 14:26.
123 Jn 16:10.
124 Jn 15:27.
125 C.K. Barrett, 'The Holy Spirit in the Fourth Gospel', JTS 1 (1950), pp. 1–15.
126 O. Betz, *Der Paraklet* (Leiden, 1963), especially pp. 36–55 which examines the
    forensic use of the term in Israelite law courts, and pp. 56–72 which looks at
    παράκλητος in the light of the Qumran literature.

and intercessor,[127] pointing out that in God's law court any spokesman also acts as an intercessor.[128] It would seem that in concentrating upon its forensic use Betz has unduly limited the meaning of παράκλητος even in the sense of intercessor. When Philo uses the word it is by no means confined to angelic mediators. God's forgiving nature, the holiness of the patriarchs and penitence are three παράκλητοι.[129] When John speaks of the paraclete it is hardly in terms of an intercessor before the throne of God. The paraclete acts as an advocate of Jesus and witnesses to him. Furthermore, its advocacy is not before God but to the disciples. In its role as advocate and witness the paraclete has Jesus as its subject and not, as one would expect if it were used in the sense of an angelic mediator, the disciples or the world. Certainly, as we have seen, witness is an important part of the paraclete's function, but it is only one of a number of functions or facets.[130] Probably it is therefore best to translate the word παράκλητος as 'helper',[131] since the others which have been suggested (advocate, intercessor, comforter) are too limiting.

In 1 John the christological content of the spirit's witness is even more emphasized than in the Fourth Gospel. Only those who acknowledge the Incarnation can be said to have the spirit.[132] In 1 Jn 5:6, 8 πνεῦμα is described as a fellow witness with blood and water. That verse 6 is a reference to events in the past, i.e. Jesus's baptism and death, is clear from the use of ἐλθών. Probably the author wished to emphasize that Christ's passion, as much as his baptism, was a witness to his Messianic identity. To both central events in the incarnate life of Christ the spirit bore testimony.[133] However, the difficulty arises in verse 8 with the statement that the witness of the water and the blood is united with

---

127 'Intercessor' would be the correct translation of παράκλητος if it were derived from παρακαλεῖν in its active sense. Thus S. Mowinckel, 'Die Vorstellung des Spätjudentums vom heiligen Geist als Fürsprecher und der johanneische Paraklet', ZNTW 32 (1933) pp.97–130, and N. Johansson, *Parakletoi* (Lund, 1940), view the Johannine Paraclete against the background of inter-testamental beliefs about angelic intercessors. The other active meaning of παρακαλεῖν, to comfort, has been upheld by J.G. Davies, 'The Primary Meaning of παράκλητος', JTS 4 (1953), pp.35–38, following E.C. Hoskyns and F.N. Davey, *The Fourth Gospel* (London, 1940), Vol. II, p.550.
128 O. Betz, op. cit., pp. 73–116.
129 Philo, Praem. 166f. Cf. Spec. Leg. 1, 235–238 where conscience is the παράκλητος of the penitent.
130 See R.E. Brown, 'The Paraclete in the Fourth Gospel', NTS 13 (1967), p. 118.
131 R. Bultmann, *The Gospel of John: A Commentary* (Oxford, 1971), pp.566–572, has seen the origin of the paraclete in the Proto-Mandean figure of Yawar, the Helper. In adopting the term 'helper' above, no acceptance of Bultmann's identification is intended. For a criticism of Bultmann's thesis see J. Behm, TWNTE V, pp.800–814, N. Johansson, *Parakletoi*, p.285, W. Michaelis, 'Zur Herkunft des johanneischen Paraklet-Titels,' *Coniectanea Neotestamentica* XI (1947, Friedricksen Festschrift), pp. 147–162.
132 1 Jn 4:2f; 5:6.
133 So A.E. Brooke, *The Johannine Epistles* (ICC Edinburgh, 1912), p.133.

that of the spirit. J.D.G. Dunn[134] has argued against those who see here a reference to the sacraments.[135] He claims that, since αἷμα is never used by itself of
the eucharist, either in the N.T. or in the writings of Ignatius which are normally
cited in favour of a eucharistic interpretation, as in verse 6 the reference here is
to the incarnate life of Christ, to which the spirit bears witness.

The Lucan, Pauline and Johannine writings may emphasize different aspects of
the work of the spirit, but all are agreed that it is the church which is the *locus*
of that spirit. They may not all reflect an identical eschatology, but they all
regard the spirit as the means by which eschatological hopes are 'realized'[136] in
the present. Furthermore, as the writers of Hellenistic Judaism claimed a special
pneumatic endowment for Israel, so the church's affirmation of her present
possession of the spirit constitutes her claim to be the eschatological community
of the new Israel.

Spirits – holy and unholy

In company with their Jewish predecessors, be they Palestinian or Hellenistic,
for N.T. writers πνεῦμα is predominantly 'the spirit of God'. This is particularly
evident in the Pauline writings where, not only does πνεῦμα θεοῦ occur eleven
times,[137] but the identification between God and the spirit is clearly made. In
1 Cor 3:16 the apostle can speak of θεός or πνεῦμα θεοῦ interchangeably. To
be the temple of God (ναὸς θεοῦ)[138] means that the spirit of God dwells in you
(τὸ πνεῦμα τοῦ θεοῦ ἐν ὑμῖν οἰκεῖ).[139] In Rom 8:11 'τὸ πνεῦμα τοῦ ἐγείραντος
τὸν Ἰησοῦν ἐκ νεκρῶν' is 'ὁ (i.e. God) ἐγείρας ἐκ νεκρῶν Χριστὸν Ἰησοῦν'.

Just as we have seen that the writers of Hellenistic Judaism used of the spirit
terms which were normally associated with and confined to God, so we can
see the same process in the Pauline letters. Ἅγιος was one of the most distinctive
attributes of God within Judaism, and Paul can sometimes use 'spirit of God'

134 J.D.G. Dunn, *Baptism in the Holy Spirit* (London, 1970), pp.200–204.
135 E.g. C.H. Dodd, *The Johannine Epistles* (MNTC London, 1946), pp. 130f.
136 See C.K. Barrett, *The Gospel According to St. John* (London, 1955), pp. 45f and
    idem, 'The Holy Spirit in the Fourth Gospel', JTS 1 (1950), pp. 1–15.
137 1 Cor. 2:12, 14; 3:16; 7:40; 12:3; 2 Cor 3:3; Rom 8:9, 11, 14; Phil 3:3; Eph 4:30.
138 See also Eph 2:20–22 where the image of the Christian community as a building is
    developed. 'You are built upon the foundation stone laid by the apostles and prophets,
    and Christ Jesus himself is the foundation stone (cf. Isa 28:16). In him the whole
    building is bounded together and grows into a holy temple (εἰς ναὸν ἅγιον) in the
    Lord. In him you too are being built with all the rest into a spiritual dwelling (εἰς
    κατοικητήριον τοῦ θεοῦ ἐν πνεύματι).' *Contra* this NEB translation, T.K. Abbott,
    The Epistles to the Ephesians and the Colossians (ICC Edinburgh, 1897), who
    translates ἐν πνεύματι as an instrumental dative, 'by the spirit', and sees here a
    reference to the agency of the holy spirit.
139 Cf. Rom 8:9 where this phrase recurs.

interchangeably with 'holy spirit'. Thus in 1 Cor 12:3 ἐν πνεύματι θεοῦ is synonymous with ἐν πνεύματι ἀγίῳ.[140] The formulation in Eph 4:30 τὸ πνεῦμα τὸ ἅγιον τοῦ θεοῦ is an unusual one. Usually in Pauline writing, to call the spirit 'holy' is the same as saying that it is τοῦ θεοῦ. However it is notice-able that Paul tends to use ἅγιος more of the ethical results produced by the activity of the spirit upon man, than of the nature of God. He speaks more of God's activity than of His essence. Thus the holy spirit is involved in the work of sanctification,[141] inspiring in the believer the justice, peace and joy of the kingdom of God.[142] It is the gifts of the spirit which are a Christian's commen-dation in 2 Cor 6:6, and that these gifts are ethical in nature is evident from the context, where they are associated with patience, kindness and love. Similarly in Rom 5:5 it is God's love[143] which 'has flooded our inmost heart through the holy spirit He has given us (διὰ πνεύματος ἀγίου τοῦ δοθέντος ἡμῖν)'.

Paul, like the writers of the O.T., connects the holy nature of God with the ethical nature of His demands upon men.[144] The sentiment of Lev 20:7f, 'Hallow yourselves and be holy, because I the Lord your God am holy . . . I am the Lord who hallows you', finds its echo in the Pauline Epistles. See for example 1 Thes 4:7f:

> For God called us to holiness, not impurity. Anyone
> therefore who flouts these rules is flouting, not man,
> but God who bestows upon us His holy spirit
> (διδόντα τὸ πνεῦμα αὐτοῦ τὸ ἅγιον εἰς ὑμᾶς).[145]

Here the author stresses the relationship between the moral nature of God and the moral effects of his spirit at work in men.

Yet precisely because of its holy nature, like Philo Paul is at pains to stress the qualitative difference between πνεῦμα and the world: 'ἡμεῖς δὲ οὐ τὸ πνεῦμα τοῦ κόσμου ἐλάβομεν ἀλλὰ τὸ πνεῦμα τὸ ἐκ τοῦ θεοῦ'.[146] In this passage there may well be an echo of the *anima mundi* belief of the Stoa. However the way

140 The NEB takes ἐν as instrumental, 'under the influence of the Spirit of God.' However, the dative can be understood as indicating sphere, i.e. in the area of the spirit's influence.
141 Rom 15:16.
142 Rom 14:17. For righteousness, peace and joy as fruits of the spirit see Gal 5:22; Rom 15:13. In 1 Thes 1:6 the holy spirit is specifically associated with joy.
143 Reading with C.K. Barrett, Romans, W. Sanday and A.C. Headlam, Romans, C.H. Dodd *The Epistle of Paul to the Romans* (MNTC London, 1932), and M-J. Lagrange, *Saint Paul Epître aux Galates* (EB Paris, 1950), ἀγαπή τοῦ θεοῦ as an objective rather than a subjective genitive, i.e. God's love for us rather than our love for God.
144 Rom 12:1; Col 1:22; Eph 1:4; 5:27.
145 The unusual use of εἰς may be due to the influence of LXX Ezek 37:14 καὶ δώσω πνεῦμα μου εἰς ὑμᾶς. The change from the future tense in Ezek (where the spirit is described as a blessing to be awaited) to the present tense in 1 Thes is significant. For Paul the promise has been fulfilled and the possession of the spirit is a present reality.
146 1 Cor 2:12.

Paul uses it denies the very basis of Stoicism – that πνεῦμα has its *locus* in the world – and stresses that it has its origin in God. Ἐκ τοῦ θεοῦ would seem to be a genitive of relationship or origin. Therefore, Paul is not asserting any dualism between a worldly *versus* a divine spirit, but affirming that it is God rather than the world who is the origin of the spirit. In other words he refutes Stoic pantheism.

For Paul, it is precisely because πνεῦμα is a signification of the divine, which is wholly 'other' and not to be confused with the material world, that natural man (ψυχικός) cannot receive τὰ τοῦ πνεύματος τοῦ θεοῦ.[147] Furthermore, Paul contrasts σάρξ and πνεῦμα in such a way as to emphasize this distinction between the human and the divine. Such a contrast has already been made by Isa 31:3, 'The Egyptians are men not gods, their horses are flesh not spirit'. Here 'flesh' represents all that is mortal and powerless over against 'spirit' which is immortal and omnipotent. In the light of this distinction between the human and the divine, Paul contrasts the divine life imparted by the spirit to Christians with the merely mortal existence of those who remain outside the sphere of the spirit's activities. 'But you are not in the flesh (ἐν σαρκί) but in the spirit (ἐν πνεύματι) if God's spirit dwells within you.'[148] A similar point is made in Rom 8:4f where being controlled by the lower nature is contrasted with being directed by the spirit.[149]

The πνεῦμα/σάρξ contrast in Gal 3:3, where Paul is discussing the question of circumcision, symbolizes the respective Christian and Jewish dispensations. Once again σάρξ represents that which is weak and powerless, as opposed to the superior life and strength of πνεῦμα. A similar point is made in Gal 4:29 where the apostle discusses the merits of the sons of Abraham. He claims that the son of Hagar is merely κατὰ σάρκα because he is the child of a slave. Whereas the son of Sarah is κατὰ πνεῦμα, since Isaac is freeborn. This same passage, Gen 21, was also used by Philo.[150] Paul's Alexandrian contemporary allegorizes the story to make Hagar the type of secular learning; the preliminary studies whose offspring is sophistry. Hagar, however, is later abandoned in favour of Sarah, the type of true wisdom, from which alone can come true revelation. It is possible that both Paul and Philo reflect a common haggadic tradition which lies behind their allegorizing of the Hagar and Sarah story. However, they refer to the story for different purposes; Philo uses it to show

---

147 1 Cor 2:14.
148 Rom 8:9, interpreting ἐν as locative, i.e. 'in the sphere of'. Blass, Debrunner, op. cit. ff.219 (4) states that this passage exhibits fluctuation between the local and the instrumental meaning of ἐν.
149 See also Rom 8:6 φρόνημα τῆς σαρκὸς opposed to φρόνημα τοῦ πνεύματος. Here φρόνημα would seem to mean 'outlook formed by'. For the πνεῦμα/σάρξ contrast in the moral sphere cf. Gal 5:16f.
150 Cher. 4–9.

the superiority of revelation over reason, whereas Paul uses it to show the superiority of Christianity over Judaism.

Of course, the πνεῦμα/σάρξ contrast can be used without this sense of opposition or antagonism. For example in Rom 1:4 Jesus is referred to as Son of David κατὰ σάρκα and Son of God κατὰ πνεῦμα. Here Paul seems to be stressing the aspectual differences rather than suggesting a contrast between Christ's human and divine natures. Looked at from a human point of view Jesus was the Son of David; from the divine viewpoint he was God's Son.[151] In spite of such exceptions Paul normally uses πνεῦμα in contrast to σάρξ to demonstrate the qualitative difference between God and the world, the creator and his creation.

The same can be said of πνεῦμα in the Fourth Gospel. There it is used of the divine rather than the earthly sphere. As R. Schnackenburg has said, 'In John, πνεῦμα means all that belongs to God and the heavenly world, in contrast to all that is earthly and human.'[152] Thus the author of the Gospel can write, 'πνεῦμα ὁ θεός'.[153] As a definition of the divine this could easily have been accepted by the Stoics. However, John has a very different concept of πνεῦμα from that held by the Stoa. His ideas of spirit are firmly entrenched in the Jewish tradition, and hence for the evangelist πνεῦμα is immaterial and θεός transcendent. Therefore, the divine πνεῦμα cannot be contained even in the Jerusalem temple.[154] It cannot be identified with a place, but must be seen as a sphere of worship – ἐν πνεύματι καὶ ἀληθείᾳ.[155] This is no 'spiritualizing' of the idea of worship, nor even is it primarily intended to stress its inward nature.[156] Rather is it a contrast between the cultic worship of the temple, which the author is claiming to be merely human, and the eschatological worship of the *Endzeit* which has its origin in God. When we come to consider the part played by πνεῦμα in the christology of the N.T. we shall see that, both in

---

151 Cf. a Deutero-Pauline work 1 Tim 3:16, where Jesus is spoken of as being manifested in the flesh (ἐν σαρκί) and justified in the spirit (ἐν πνεύματι). This particular verse is capable of several interpretations: a) Christ was vindicated by the spirit (presumably at his resurrection), b) He was kept sinless through the action of the spirit, or c) Jesus was justified in his claims to be the Christ by virtue of his possession of the spirit. Whichever, a contrast between the divine and human elements is not intended.
152 R. Schnackenburg, *The Gospel According to St. John* (London and New York, 1968), Vol. I, p.439.
153 Jn 4:24.
154 Jn 4:24. Cf. 3 Kgdms 8:27.
155 Cf. Ps 144 (MT 145): 18 'The Lord is near to those who call upon Him ἐν ἀληθείᾳ'.
156 Such 'spiritualizing' of worship had been undertaken by Philo. Plant. 108, 'God delights in altars, beset by a choir of Virtues, albeit no fire burn on them'. Cf. V.Mos.11, 108; Spec. Leg. 1, 271f.

Johannine and Pauline thought, this divine eschatological sphere is located in the person of Jesus; that to be ἐν πνεύματι is to be ἐν Χριστῷ and *vice versa*.[157]

That the spirit is the medium of the new life of the eschaton is the major theme of the discourse with Nicodemus in John 3:1–15. It is birth ἐξ ὕδατος καὶ πνεύματος which is necessary before one can enter the kingdom of God.[158] 'It is spirit that gives birth to spirit (ἐκ τοῦ πνεύματος πνεῦμά ἐστιν).'[159] To be begotten of the spirit is synonymous with being begotten of God – being born ἄνωθεν.[160] Such metaphors of rebirth[161] were common in Hellenistic pagan writings, but the Johannine literature uses them to express a Jewish theology of the dawning of the new age. It is from Judaism that the author of the Fourth Gospel has inherited the association of πνεῦμα with life. In contrast to that of σάρξ this is the new life of the eschaton 'τὸ πνεῦμά ἐστιν τὸ ζωοποιοῦν'.[162]

'The spirit, like the wind, is entirely beyond both the control and the comprehension of man. It breathes into the world from another',[163] writes C.K.Barrett on John 3:8.

For both John and Paul πνεῦμα is therefore associated with the dawning of the Messianic Age which they were convinced had come in the person of Jesus of Nazareth. As such it is πνεῦμα ἅγιον or πνεῦμα θεοῦ breaking into human history in a unique and final way.

However in the Synoptic Gospels there are frequent references to unclean or demonic spirits. Of the 22 occurrences of πνεῦμα in Mark, 13 fall into this category. Mark's Gospel usually refers to ἀκάθαρτον πνεῦμα although sometimes the author prefers τὸ δαιμόνιον.[164] These unclean spirits are normally referred to in the context of an exorcism performed by Jesus where the disorder is attributed to demonic possession. These stories no doubt reflect the hag-ridden nature of the ancient world. Certainly a belief in evil spirits was a part of the *Weltanschauung* of Jews as well as pagans judging from such literature as *Enoch, Jubilees* and the *Testament of the Twelve Patriarchs.* These books reflect the remarkable development of ideas with respect to the spirit world which took

---

157 Cf. R. Bultmann, *The Gospel of John: A Commentary* (Oxford, 1971), p. 190, n.4, E. Schweizer, *The Spirit of God*, p.91, C.K. Barrett, *The Gospel According to St.John* (London, 1955), p. 47.

158 Jn 3:5.   159 Jn 3:6.

160 Jn 3:3. Cf. 1Jn 4:13 where the possession of πνεῦμα is a sign of mutual indwelling; 1 Jn 3:21 the spirit is the sign of the indwelling of God.

161 See also 1 Jn 3:9 where the 'divine seed' is mentioned.

162 Jn 6:63. Cf. Gen 2:7. For the lifegiving role of πνεῦμα see also Rev 11:11 about the new life which eventually will be afforded the martyrs. A special life-giving power is also attributed to the words of Jesus (Jn 5:24) because it is the spirit which enables him to speak the words of God (Jn 3:34).

163 C.K. Barrett, John, p. 176.   164 e.g. Mk 7:30.

place in the period.[165] If demonology can be properly said to have had a hey-
day then the epoch immediately prior to and contemporary with the beginnings
of Christianity was certainly it![166] Pagan Hellenistic literature produced its
stories of exorcisms,[167] but by the time of Josephus the ability to cast out
demons was held in such esteem by Jews also that he attributes these powers
to Solomon.[168]

What is particularly significant about Mark's portrayal of Jesus as an exorcist is
not that he is shown to have possessed the ability, but that the evangelist claims
that his power is a sign of the new age. Jesus's exorcisms are shown to be part
of his eschatological, Messianic activity. *The Testament of the Twelve Patriarchs*
provides evidence of a belief in the coming Messiah's ability to cast out demons,[169]
that evil will shun the good. 'If ye do well even the unclean spirit will flee from
you.'[170] 'Every spirit of Beliar shall flee from you.'[171] How far the *Testament
of the Twelve* may be taken as an indication of pre-Christian thought is disputed,
however. R.H. Charles recognized that in its present Greek version the *Testament of the Twelve* contains Christian interpolations.[172] M. de Jonge has gone
further and suggested that the *Testament of the Twelve*, in the form in which
we have it, is a second century A.D. Christian work, the authors of which may
have utilized an earlier Jewish Testament.[173] Caves I and IV at Qumran have
provided us with proof of the existence of the *Testaments of Levi* and *Naphthali*,
prior to the Christian era.[174] The former is in Aramaic[175] and the latter in Hebrew.
However, although fragmentary, both are longer than the Greek version, and

---

165 Cf. Strack-Billerbeck, op. cit., Vol. IV, pp. 501–535, J. Bonsirven, op. cit., pp.
    239–246, D.S. Russell, *The Method and Message of Jewish Apocalyptic* (London,
    1964), pp. 235–262.
166 For a general analysis of demonology in the O.T. see E. Langton, *Essentials of Demon-
    ology* (London, 1949). J. Kallas, *The Significance of the Synoptic Miracles* (London,
    1961), stresses the centrality of demonology to N.T. eschatology, and G.B. Caird,
    Principalities and Powers (Oxford, 1956), has shown its importance in Pauline theology.
    Cf. also T. Ling, *The Significance of Satan* (London, 1961), who detects in the N.T. a
    process of centralizing the many evil powers into the one Satan.
167 See for example Philostratus's *Life of Appolonius of Tyana*, and the Magic Papyri.
    For an outline of the main features of Hellenistic Magic see J.M. Hull, *Hellenistic
    Magic and the Synoptic Tradition* (London, 1974), pp. 20–45.
168 Ant. VIII, 45–49.
169 Test. Lev. 18:11f; Reub. 6:10–12; Jud. 25:3; Zeb. 9:8.
170 Test. Ben. 5:2.   171 Test. Iss. 7:7.
172 R.H. Charles, op. cit., Vol. II, p. 291.
173 M. de Jonge, *The Testaments of the Twelve Patriarchs, A Study of their Text, Compo-
    sition and Origin* (Assen, 1953), pp. 118 n.16 121–125, 130–131.
174 See J.T. Milik, *Ten Years of Discovery in the Wilderness of Judea* (London, 1959),
    pp. 34–35, and F.M. Cross, Jr., *The Ancient Library of Qumran* (New York, 1961),
    p. 44, and A-M. Denis, Introduction, pp.59–69.
175 See J.T. Milik, 'Le Testament de Levi en Araméen, RB (1955), pp. 398–406.

the exact relationship between these semitic Testaments and the Greek *Testament of the Twelve* has yet to be established. Therefore we cannot use Test. Lev. 18:11f as evidence of a Palestinian, pre-Christian belief in the Messiah's role as exorcist. We can only suggest the possibility. Such a belief would certainly provide a meaningful background for the presentation of Jesus as possessing ἐξουσία over unclean spirits, so that they are forced to submit.[176] In fact Mark presents the entire ministry of Jesus as a battle between the holy spirit and the unclean spirits. In this conflict Jesus's holy spirit is recognized for what it is by the unholy spirits. The unforgivable sin is the refusal to recognize the nature of Jesus's ἐξουσία, for that is to sin against the holy spirit.[177]

The Marcan account of the healing of the Gerasene demoniac[178] reflects current beliefs in tombs as the abode of demons.[179] But some parts of the O.T. also associate such demon possession of certain sites with idolatrous practices carried on in those places. In Isa 65:1–4 the wastes laid bare by the judgement of God have previously been the sites of idolatry. Ps 67:6 (MT 68:6) mentions tombs as the abode of the rebellious.

Mark's use of the concept of unclean spirits not only reflects popular demonological beliefs, but also has a strong eschatological orientation and conveys a particular christological claim.

In contrast, Matthew's Gospel rarely refers to πνεῦμα as ἀκάθαρτον. Of 19 usages of the term πνεῦμα only 4 are so described. In keeping with his tendency to cut or abbreviate Mark's exorcisms Matthew omits Marcan references to unclean spirits.[180] The πνεῦμα ἀκάθαρτον of Mark 5:2, 8, 13 becomes δύο δαιμονιζόμενοι in Mt 8:28 and δαίμονες in Mt 8:30. The πνεῦμα ἀκάθαρτον of Mk 7:25 is replaced by δαιμονίζεται in Mt 15:22.[181] It is true that Mt 10:1 follows Mk 6:7 and retains πνεῦμα ἀκάθαρτα, although Mt 10:8 reverts to the author's preferred δαιμόνια. It is therefore evident that Matthew prefers δαίμων and cognates to πνεῦμα. He only uses ἀκάθαρτον πνεῦμα if it is in his sources.[182]

This is also borne out by Matthew's use of Q. Mt 12:43–45 in common with Lk 11:24–26[183] retains ἀκάθαρτον πνεῦμα and πνεῦμα πονηροτέρα. However,

---

176 Mk 1:27   177 Mk 3:28–30

178 Mk 5:1–20.

179 For a discussion of the Jewish idea of the wilderness being a haunt of demons see Strack-Billerbeck, op. cit., Vol. IV, p.516.

180 See Mk 1:26, 27; 3:11; 9:17, 20, 25.

181 Although Mk himself refers to πνεῦμα as δαιμόνιον in Mk 7:30.

182 With the exception of Mt 8:16, where πνεύματα/δαιμονιζομένους are introduced although they are not in the Marcan parallel.

183 This is the parable of the return of the evil spirits. For the δαιμόνια who inhabit the deserted wastes see LXX Isa 31:21. Cf. Isa 34:14 for δαιμόνια and satyrs finding rest in deserted places, and Baruch 4:35 for a similar idea.

along with the LXX translators,[184] Matthew seems to prefer to use δαίμων rather than πνεῦμα when he wishes to describe something evil.

A similar tendency can be detected in the Lucan writings. Out of a total of 36 references to πνεῦμα in Luke's Gospel, 12 refer to evil or unclean spirits. This is a higher incidence than in Matthew, but even so we can see that the author tends to substitute or even add δαιμόνιον in place of the Marcan πνεῦμα ἀκάθαρτον. For example the unclean spirit in Mk 1:23 becomes ἔχων πνεῦμα δαιμονίου ἀκαθάρτου[185] in Lk 4:33 and made plural – ἀκάθαρτα πνεύματα – in Lk 4:36. Lk 6:18 retains the Marcan πνεῦμα ἀκαθάρτον of Mk 3:11, as does Lk 8:29 (= Mk 5:2, 8, 13).[186] However the πνεύματα of Mk 6:7 become δαιμόνια in Lk 9:1. The dumb spirit (πνεῦμα ἄλαλον) of Mk 9:17, 20, 25 becomes the πνεῦμα who seizes the boy in Lk 9:39, but a few verses later (Lk 9:42) Luke reverts to δαιμόνιον as a synonym for τὸ πνεῦμα τὸ ἀκάθαρτον. The Marcan pericope of the Syro-Phoenician woman who had πνεῦμα ἀκάθαρτον is not recorded by Luke at all.

In Luke's version of the visit of John the Baptist's disciples (Lk 7:18–23 = Mt 11:24–26) Lk 7:21 adds the statement that Jesus there and then cured those who had diseases and πνεύματα πονηρά. T.W. Manson[187] is probably right in regarding this as an editorial insertion intended to provide the messengers with first hand evidence with which to answer their own question, 'Are you the one who is to come, or are we to expect some other?'

In the material peculiar to Luke there are references to unclean spirits. In Lk 8:2 we are told that, apart from the twelve, Jesus was accompanied by a number of women who had been set free ἀπὸ πνευμάτων πονηρῶν καὶ ἀσθενειῶν.[188] One of these was Mary of Magdala from whom he had cast out seven devils (δαιμόνια). When the seventy return from their mission[189] it is with the news that τὰ πνεύματα had submitted to them. However, once again Luke seems to intend to make it perfectly clear what sort of πνεύματα they are. Hence, in verse 17 of the same chapter he describes them as δαιμόνια.

Unlike Mark, Luke seems to use the term ἀκάθαρτον πνεῦμα of disease in general and not simply of demon possession. This is in spite of the fact that the battle against disease waged by Jesus and his disciples is portrayed in the

---

184 There are some references to πνεῦμα πονηρόν in the LXX, e.g. 1 Kgdms 16:16; Judg 9:23.
185 Cf. Lk 4:35 δαιμόνιον.
186 Yet N.B. Lk 8:26, 30, 33 where πνεῦμα becomes δαιμόνια.
187 T.W. Manson, *The Sayings of Jesus* (London, 1949), p. 61.
188 See also Lk 13:11 where it is πνεῦμα ἀσθενείας which has crippled the woman for eighteen years.   189 Lk 10:17–30.

Lucan writings as a sign of Messianic power. This is particularly true of Acts where this power is the possession of the church. Of the 71 references to πνεῦμα in Acts, 8 are used of unclean or evil spirits, and they all occur within the context of exorcisms and healings performed by the apostles. In Acts 5:16 those with πνεύματα ἀκάθαρτα come to the apostles for exorcism. Similarly Acts 8:7 tells of Philip exorcizing unclean spirits. Paul's healing miracles are described in terms of overcoming πνεύματα πονηρά.[190] It was πνεῦμα τὸ πονηρόν which overpowered the Jewish exorcists who had been using the name of Jesus.[191] Finally in Acts is the πνεῦμα Πύθωνα[192] which Paul exorcized from the slave girl at Philippi. This is probably a reference to the Python god, Apollo, who had his shrine at Delphi and who was believed to deliver oracles to the priestess at his sanctuary. Πνεῦμα Πύθωνα is probably used here as a designation of oracular possession in general, since it is unlikely that Luke was suggesting that the girl was a priestess from the Delphic oracle.[193]

It would appear therefore that references to unclean spirits in Luke–Acts are placed within the general context of wonder working, whether it be performed by Jesus or the apostles. Although the miraculous is regarded by the author as part of the Messianic Age, the eschatological 'edge' of Marcan usage has become less keen, and the sense of cosmic struggle between the holy spirit and the unholy spirits has receded.

The only other place where πνεῦμα is used of the unclean in the N.T. is Rev 16:13f, where it is applied to the Imperial cult:

> Then I saw coming from the mouth of the dragon, the mouth
> of the beast, and the mouth of the false prophet, three foul
> spirits like frogs (πνεύματα τρία ἀκάθαρτα ὡς βάτραχοι).

This satanic trinity has been described by G.B. Caird as a 'triad of political disaster',[194] symbolizing internal anarchy, external invasion and total collapse, which the seer predicts as the fate of the Roman Empire. In verse 14 of this chapter the unclean spirits are specifically equated with δαιμόνια[195] and are attributed with the power to work miracles. We have already noted[196] that δαίμων rather than πνεῦμα is the word normally chosen by the LXX translators

---

190 Acts 19:12f.   191 Acts 19:15f.   192 Acts 16:16.

193 Plutarch, *De Defectu Oraculorum* IX, 414E, describes oracular possession in terms of ventriloquism – ἐγγαστριμύθους. This suggests that the person has entirely been taken over by the god. A similar understanding seems to lie behind the LXX use of ἐγγαστριμύθος about the Witch of Endor in 1 Kgdms 28:7ff. See also Rev 13:15 where the monster from the land (= the Asiarchs of the Imperial cult) are said to give πνεῦμα to the image of the beast. This may be a reference to a similar ventriloquism whereby they speak through the idol. On the other hand it is more likely to be a general metaphor indicating that the Asiarchs are the mouthpiece of the cult.

194 G.B. Caird, *The Revelation of St. John the Divine* (BNTC London, 1966), p. 204.

195 Cf. Lk 4:33.   196 See part I, pp. 16, 33f.

when they refer either to false gods[197] or false prophets.[198] Following Septua-gintal usage most N.T. writers – with the notable exception of Mark – do likewise. In this they are in accord with the writers of Hellenistic Judaism, who, in the interests of retaining πνεῦμα as a designation of the divine, and in an attempt to refute any suggestion of evil or impurity in God's nature, eschew the term altogether of anything unholy or demonic. The N.T. does not quite go this far, but an examination of Matthew and Luke and their modifications of Mark and Q indicates a tendency to prefer δαίμων rather than πνεῦμα in this context.

What is all the more striking is that the same tendency can be seen in the Pauline Letters and John's Gospel. Both of these bodies of work are concerned with the conflict between good and evil and both see this struggle in terms of Jewish eschatological thinking. And yet for both Paul and John πνεῦμα is only associated with one side of the struggle, that of God. It is never used of the opposing forces of evil.

In Gal 5:17 this conflict is posed in terms of πνεῦμα versus σάρξ:

> That nature (i.e. σάρξ) sets its desires against the spirit
> (κατὰ τοῦ πνεύματος) while the spirit (πνεῦμα) fights against it
> (κατὰ τῆς σαρκός). They are in conflict with one another so
> that what you will to do you cannot do.

Man is the helpless battlefield. As in Rom 7 Paul depicts the conflict going on within man himself. This may well reflect a belief in the two *yeserim* of rabbinic Judaism, but what is worthy of note is that σάρξ rather than πνεῦμα ἀκάθαρτον is the term chosen.

Most commentators have interpreted τὸ πνεῦμα τοῦ κόσμου in 1 Cor 2:12 as a reference to Satan.[199] The apostle has been contrasting human wisdom with God's wisdom, the powers of the age (οἱ ἄρχοντες τοῦ αἰῶνος τούτου)[200] with the power of God. Those who see in verse 12 a demonic reference do so in the light of a similar contrast, this time between the satanic spirit and the divine spirit. If such an interpretation is correct, however, it is the only occasion upon which Paul uses πνεῦμα as a reference to an evil power. We have already seen that, in keeping with its previous uses in Hellenistic Judaism, the apostle retains πνεῦμα for that of the divine, and it is possible to maintain that this particular passage is no exception. Κόσμος need not be seen as a pejorative term, but could be being used by the apostle to emphasize that the world, like the flesh,

---

197 Deut 32:17.   198 Zech 13:2; 3 Kgdms 22:22f.
199 E.g. E. Evans, *The Epistles of Paul to the Corinthians* (London, 1922), and E.Edwards, *The First Epistle of St. Paul to the Corinthians* (London, 1885).
200 Cf. 1 Cor 15:24. G.B. Caird, *Principalities and Powers* (Oxford, 1956), p.16, describes these as 'angelic powers behind the pagan world order'.

is a sphere of what is mortal and weak rather than demonic. We have already suggested that the genitive here is one of relationship or origin,[201] and is used within the context of Paul's argument to stress that God rather than the world is the origin of πνεῦμα. In the preceding verses he has made a similar claim for σοφία, which he asserts does not have its source in οἱ ἄρχοντες τοῦ αἰῶνου τούτου but in God. Just as God rather than the powers is the author of wisdom, so God rather than some satanic *anima mundi* is the source of πνεῦμα which is ἐκ τοῦ θεοῦ rather than τοῦ κοσμοῦ.

It is therefore only in the Deutero-Paulines that πνεῦμα is used of the demonic. In Eph 2:2 reference is made to ἄρχων τῆς ἐξουσίας τοῦ ἀέρος as πνεῦμα 'now at work among God's rebel subjects'.[202] The continuing fight is not against 'human foes, but against cosmic powers (πρὸς τὰς ἀρχάς), against the authorities and potentates of this dark world (πρὸς τὰς ἐξουσίας, πρὸς τοὺς κοσμοκράτορας τοῦ σκότους τούτου), against superhuman forces of evil in the heavens (πρὸς τὰ πνευματικὰ τῆς πονηρίας ἐν τοῖς ἐπουρανίοις).'[203] This passage reflects the popular belief in the air as the abode of demons.

1 Tim 4:1 predicts the arising of false teachers. These are described as 'subverting spirits' (πνεύματα πλάνα) and their doctrines as those of devils (διδασκαλίας δαιμονίων). Here πνεῦμα and δαίμων are closely related and possibly synonymous. This would accord with Septuagintal usage, where πνεῦμα and δαίμων are sometimes associated with false prophecy.

Apart from these passages, whose Pauline authorship has been disputed on other grounds, πνεῦμα is nowhere used of the demonic in Paul's letters. In this he is truly a son of the Diaspora.

Can the same be said of the Johannine writings? Certainly the Fourth Gospel, unlike the Synoptic Gospels, does not record any cases of demonic possession, neither does it portray Jesus as an exorcist. Moreover, 1 Jn 4:6 is the only instance in the Johannine writings of πνεῦμα being associated with the unholy. There the author contrasts τὸ πνεῦμα τῆς ἀληθείας with τὸ πνεῦμα τῆς πλάνης, the former recognizing that 'we belong to God', whilst the latter 'refuses us a hearing'. This is a statement of the old contrast between true and false prophecy and does not represent any ontological dualism between two cosmic powers.

---

201 See p. 98.
202 Literally 'sons of disobedience' (υἱοὶ τῆς ἀπειθείας). E.F. Scott, *The Epistles of Paul to Philemon and to the Ephesians* (MNTC London, 1930), regards them as Gentiles who refuse to acknowledge God. Cf. Rom 1:18 f.
203 Eph 6:12.

It is possible to see in the Johannine πνεῦμα τῆς ἀληθειάς[204] an implied dualism between it and the spirit of evil or falsehood. As another paraclete,[205] the spirit comes from the Father at Jesus's request eternally to abide with the disciples. It will bear witness to Jesus and be a guide into all truth. Is this the same good spirit, the spirit of truth to which there are references[206] in the Qumran literature? There it is seen in opposition to the spirit of falsehood which will be conquered only in the final judgement, when men will be refined, purged and purified.[207] The Test. XII also has a similar idea of the two *yeserim* in man.[208] Test. Jud. says that man possesses a spirit of truth and a spirit of deceit.[209] The spirit of truth is also portrayed as acting as man's accuser, just as the Johannine paraclete is shown to function as the convincer or convictor of sin.[210]

O. Betz[211] has seen in the 'spirit of truth' the influence of Iranian dualism. He believes that this influence is to be detected in the *Dead Sea Scrolls*, where the spirit of truth is linked with angels in general and the archangel Michael in particular, waging war against the spirits of evil. Betz argues that John has equated the angelic advocate Michael with this spirit of truth.[212] Furthermore he has identified the paraclete with Michael,[213] and, Betz claims, it is precisely because the Johannine paraclete is the product of these two strands − 'the spirit of truth' and the archangel Michael − that it displays both personal and impersonal characteristics. In Betz's view behind the concept of the 'spirit of truth' lies an essential dualism. This he contrasts with the monotheistic tradition which is at the heart of the idea of 'the holy spirit'.

However, there are a number of points which can be raised against Betz. It is by no means certain that 'the spirit of truth' in the Dead Sea Scrolls owes its origins to Persia. Coppens[214] has argued that it is to the figure of wisdom in the O.T. that we must look for parallels to the role played by the spirit in the

204 Jn 14:17; 15:26; 16:13. Cf. 1Jn 5:6 τὸ πνεῦμά ἐστιν ἡ ἀλήθεια and Jn 14:6 where Jesus himself is ἡ ἀλήθεια.
205 Jn 14:16. Cf. Jn 15:26.
206 E.g. 1QS 111, 6f; 1QS 111, 13−IV, 26.
207 M. Black, *The Scrolls and Christian Origins* (London, 1961), p.134, has seen affinities between this and the purging function of the paraclete in John's Gospel.
208 Test. Ash. 1:5.   209 Test. Jud. 20:1−5.
210 Jn 16:8 where ἐλεγχώ is used.
211 O. Betz, *Der Paraklet* (Leiden, 1963), pp. 165−169.
212 O. Betz, op. cit., p. 156.
213 Cf. Rev 12:7. G. Johnston, *The Spirit-Paraclete in the Gospel of John* (Cambridge, 1970), pp. 119−126, although agreeing with Betz that in late Judaism the spirit of truth was identified with Michael, disagrees as to John's purpose in combining the spirit of truth with Michael in the paraclete. It was not to emphasize a similarity of role between Jesus and Michael, but to rebut such tendencies which were docetic in tone and a threat to orthodoxy.
214 J. Coppens, op. cit., p. 220.

thought of the Covenanters. Similarly it is to the role of wisdom that we can look for parallels to the Johannine 'spirit of truth', i.e. the spirit which communicates truth.[215] In Sap Sol 9:11 wisdom is depicted as knowing and understanding all. She is Israel's guide. She grants knowledge of holy things and guides into the right paths.[216] A similar metaphor of guiding to truth is used by Philo of the νοῦς of which he says, 'Θεῖον ἦν πνεῦμα τὸ ποδηγετοῦν πρὸς αὐτὴν τὴν ἀλήθειαν'.[217]

It can therefore be maintained that it is not to Iranian dualism, nor to the rabbinic doctrine of the *yeserim* (which may itself have been influenced by Zoroastrianism) that we must look for an understanding of the 'spirit of truth' in John, but to Jewish ideas of wisdom. The fact that the Gospel has no reference to evil or wicked spirits would tell against the former view. The absence of such an expression is all the more striking when we remember that John does depict a dualistic eschatology, but chooses to do so in terms of a conflict between light and darkness, God and the world, or God and the prince of this world.[218] As in Paul, in the Fourth Gospel πνεῦμα is entirely on the Godward side of the struggle.

Whether the same can be said of the use of πνεῦμα in 1 Peter is another matter. Our conclusions will depend upon the interpretation of a notoriously difficult passage, 1 Pet 3:18–4:6.[219] For our purposes the major issue is to whom the πνεύματα of 1 Pet 3:18f refer:

Θανατωθεὶς μὲν σαρκὶ ζωοποιηθεὶς δὲ πνεύματι
ἐν ᾧ καὶ τοῖς ἐν φυλακῇ πνεύμασιν πορευθεὶς ἐκήρυξεν.

Some commentators[220] see here a reference to human beings who perished in the flood. Josephus reflects the tradition that those who lived in the era immediately prior to the flood were especially sinful, and hence brought upon themselves God's judgement.[221] To support this identification it is possible to cite instances of πνεῦμα being used of the dead. The N.T. itself provides some of these. Lk 24:37 records that when Jesus appeared to the eleven in Jerusalem they thought he was a ghost (πνεῦμα). Verse 39 of the same chapter goes on

215 C.K. Barrett, 'The Holy Spirit in the Fourth Gospel', NTS 1 (1950), p. 8.
216 Sap Sol 10:10. Cf. Sap Sol 10:17.
217 V Mos. II, 265.
218 Jn 12:31.
219 For a full discussion of this passage see E.G. Selwyn, *The First Epistle of St. Peter* (2nd ed. London, 1947), pp. 314–362.
220 E.g. C. Bigg, *The Epistles of St. Peter and St. Jude* (ICC Edinburgh, 2nd ed. 1909), F.W. Beare, *The First Epistle of Peter* (Oxford, 2nd ed. 1958), and C.E.B.Cranfield, *1 and 2 Peter, Jude* (TBC London, 1960). See also E. Schweizer, *The Spirit of God* (London, 1960), pp. 101f.
221 Josephus, B.J. VII, 62.

to say that πνεύματα do not have flesh and bones, i.e. they are disembodied beings. Heb 12:23 describes the righteous who have died as 'the spirits of good men made perfect (καὶ πνεύμασι δικαίων τετελειωμένων)'.[222] However, πνεῦμα is rarely used of a disembodied being. The more usual term is ψυχή, as can be seen for example in Sap Sol 3:1 where it is the δικαίων ψυχαί which are in the hands of God, and Rom 6:9ff where the martyrs are ψυχαί.

A more likely interpretation of the πνεύματα of 1 Pet 3:19 is to see here a reference to the disobedient angels of Gen 6 whose sinfulness was thought to have caused the flood.[223] These are mentioned in 2 Pet 2:4 as having sinned and been consigned to hell.[224] The contrast σάρξ/πνεῦμα is taken up again in 1 Pet 4:6. In 1 Pet 3:18 it is applied to Christ rather than to Christians who have died, but it seems to stress the same point; that although in the physical sphere Christ died, in the spiritual sphere[225] he lives. The ἐν ᾧ of the next phrase would then mean 'in which sphere of the spirit[226] he went and made proclamation to the imprisoned spirits'.

Rendel Harris put forward the suggestion that ἐν ᾧ καὶ is a misreading of the original Ἑνώχ.[227] It is quite possible that the idea of the risen Christ preaching to the dead could have been patterned on the Enoch tradition. However, Harris's conjecture of an original reference to Enoch has no textual evidence to substantiate it.[228]

If in fact the πνεύματα of 1 Pet 3:19 are the fallen angels then we have here the *Christus Victor* theme of Christ entering heaven 'after receiving the submission of angelic authorities and powers'.[229] In which case, like Mark, the

---

222 E.G. Selwyn, op. cit., W.J. Dalton, *Christ's Proclamation to the Spirits* (Rome, 1965) and E. Best, *1 Peter* (London, 1971), take 1 Pet 4:6 as a reference to Christians who have died; who κατὰ ἀνθρώπους σαρκί, i.e. in the estimation of man, are dead, but who κατὰ θεὸν πνεύματι, i.e. in the divine sphere, continue to live. J. Héring, *L'Epître aux Hébreux* (Neuchâtel, 1954), identifies them in Heb 12:23 with Christian martyrs. However against such an interpretation Heb 12:4 states that the community have not yet had to suffer physical persecution.

223 So E.G. Selwyn, *1 Peter*, J.N.D. Kelly, *The Epistles of Peter and of Jude* (BNTC London, 1969), E. Best, *1 Peter*, and B. Reicke, *The Epistles of James, Peter and Jude* (New York, 1964).

224 See En. 6; Jub. 5; En. 10:11–14. Cf. Jud 6.

225 A.R.C. Leaney, *The Letters of Peter and Jude* (Cambridge, 1967), p. 51.

226 So W.J. Dalton, op. cit., pp. 137–143, J.N.D. Kelly, op. cit., pp. 152–157; *contra* E.G. Selwyn, who takes it as a reference to the spirit which raised Jesus from the dead, B. Reicke, who translates the 'on which occasion' to mean after the resurrection, and E. Schweizer, *The Spirit of God*, p. 102, who regards it merely as a connecting phrase 'and so'.

227 R. Harris, Expos. VI, 4, pp. 364ff and 5, pp. 317f.

228 Although this conjecture was accepted by J. Moffatt, *The General Epistles* (MNTC London, 1928), pp. 141f.

229 1 Pet 3:22.

author of 1 Peter has associated πνεῦμα not only with the holy spirit of God at work in Christ, but with the cosmic forces of evil – in this case represented by the fallen angels – against whom God's Messiah is ultimately victorious.

Πνεύματα is used in the N.T. of angelic beings.[230] This is not surprising since the inter-testamental period was one in which there was a remarkable development in Jewish thinking about the whole spirit world – good as well as bad. We know that the existence of angels was one of the points at issue between the Pharisees and the Sadducees. The author of Acts 23:8f tells us, Σαδδουκαῖοι γὰρ λέγουσιν μὴ εἶναι ἀνάστασιν μήτε ἄγγελον μήτε πνεῦμα, Φαρισαῖοι δὲ ὁμολογοῦσιν τὰ ἀμφότερα.[231] If ἀμφότερα here means 'both'[232] then it could be argued that ἄγγελος and πνεῦμα are used here as synonyms, i.e. that the Pharisees accept both the resurrection and the existence of angels/spirits. This would accord with what we know of Palestinian usage of *ruach*, where sometimes angels are so designated.[233] Similarly, in Hellenistic Judaism πνεύματα can be a term for angels,[234] although this is rare.

Some have seen in the seven spirits of Revelation[235] a similar reference to angels. R.H. Charles regards the seven spirits as angelic beings,[236] whose activities in the Apocalypse have their counterpart in the Jewish angelology of the inter-testamental period.[237] They are therefore seven in number, as were the archangels of *1 Enoch* and the Test. Lev.[238] Rev 1:4 describes them as throne angels[239] and in Rev 4:5 they are equated with seven flaming torches, reminiscent of holy beings of flame and fire before the throne of God in 2 Bar. 21:6.

230 We have already noted that the LXX may be ultimately responsible for this use of πνεῦμα. See Part I, p.14.
231 Cf. Josephus, B.J.II, 164ff, where the Sadducees do not believe in the survival of the ψυχή, and Ant. XVIII, 16 they think that the ψυχή perishes along with the σῶμα.
232 Rather than 'all' as in Acts 19:16. 'Both' would seem to be borne out by Acts 23:9 where angel and spirit are clearly synonymous.
233 E.g. Jub. 1:25; 15:31f; 1 En. 61:12; 2 Esdr 6:41.
234 Cf. Philo, Qu.Gen. 1, 92; Abr. 113; Josephus, Ant. IV, 108; 2 En. 12:1 (B); 16:7.
235 Rev 1:4; 3:1; 4:5; 5:6.
236 R.H. Charles, *The Revelation of St. John* (ICC Edinburgh, 1920), Vol. 1, p. 78. So also T. Holtz, *Die Christologie der Apokalypse des Johannes* (Berlin, 1962), pp. 138–140.
237 For angels in late Judaism see G.F. Moore, op. cit., Vol. 1, pp. 401–413, and J. Bonsirven, *Le Judaisme Palestinien au temps Jésus-Christ* (Paris, 1934–35), Vol. 1, pp. 222–239.
238 1 En. 90:21;Test. Lev. 8:2. Cf. 1 En. 20:1–8.
239 Although R.H. Charles, op. cit. Vol. 1, pp.11–13 regards καὶ ἀπὸ τῶν ἑπτὰ πνευμάτων as an interpolation into the text, introduced for trinitarian motives. In spite of the lack of textual evidence to support his contention, Charles believes that angels could not possibly have ranked along with God and Christ in the original, since the author has a polemic against angel worship. See 2 En. 12:1(B) for a description of πνεύματα as chariot angels.

The spirits of Rev are also equated with stars[240] and behind such an image Bousset[241] sees the astral deities of Babylonia, adopted by Judaism and, in the interests of monotheism, converted into angels. Astrological speculations certainly played some part in Judaism. Philo was not afraid to see an astral significance in the seven branched candelabra,[242] which he allegorized into the seven planets. However, one need not look beyond the O.T., either to Babylonia or to Philo to find the seven branched candelabra of the author of Revelation. Zech 4:2 had already equated the candelabra with Israel and it is to Zechariah that the seer is indebted for his imagery.[243]

However, although the language employed owes much to the picture of throne angels in Judaism, from the close identification of the seven spirits with the risen Christ[244] it would seem unlikely that in Rev they are meant to represent angels. As Caird has pointed out,[245] in Rev 3:1 the spirit addresses the angels of the churches and therefore cannot be identified with an angelic being. He takes the number seven to be a symbol of completeness[246] and the seven spirits to signify 'the spirit of God in the fullness of his activity and power'.[247] In which case the seven spirits of Rev represent the one, holy spirit of God in its various aspects[248] rather than angelic beings who serve Him.

The Epistle to the Hebrews, unlike the Apocalypse, undoubtedly has references to πνεύματα in the sense of angels. Heb 1:7 seems to depend upon the double meaning of πνεύματα as angels as well as winds. So it quotes the LXX of Ps 103:4 (MT 104:4), 'He who makes his angels and his ministers a fiery flame' (ὁ ποιῶν τοὺς ἀγγέλους αὐτοῦ πνεύματα, καὶ τοὺς λειτουργοὺς αὐτοῦ πυρὸς φλόγα).[249] Heb substitutes πυρὸς φλόγα for the πῦρ φλέγον of the LXX. Probably this change has been made by the author in the interests of achieving a perfect parallelism with πνεύματα.[250] The passage may intend to call to mind

---

240 Rev 3:1. Cf. 2 En. 30:14 which possibly refers to the four stars as ministering angels appointed to wait upon Adam.

241 W. Bousset, *Die Offenbarung Johannes* (Göttingen, 1906), pp.186, 248.

242 Heres. 221f; V.Mos.II, 102f; Qu.Ex.II, 75f. Cf. Josephus, Ant.III, 6f.

243 Cf. Zech 4:6 'by my spirit'.

244 E.g. Rev 3:1, where the spirits are held in the hand of Christ (cf. Rev 1:6) and Rev 5:6, where the spirits are the seven eyes of the lamb.

245 G.B. Caird, *The Revelation of St. John the Divine* (BNTC London, 1966), p.48.

246 G.B. Caird, op. cit., p.14.

247 G.B. Caird, op. cit., p.15. However, H.B. Swete, *The Holy Spirit in the New Testament* (London, 1909), p.274, thinks they are seven because there are seven churches addressed.

248 Thus H.B. Swete, op. cit., p.274, E.B. Allo, *Saint Jean L'Apocalypse* (4th ed. Paris, 1933), and F.F. Bruce, 'The Spirit in the Apocalypse', *Christ and Spirit in the N.T.* ed. B. Lindars and S. Smalley (Cambridge, 1973), p. 336.

249 The MT reads 'who makest the winds thy messengers and the flames of fire thy servant'. Thus the LXX has made a significant alteration, making winds and flames of God's angels rather than *vice versa*.

250 So K.J. Thomas, 'The O.T. Citations in Hebrews', NTS 11 (1965), p. 304.

the appearance of the angel to Moses in the burning bush[251] or the fire from which God spoke in giving the law at Sinai.[252]

These angels are contrasted with the eternal son[253] in the light of whom they are 'insubstantial and mutable as wind and fire'.[254] So unstable is their nature that God can reduce them to the elemental forces of wind and fire.[255] Furthermore, in contrast to the sovereign Christ, they are merely λειτουργικὰ πνεύματα.[256] This subordinate nature of angels was one of the themes of inter-testamental literature. Unlike the angel of the presence or the angel of the Lord,[257] they are no longer merely a periphrastic way of referring to Jahweh,[258] but are subordinate beings. Their task is to serve God[259] and to intercede for men.[260]

For the author of Hebrews the status of angels is below that of Christ. He is 'as far above angels, as the title he has inherited is superior to theirs. For God never said to any angel, "Thou art my son" '.[261] A. Bakker[262] thinks that Hebrews' stress upon the inferiority of angels represents an attempt to assert the humanity of Christ. Opposing any docetic tendencies the author was claiming that Jesus was σάρξ rather than πνεῦμα. A similar point is made in Tertullian's *De Carne Christi* 6. Spicq,[263] on the other hand, sees no particular polemical motive in this passage on angels. They are mentioned, not because anyone in the Christian church was claiming that they were superior, nor because of the presence of docetic tendencies which needed to be combatted, but because mediation is the central theme of the work and angels were thought to have been mediators of the old dispensation.

This would certainly seem the most likely interpretation, especially in view of the beginning of Heb 2 which stresses the superior nature of the revelation granted through Christ to that mediated through angels (i.e. the law). Their mediatorial, ministering role would then be seen largely in the light of their revelation of the law. Precisely in that they are inferior to Christ – the new Torah.

---

251 Ex 3:2 LXX.   252 Deut 4:12.   253 Heb 1:8f.
254 H. Montefiore, *The Epistle to the Hebrews* (BNTC London, 1964), p. 47.
255 Cf. 2 Esdr 8:21, 'before whom (heaven's) hosts stand trembling and at thy word change to wind and fire'.
256 Heb 1:14.   257 Isa 63:9.   258 E.g. Gen 31:11,13.
259 Philo speaks of ἄγγελοι λειτουργοί in Virt. 74 and describes them as διάκονοι in Gig.12. Spicq, op. cit. Vol. I, p. 48, thinks this Philonic usage may have influenced Hebrews. *Contra* R. Williamson, *Philo and the Epistle to the Hebrews* (Leiden, 1970), p. 197, argues that the role played by angels in Philo is very different from that in Heb. In the former they have a mediatorial role, whereas in Heb Christ is the only true mediator. But is not this a reflection merely of the fact that the author of Heb was a Christian whereas Philo was not?
260 Zech 1:12; Job 5:1; 1 En. 9:3; 15:2; Test. Lev. 3:5.   261 Heb 1:4f.
262 A. Bakker, 'Christ an angel?', ZNTW 32 (1933), pp. 255–265.
263 Spicq, op. cit., Vol. II, pp. 52f.

10
ΠΝΕΥΜΑ AND CHRISTOLOGY

The spirit of Christ

We have seen that, for Paul, possession of the spirit was part of the unique claim of the Christian church, distinguishing her from the old Israel and constituting an eschatological sign of her faith. Since it is an expression of the life of God Himself,[1] πνεῦμα is characterized by holiness and power, in contrast to all that is unholy and impotent. In 2 Cor 3 Paul juxtaposes the life-giving nature of the spirit over against the powerlessness of the old dispensation. The Corinthians are 'a letter written not with ink but with the spirit of the living God'.[2] The new covenant is 'expressed not in a written document, but in a spiritual bond: for the written law condemns to death, but the spirit gives life'.[3] This new dispensation – ἡ διακονία τοῦ πνεύματος – will be ἐν δόξῃ;[4] an even greater glory than that which accompanied the giving of the law. The apostle then goes on with his midrash of Ex 34: 29–35[5] to assert that the Lord of Ex 34:34 is none other than the spirit of Christian experience,[6] which removes the veil between God and man, breaking down all barriers.

Although in this passage in 2 Cor 3 the spirit and Christ are not identified, there are other occasions when Paul does not distinguish between the spirit of God and Christ. This is because, for Paul, the experience of union with God has been mediated through the person of Jesus. Therefore, he makes no rigid distinction between the source and the agent of the spirit. In Rom 8:9f πνεῦμα θεοῦ, πνεῦμα Χριστοῦ, and Χριστὸς ἐν ὑμῖν are clearly synonymous expressions of the same reality.

Yet Jesus and the spirit are not simply equated. Baptism is 'ἐν τῷ ὀνόματι τοῦ κυρίου Ἰησοῦ Χριστοῦ καὶ ἐν τῷ πνεύματι τοῦ θεοῦ ἡμῶν'.[7] Paul exhorts the

---

1 Cf Rom 8:11 where the indwelling spirit is the spirit of God.
2 2 Cor 3:3 'ἐνγεγραμμένη οὐ μέλανι ἀλλὰ πνεύματι θεοῦ ζῶντος'.
3 2 Cor 3:6 'οὐ γράμματος ἀλλὰ πνεύματος' τὸ γὰρ γράμμα ἀποκτείνει, τὸ δὲ πνεῦμα ζωοποιεῖ'.   4   2 Cor 3:8.
5 See J.D.G. Dunn, '2 Cor.III. 17 "The Lord is the Spirit" ', JTS 21 (Oct. 1970), pp. 309–320.
6 2 Cor 3:17f. Therefore ὁ κύριος τὸ πνεῦμά ἐστιν is not an identification of Christ with the spirit. See J.D.G. Dunn, op. cit., *passim*, and C.F.D. Moule, '2 Cor 3:18ᵇ', *Neues Testament und Geschichte* (Oscar Cullmann zum 70 Geburtstag) hg. von H. Baltensweiler, Bo Reicke (Zürich, 1972), pp. 231–237.
7 1 Cor 6:11. Cf. Mt 28:19.

Romans 'διὰ τοῦ κυρίου ἡμῶν Ἰησοῦ Χριστοῦ καὶ διὰ τῆς ἀγάπης τοῦ πνεύματος'.[8] Furthermore, a trinitarian formula occurs in the grace which closes 2 Cor.[9]

The same close relationship between Christ and the spirit can be seen in Revelation. Here the spirit which addresses the churches[10] is none other than the risen Christ – 'the one who holds the seven stars in his right hand and walks among the seven lamps of God'.[11] Rev 5:6 speaks of the seven eyes of the lamb which are the seven spirits sent throughout the world.[12] Omniscience, normally strictly the prerogative of God, is attributed here to the risen Christ. Similarly πνεῦμα, usually only predicated of God, can be used of Christ, since he is the agent of God's revelation.

Yet, as with Paul, in Rev the spirit which proceeds from the risen Christ is also distinguished from the Lord himself. 'I, Jesus, have sent my angel (ὁ ἄγγελός μου) to you with this testimony for the churches . . . "Come" say the spirit (πνεῦμα) and the bride.'[13] The angel and the spirit are here described as though they were separate from Jesus. This is hardly surprising, since for Jews, 'spirit' was a term often used of God Himself. Therefore it is not the distinction between Christ and the spirit which warrants comment; it is the connection between Christ and πνεῦμα which we find in the N.T. Here the Jewish understanding of πνεῦμα θεοῦ has undergone a re-orientation. So completely has the N.T. writers' understanding of πνεῦμα been shaped by their beliefs about the person of Christ, that πνεῦμα θεοῦ can become πνεῦμα Χριστοῦ. Hence the pneumatology of the N.T. cannot be divorced from its christology.

This is evident if we look at πνεῦμα in the Synoptic Gospels. We have already noted that in Mark there are Messianic claims to ἅγιον πνεῦμα implicit in the exorcisms of ἀκάθαρτον πνεῦμα.[14] These claims are made explicit in the Marcan passages which actually mention the divine πνεῦμα. In the story of Christ's baptism in Mk 1, John's baptism with water is contrasted with the coming baptism πνεύματι ἁγίῳ.[15] The Q version of this pericope adds καὶ πυρί.[16] Bultmann, in keeping with his view that a reference to the spirit was not original to the saying and reflects later Christian baptismal practice, believes that a

---

8 Rom 15:30, i.e. love created by the spirit, rather than love directed towards the spirit.
9 2 Cor 13:14 'The grace of the Lord Jesus Christ and the love of God and fellowship in the holy spirit be with you all'.
10 Rev 2:7, 11, 17, 29; 3:6, 13, 22.
11 Rev 2:1.
12 Cf Zech 4:10 where seven eyes represent wisdom.
13 Rev 22:16f.
14 See pp. 100ff.
15 Mk 1:8 Ἐγὼ ἐβάπτισα ὑμᾶς ὕδατι, αὐτὸς δὲ βαπτίσει ὑμᾶς πνεύματι ἁγίῳ.
16 Mt 3:11; Lk 3:16.

baptism by fire was what was predicted.[17] J.C. Fenton, on the other hand, maintains that the Marcan pericope is more original and that καὶ πυρί is the later addition.[18]

It can be argued, however, that the Q version of the pericope is probably more original, and that both πνεῦμα and πῦρ were part of the saying.[19] In that case the baptism foretold is not that of the gift of the spirit as an effusion of divine grace, but a baptism of judgement and cleansing. In Isa 4:4 (LXX) πνεῦμα had already been associated with washing as well as burning — 'ἐν πνεύματι κρίσεως καὶ πνεύματι καύσεως'[20] — and this may well have helped bring about the birth of a new metaphor — baptism in the spirit. The Dead Sea Scrolls may also throw some light on this pericope. 1 QS IV, 21 speaks of 'cleansing by the holy spirit'. A.R.C. Leaney[21] and M. Black[22] take this as a reference to the purifying fire of Mal 3:2f.

If, in its original form, this saying was a prophecy of impending judgement rather than a promise of divine power, then it would fit in with what we know of Messianic beliefs in the inter-testamental period. We have noted the few references to the Messiah as possessor of the spirit.[23] Even fewer, however, are the hints that the Messiah was to be the bestower of the spirit. One such is to be found in Test. Lev. 17:11, 'And he shall give to the saints to eat from the tree of life, and the spirit of holiness shall be on them.'[24] If the Q version of this particular pericope in the Synoptics is the more original, then Jesus is depicted in it as the agent of God's judgement, and as such it is he rather than John who is the one who is to come.

Jesus's baptism is portrayed as a Messianic anointing with the spirit. Bultmann regards it as a 'baptismal legend' which has its origins in Hellenism. In its present form, he claims, it arose from the combination of two beliefs: a) that the Messiah was consecrated by πνεῦμα, and b) that baptism bestows πνεῦμα.[25] As evidence of its non-Palestinian origin Bultmann relies upon Dalman's statement that 'spirit' is never used without a qualifying adjective to mean God or

17 R. Bultmann, Synoptic Tradition, p. 246. Cf. also J.M. Creed, *The Gospel According to St. Luke* (London, 1930), p. 54, T.W. Manson, Sayings, p. 44, and M. Dibelius, *Die urchristliche Überlieferung von Johannes dem Täufer* (Göttingen, 1911).
18 J.C. Fenton, *St. Matthew* (PGC Harmondsworth, 1963), p. 57.
19 So F.W. Beare, *The Earliest Records of Jesus* (Oxford, 1964), pp. 39–40, C.H. Kraeling, *John the Baptist* (New York, 1951), pp. 274–279, E. Schweizer, *Spirit of God*, pp. 27–29.
20 See also the breath (πνεῦμα) of God which slays the wicked, Isa 11:4.
21 A.R.C. Leaney, *The Rule of Qumran and its Meaning* (London, 1966), p. 159.
22 M. Black, *The Scrolls and Christian Origins* (London, 1961), p. 135.
23 E.g. Isa 11:2.
24 We have already noted, however, the problems involved in accepting the Test.XII as evidence of pre-Christian belief. See p. 101f.
25 R. Bultmann, *The History of the Synoptic Tradition* (2nd ed. Oxford, 1968), p. 250.

the divine. 'In Jewish literature it is so unheard of to speak of "the spirit" when the Spirit of God is meant, that the single word "spirit" would much rather be taken to mean a demon or wind.'[26] Dalman can no longer go unchallenged, however. He came to his conclusions from a study of *ruach* in the Targums. It is not true of *ruach* in the Dead Sea Scrolls nor of *ruach* in inter-testamental literature. Cf. 2 Bar 21:4, 'He hath made firm the height of heaven by the spirit', and En. 91:1, 'For the word of God calls me and the spirit it is poured out upon me'. Furthermore it is not true of πνεῦμα, as the literature of Hellenistic Judaism confirms. Pre-Christian Hellenistic Jewish usage could have influenced Palestinian Judaism even before the birth of the church. Therefore, one cannot base any judgement of the baptism pericope in the Synoptic Gospels upon Dalman's assertion concerning the use of 'spirit' in the Targums.

The event, as described by the Synoptists, carried with it implicit Messianic overtones. Jesus is anointed with the spirit at the outset of his ministry. Mk 1:10, 'καὶ τὸ πνεῦμα ὡs περιστερὰν καταβαῖνον εἰs αὐτόν'.[27] Probably this originally referred to the dove-like descent of the spirit,[28] which later, as reflected in the Lucan σωματικόs,[29] came to be interpreted adjectivally. Various theories have been put forward as to the origin of the dove symbolism. Some scholars have seen it as a reflection of O.T. and rabbinic beliefs. Thus M-J. Lagrange[30] and G.W.H. Lampe[31] regard it as an echo of Noah's dove – the symbol of reconciliation and peace and the harbinger of another covenant. J.C. Fenton,[32] H.B. Swete[33] and V. Taylor[34] point to rabbinic commentators on Gen 1:2 who interpret the spirit hovering on the face of the waters as brooding like a bird. Strack and Billerbeck cite instances of the *bath qol* being likened to the chirping of a bird.[35] The Targum on Cant. II, 12 compares the voice of the turtle dove to 'the voice of the Holy Spirit of salvation', but Strack and Billerbeck have pointed out that this is of late date.[36]

---

26 G. Dalman, *The Words of Jesus* (Edinburgh, 1902), p. 203.
27 Cf. Mt 3:16 'τὸ πνεῦμα θεοῦ . . . ἐπ' αὐτόν', and Lk 3:22 'τὸ πνεῦμα τὸ ἄγιον · · · ἐπ' αὐτόν'. By replacing the Marcan εἰs with ἐπι Mt and Lk have played down the suggestion of spirit possession.
28 So D.E. Nineham, *St. Mark* (PGC Harmondsworth, 1963), p. 61 and L.E. Keck, 'The Spirit and the Dove', JTS 17 (Oct. 1970), pp. 41–67.
29 Lk 3:22.
30 M-J. Lagrange, *Evangile selon Saint Marc* (EB 3rd ed. Paris, 1920).
31 G.W.H. Lampe, *The Seal of the Spirit* (2nd ed. London, 1967), p. 37, n. 3.
32 J.C. Fenton, *St. Matthew* (PGC Harmondsworth, 1963), p. 57.
33 H.B. Swete, *The Holy Spirit in the New Testament* (London, 1909), p. 9.
34 V. Taylor, *The Gospel According to St. Mark* (London, 1952), p. 161.
35 Strack-Billerbeck, op. cit., Vol. 1, pp. 126f. Cf. I. Abrahams, *Studies in Pharisaism and the Gospels* (Cambridge, 1917), Vol. 1, pp. 47–49.
36 Strack-Billerbeck, op. cit., Vol. 1, p. 123.

An older generation of scholars[37] looked to Hellenistic Judaism for the origin of the dove symbolism. They pointed to a passage in Philo in which the birds of Gen 15:9 are allegorized. Philo distinguishes between the περιστέρα, the tame sociable pigeon, and τρυγών, the solitary dove. The former he identifies with human wisdom, as distinct from the dove, which represents divine wisdom.[38] However, if this allegorizing were behind the Synoptists' account of the descent of the spirit on Jesus, signifiying his reception of the divine wisdom, we would surely expect to find the word τρυγών rather than περιστέρα.

Even more unlikely are the suggestions of a pagan origin for this symbol. E.P. Gould thought that, since the dove was sacrosanct among Philistines and Phoenicians and regarded by them as a divine messenger and helper, so it was used in the Gospels.[39] On the other hand, H. Leisegang has identified the dove with the female principle which begets the soul of Jesus at his baptism.[40] Bchind the baptism story therefore lie pagan ideas of divine begetting. The dove as the female spirit gives birth to the pneumatic Christ. 'Ebenso wie die Geburtsgeschichten tragen auch die verschiedenen Berichte von der Taufe Jesu im Jordan den Charakter eines erbaulichen Mythus, in den eine religiöse Spekulation hineingearbeitet ist.'[41] Such speculation on Leisegang's part is both unproven and unnecessary. Possibly the origins of the dove symbolism remain unknown,[42] but it seems most unlikely that we should need to look further afield than Judaism itself.

Mark uses language which suggests the pneumatic possession of Jesus at his baptism. The spirit not only 'enters into' rather than 'rests upon' him, it also drives him (ἐκβαλλεῖν) into the wilderness. Like the prophets of old he is under the compulsion and irresistible power of the spirit.[43] Matthew[44] and Luke[45] use less forceful verbs – ἀναγεῖν and ἀγεῖν. In the Q account of the temptations[46] further Messianic claims are made. Jesus who has been declared Son of God by virtue of his pneumatic anointing must now face the πειρασμός. Thus we can see that in the view of the Synoptic writers, Jesus's possession of the spirit and his claim to be Messiah are inextricably intertwined.

37 E.g. F.C. Conybeare, 'N.T. Notes (1) The Holy Spirit as a Dove', Exp. T. 9 (1894), pp.51–58, and E. Nestle, 'Zur Taube als Symbol des Geistes', ZNTW 7 (1906), pp.358f.
38 Heres. 126f.
39 E.P. Gould, *The Gospel According to St. Mark* (ICC Edinburgh, 1896).
40 H. Leisegang, *Hagion Pneuma* (Leipzig, 1922), pp. 80–95.
41 Leisegang, op. cit., p. 80.
42 So E. Schweizer, *Spirit of God*, p. 40 and D.E. Nineham, Mark, p. 61.
43 Cf. 2 Kgs 2:16; Ezek 8:3; 11:1 etc. This compulsive force of the spirit is emphasized even more in the *Gospel to the Hebrews*, Origen, Com. on Jn II, 12, 'My mother the holy spirit seized me by one of my hairs and carried me away to Mount Tabor'.
44 Mt 4:1.
45 Lk 4:1.
46 Mt 4:1–12; Lk 4:1–12.

It is the spirit which authenticates Jesus's Messianic claims. To fail to recognize this spirit is, therefore, to commit a blasphemy for which there is no forgiveness. In the Marcan version of the pericope,[47] by slander εἰς τὸ πνεῦμα τὸ ἅγιον, the refusal to recognize the spirit as the authenticating sign of Jesus's Messiahship is clearly intended. However, in the form in which the pericope occurs in Matthew and Luke the christological emphasis has undergone a certain modification and, in the process, become less clear. The blasphemies committed by 'the sons of men' in Mk 3:28 have become those spoken against the 'Son of Man' in Lk 12:10 and Mt 12:32. In the Q version there is therefore a distinction made between blasphemy against the Son of Man, for which forgiveness is possible, and blasphemy against the holy spirit, for which there is no forgiveness. This seems to cut across the Marcan tradition where the closest possible relationship is maintained between Jesus and the spirit, since the latter is the sign of Jesus's Messiahship. Most scholars accept the Marcan version of this pericope as more original.[48] But it is difficult to explain why, as opposed to how, such a distinction between the spirit and the Son of Man came about. Schweizer has suggested that in its Q form the pericope was used as a missionary slogan addressed to the Jews.[49] Certainly it seems to reflect the church's conviction that she alone possessed the spirit and that one fails to respond to this spirit at one's peril. Possibly it is a statement to the effect that the identity of the Son of Man may have been obscure during his earthly life, but now, in the guise of the spirit at work in the church, there is no excuse for rejection. Πνεῦμα as the credential of Jesus in Mark has become πνεῦμα the credential of the church in Matthew and Luke.

This is not to suggest that Mark has no reference to the spirit being promised to the church. It is specifically promised to meet needs which will arise in time of persecution. 'So when you are arrested and taken away, do not worry beforehand about what you will say, but when the time comes say whatever is given you to say; οὐ γάρ ἐστε ὑμεῖς οἱ λαλοῦντες ἀλλὰ τὸ πνεῦμα τὸ ἅγιον.'[50] Mt 10:20 substitutes τὸ πνεῦμα τοῦ πατρὸς for τὸ πνεῦμα τὸ ἅγιον. This phrase is unique in the New Testament.[51] In the Lucan version any idea of spirit possession has

---

47 Mk 3:28–30.
48 E.g. V. Taylor, op. cit., p. 242, R. Bultmann, Synoptic Tradition, p. 131, A.H. McNeile, Matthew, pp. 177–179, T.W. Manson, Sayings, p. 109. A.E.J. Rawlinson, *St. Mark* (WC London, 1925), pp. 44–45 thinks that the Q 'Son of Man' was not originally intended as a Messianic title, but was used as a periphrasis for 'I'. Accepting this interpretation he sees no reason for preferring the Marcan pericope.
49 E. Schweizer, *Spirit of God*, pp. 25–26.
50 Mk 13:11. Cf. Rom 8:15, 26; Gal 4:6 for the idea of the spirit praying in and through the supplicant.
51 Hence V. Taylor, Mark, p. 509 thinks it more likely to be original. *Contra* T.W. Manson, Sayings, p.110, who supports 'holy spirit' on the grounds that the Matthean version is a conflation of Mk and Lk.

been avoided by the substitution of διδάξει ὑμᾶς for the spirit speaking (λαλεῖν) through the disciples.[52]

Nor would it be true to suggest that Mt and Lk confine the spirit to the era of the church. Both make even more explicit the Christian belief in Jesus as the unique possessor of the spirit. This they do by including birth narratives in which Jesus's conception is attributed to the holy spirit.[53] 'Πνεῦμα ἅγιον ἐπελεύσεται ἐπὶ σέ, καὶ δύναμις 'Υψίστου ἐπισκιάσει σοι.'[54] We have seen that πνεῦμα had been associated with new life – especially the new eschatological life promised to a purified Israel.[55] The creative power of the spirit was a concept with which Judaism was familiar in the inter-testamental period. But in the Gospels, more than an affirmation of the divine spirit at work in the life of Jesus is made; his very conception is attributed to the spirit. For John the Baptist Luke can claim that he was full of the holy spirit even from his mother's womb;[56] that as the forerunner he was 'possessed by the spirit and power of Elijah (ἐν πνεύματι καὶ δυνάμει 'Ηλεία)'.[57] However, for the birth of Jesus Luke makes a greater claim; that it was brought about by divine paternity. D. Daube has put forward the suggestion that ἐπισκιαζεῖν is here used, as in Ruth 3:9, to mean 'spread one's wings over', i.e. to have sexual intercourse with.[58] However, ἐπισκιαζεῖν can also be used of the *shekinah*[59] and may here have no overt sexual reference. In fact it is extremely unlikely that any suggestion of sexual intercourse between God and Mary was intended. Ideas of divine paternity and virgin birth were quite common in pagan Hellenism,[60] but are not to be found in Jewish thought.[61] The O.T. does contain stories of miraculous conception by women such as Sarah, who were previously barren.[62] But there is no suggestion of divine paternity as such.

---

52 Lk 12:12 'τὸ γὰρ ἅγιον πνεῦμα διδάξει ὑμᾶς ἐν αὐτῇ τῇ |ὥρᾳ ἃ δεῖ εἰπεῖν'. Cf. Lk 21:15 'ἐγὼ γὰρ δώσω ὑμῖν στόμα καὶ σοφίαν'. This theme of the disciples' power to defend their faith before synagogue and courts is taken up in Acts.
53 Mt 1:18, 20 ἐκ πνεύματος ἁγίου.   54 Lk 1:35.
55 E.g. Ezek 37:14; Jud 16:14; 2 Bar. 21:4 etc.
56 Lk 1:15. Cf. Ps 22:10 'Thou art my God even from my mother's womb'.
57 Lk 1:17. For the idea of Elijah as the forerunner see Mal 3:1; 4:5; Ecclus 48:10. Yet in inter-testamental writing Elijah is to be the forerunner of God Himself and not of the Messiah. Cf. Test. Sim. 6:5–8 where it is God Himself who will come and subdue evil spirits etc.
58 D. Daube, *The New Testament and Rabbinic Judaism* (London, 1956), pp. 27–36.
59 See Mk 9:7; Lk 9:34; Mt 17:5 where ἐπισκιαζεῖν is used of the cloud at the transfiguration. Cf. Ex 40:35.
60 See E. Norden, *Agnostos Theos* (Berlin, 1913), pp. 76–116 and W. Bousset, *Kyrios Christos* (2nd ed. Göttingen, 1921), pp. 268–270. R. Bultmann, Synoptic Tradition, p. 292 draws parallels between the Matthean birth narrative and the Arabian cult of Dusares which celebrated the birth of God from a virgin mother and at which festival gifts were offered.   61 Cf. Strack-Billerbeck, Vol. I, pp. 49f.
62 E.E. Ellis, *The Gospel of Luke* (CB London, 1966), p. 72, regards these O.T. stories as the direct antecedents of the birth narratives in the Gospels.

The LXX translators who chose to use παρθένος for *almah* in Isa 7:14 had paved the way for such an interpretation. Certainly if the LXX had not introduced the idea of virginity into the text, Matthew would not have been able to use it as a proof text.[63] Furthermore, the LXX had also introduced the concept of virginity into Jer 3:4, where God is 'πατέρα καὶ ἀρχηγὸν τῆς παρθενίας '. This passage is quoted by Philo, who interprets it in terms of God being the husband of wisdom. It is interesting to note that Philo reads ἀνήρ in place of the LXX ἀρχηγός.[64] He does not hesitate to use sexual imagery to convey the idea of God as father and source. Hence he can speak of virtue in man as the divinely implanted seed.[65] Elsewhere he alludes to God as father, and wisdom (σοφία or ἐπιστήμη) as mother.[66] Such passages illustrate the daring with which Philo can adopt essentially pagan images, using them as vehicles of Jewish theology. However, they do not throw direct light upon the conceptions of divine paternity and virgin birth as they occur in the New Testament. Philo's sexual imagery is employed in the context of allegory, whereas the birth narratives in the Gospels are of a wholly different *genre.*

Leisegang has attempted to connect these Philonic allegorizings with the birth narrative in Luke.[67] Behind the Gospel he claims to detect ideas of the union of the soul with God, which confers supernatural power. In pagan Hellenism this was the prime understanding of prophecy, and Leisegang asserts that Philo had adopted this point of view from non-Jewish sources.[68] Such mystical experience gives rise to religious enthusiasm in general and ecstatic speech in particular. According to Leisegang, behind Luke's account of Christ's birth lie ideas of μανία as the fructifying power of God which comes upon the prophet. He claims that into this Hellenistic myth of the divine paternity of prophecy, the holy spirit has been introduced, since Jews would not tolerate the suggestion of God Himself fructifying the soul.[69]

We have noted that in Lucan theology the spirit is predominantly the prophetic spirit, and the outburst of prophecy which accompanies the birth of Jesus is seen as evidence of the dawning of a new age. We have also observed that in Luke–Acts, prophecy is portrayed as an ecstatic phenomenon. However, there is no evidence of the mystical ideas which Leisegang claims to detect in the Lucan birth narrative. Undoubtedly language of divine begetting, and an emphasis upon virginity, are pagan rather than Jewish in origin. However, these ideas had already been moulded by the theologians of the Dispersion to become

---

63 Mt 1:23.   64 Cher. 49.   65 Cher. 40–52.
66 Fug. 108f; Ebr. 30, 33–34; Leg. Alleg. II, 49–51.
67 H. Leisegang, *Hagion Pneuma*, p. 67.
68 See pp. 49–51 for a refutation of Leisegang's contention that Philo adopted an ecstatic view of prophecy from pagan sources.
69 H. Leisegang, op. cit., pp. 14–19.

vehicles of Jewish thought. Similarly the role played by the spirit in the birth narratives lies wholly within a Jewish eschatological and Messianic *milieu*.[70] Like the baptism, the events of Jesus's birth are primarily intended as a proclamation of his endowment with the spirit. By associating this pneumatic anointing, not merely with Jesus's baptism but with his birth, Mt and Lk are pushing their Messianic claims for him as far back as his conception.

It has been suggested by Schweizer[71] that Luke has deliberately avoided any impression of the spirit's supremacy over Jesus, since he wishes to portray him, not so much as a man of the spirit, as Lord of the spirit. Certainly it is true that in Luke's account the spirit is no mere transient inspiration. Jesus is 'filled' with the spirit from the very beginning. J.H.E. Hull[72] has seen a particular significance in the substitution for the Marcan ἐκβαλλεῖν[73] of 'πλήρης πνεύματος ἁγίου . . . καὶ ἤγετο ἐν τῷ πνεύματι'.[74] Hull thinks that this is done with the intention of asserting the lordship of Jesus over the spirit. A similar motive is detected by J.D.G. Dunn[75] in the Lucan version of the pericope about the eschatological significance of Jesus's power to exorcize demons. In Luke 11:20 this reads: 'But if it is by the finger of God (ἐν δακτύλῳ θεοῦ) that I drive out devils, then be sure the kingdom of God has already come upon you'. On the other hand in Mt 12:28 we have: 'εἰ δὲ ἐν πνεύματι θεοῦ ἐγὼ ἐκβάλλω τὰ δαιμόνια'. Dunn believes that the Matthean version is more original[76] and that Luke has substituted δάκτυλος to avoid any suggestion of Jesus's subordination to the spirit. The evidence would seem to favour the originality of πνεῦμα. However, this does not necessarily mean that Luke had this particular motive. If his main concern had been to assert Jesus's supremacy over the spirit, it is difficult to account for his including Christ's pneumatic conception, which if anything stresses his dependence upon the spirit for his very being. It seems more probable that Luke chose to use 'finger' to echo the δάκτυλος of Ex 8:19[77] by which God inflicted the plagues upon Egypt. It is the self-same power at work in the new Moses – Jesus.

70 See E. Schweizer, *Spirit of God*, p. 36, 'All statements about the nature of the spirit are there purely for their Christological importance.' So also C.K. Barrett, *The Holy Spirit and the Gospel Tradition* (2nd ed. London, 1966), p. 23.
71 E. Schweizer, op. cit., pp. 37–39. So also H. Conzelmann, *The Theology of Luke*, p. 179.
72 J.H.E. Hull, *The Holy Spirit in the Acts of the Apostles* (London, 1967), p. 37.
73 Mk 1:12.   74 Lk 4:1.
75 J.D.G. Dunn, 'Spirit and Kingdom', Exp. T. 82 (Nov., 1970), pp. 36–40.
76 So also J.E. Yates, *The Spirit and the Kingdom* (London, 1963), p. 91, C.S. Rodd, 'Spirit and Finger', Exp.T.72 (1961), pp. 157f. *Contra* C.K. Barrett, *The Holy Spirit and the Gospel Tradition*, p. 63, E. Schweizer, op. cit., p. 26, A.H. McNeile, Matthew, p. 176, T.W. Manson, Sayings, p. 186.
77 Cf. also Deut 9:10 and Ps 8:3.

The claims of Schweizer, that Jesus is depicted as Lord of the spirit in Luke, have their counterpart in H. Windisch's contentions about the Fourth Gospel. Windisch asserts that for John, Jesus 'als Sohn Vaters hat er nicht Geist . . . er über den Geist'.[78] Hence, whilst in the baptism story the Synoptic writers make Jesus subordinate to the spirit, in John πνεῦμα is subordinate to Jesus. During his earthly ministry he alone has the spirit. It is not until his glorification that it is bequeathed to the disciples.[79] Windisch believes that this assertion of Christ's Lordship over the spirit reflects a process of 'Christianizing', which had already begun in the Synoptics and which John takes further. The primitive tradition in which Jesus was known as *Geistträger* and *Geisttäufer* has been taken up into an assertion of Christ as Lord of the spirit.[80] Thus in the Fourth Gospel Jesus's baptism[81] does not confer sonship upon him. The Prologue has made it clear that the pre-existent Logos was already Son of God.[82] As the one sent from God, Jesus 'utters the words of God οὐ γὰρ ἐκ μέτρου δίδωσιν τὸ πνεῦμα'.[83]

Even after Jesus's death the spirit-paraclete is closely connected, if not identified, with him. John uses similar language with which to describe the paraclete and the earthly Jesus, and he also shows them performing parallel tasks. Both were sent by[84] or proceeded from[85] the Father; both are visible only to the believer[86] and are rejected by the world. Just as Jesus taught the truth,[87] so the paraclete's function will be to lead to all truth.[88] Both bear witness,[89] since they do not speak on their own account.[90] The ministry of both is to convict the world of sin.[91] In relation to the disciples both Jesus and the spirit perform the role of παράκλητος, i.e. helper. The spirit's task is to continue this same helping function as Jesus and it is therefore called ἄλλος παράκλητος.[92] It is possible with Bornkamm[93] to describe Jesus as the forerunner of the paraclete, if by 'forerunner' one does not imply any subordination, but wishes to stress the element of continuity between Jesus and the spirit.

---

78 H. Windisch, 'Jesus und der Geist im Johannesevangelium', *Amicitiae Corolla:* Essays for Rendel Harris's 80th Birthday (London, 1933), p. 315.

79 Jn 7:39. The use of παραδίδωμι about Jesus's giving up his spirit at death may intentionally echo the 'handing over' of the spirit to his disciples in Jn 20:22.

80 H. Windisch, op. cit., pp. 317–318.   81 Jn 1:32.   82 Jn 1:1–14.

83 Jn 3:34. After δίδωσιν D Θ and some mss. add ὁ θεός. Cur. adds ὁ πατήρ. Sin. adds θεὸς ὁ πατήρ. Τὸ πνεῦμα is omitted by B and Sin. Syr. Cf. Jn 6:63 'τὰ ῥήματα ἃ ἐγὼ λελάληκα ὑμῖν πνεῦμά ἐστιν καὶ ζωή ἐστιν'. This verse is omitted by ℵ and may be an interpolation.

84 Jn 14:16; 5:30; 8:16. Cf. Lk 11:13.

85 Jn 15:26; 8:42; 13:3.   86 Jn 14:17; 1:10, 12; 8:14, 19; 17:8.

87 Jn 7:16f; 8:32, 40–42. Cf. Lk 12:12.   88 Jn 14:26; 16:13.

89 Jn 8:14, 18; 15:26. Cf. Acts 5:32.   90 Jn 16:13; 7:16f; 12:49f; 14:24.

91 Jn 3:20; 7:7; 15:26; 16:8.   92 Jn 14:17.

93 G. Bornkamm, 'Der Paraklet im Johannesevangelium', *Festschrift Rudolf Bultmann zum 65 Geburtstag überreicht* (Stuttgart, 1949), pp. 12–35. So also R.E. Brown, 'The Paraclete in the Fourth Gospel', NTS 13 (1967), p. 123.

H. Windisch[94] largely based his contention that the references to the paraclete were originally independent blocks of material which in their previous form did not refer to the spirit at all, upon the fact that 'another paraclete' is mentioned in Jn 14:17. He claimed to be able to isolate five paraclete passages apart from which we would simply be left with Jesus's promise to return again. According to Windisch the paraclete was an independent figure who was to represent the absent Christ and especially to stand by believers in times of particular need. This figure was later combined with the holy spirit in order to identify the sending of the spirit with the return of Jesus.

There is no textual evidence which would support a theory of interpolation with regard to these 'paraclete passages'. However, Windisch's main thesis is that the author of the Fourth Gospel drew upon conceptual sources in which the paraclete was a separate and distinct figure, neither identified with the spirit nor with Jesus, prior to John's treatment. Concerning the pre-Christian history of the paraclete Windisch may be right, but the basis upon which he arrives at his conclusions cannot rest upon the ἄλλος παράκλητος of Jn 14:17. Far from attempting to point to a different figure, the author appears to be stressing the identity of function between the earthly Jesus and the abiding spirit. Hence he can say in the next verse, 'I will not leave you bereft; I am coming back to you'.[95] Against Windisch it can be maintained that whatever its pre-history, παράκλητος is, in John's understanding, more the personification of a function, i.e. that of helper or representative, than any separate hypostasis.[96]

But does this mean that the paraclete is actually identified with the risen Christ? E.F. Scott[97] thinks that it is, and although Schweizer states that the two are not simply identical, he goes on to say, 'In the Paraclete Jesus comes himself . . . indeed one might be tempted to say that there is really no place in John for the Spirit'.[98] Certainly it is the portrayal of the spirit-paraclete as Christ's *alter ego* and an emphasis upon their correspondence in function which is the most striking feature of Johannine pneumatology. R.E. Brown[99] attributes this to the author's need to show a connection between Christ and the church in view of the delay of the parousia and the death of eye-witnesses.

---

94 H. Windisch, 'Die fünf johanneischen Parakletspruche', *Festgabe für A. Julicher* (Tübingen, 1927), pp. 110–137.
95 Jn 14:18.
96 So G. Johnston, *The Spirit-Paraclete in the Gospel of John* (Cambridge, 1970), p. 35.
97 E.F. Scott, *The Spirit in the New Testament* (London, 1923).
98 E. Schweizer, *Spirit of God*, p. 96. Cf. W.F. Lofthouse, 'The Holy Spirit in the Acts and the Fourth Gospel', Exp.T. 52 (1941), p. 336, 'the master himself, *en permanence*'.
99 R.E. Brown, 'The Paraclete in the Fourth Gospel', NTS 13 (1967), pp. 128–232 and idem, *The Gospel According to John* (New York, 1970), Vol. II, pp. 142f.

G. Johnston[100] sees a different motive at work, however. He contends that in order to combat the de-historicizing tendencies of docetism, John associates the spirit with Christ in such a way as to ground πνεῦμα in the historical ministry. Furthermore, Johnston believes that it is to deny the supremacy of angelic mediators that the Fourth Gospel always makes the paraclete subordinate to and representative of Christ. Whether or not the threat of docetism lies behind John, the author, in keeping with the earlier Pauline tradition, maintains the closest possible relationship between the spirit and Christ.

For all N.T. writers the power and presence of God, signified by πνεῦμα, is grounded exclusively in Jesus, the Christ. Therefore, pneumatology and christology are inextricably bound up with each other, since the church's concept of the spirit of God has become conditioned by its beliefs about Jesus. Πνεῦμα θεοῦ has become Πνεῦμα Χριστοῦ.

Πνεῦμα and the Christian hermeneutic

The writers of the New Testament lay claim to the Jewish scriptures as their own. Just as the Jews of the Dispersion asserted the supremacy of the O.T. over against any pagan claims to inspiration, so the early church accepted its revelatory nature, and, in keeping with Hellenistic Jewish practice, expressed this conviction in terms of πνεῦμα.[101] Thus, to ascribe the scriptures to the holy spirit is to claim for them supreme revelation. So Mark introduces a quotation from Psalm 109 (110) with the words: 'αὐτὸς Δαυειδ εἶπεν ἐν τῷ πνεύματι τῷ ἁγίῳ'.[102] A similar formula is used in Acts to introduce O.T. quotations.[103] 2 Peter 1:20 f also attributes the prophecies of the O.T. to the inspiration of the spirit: 'οὐ γὰρ θελήματι ἀνθρώπου ἠνέχθη προφητεία ποτέ, ἀλλὰ ὑπὸ πνεύματος ἁγίου φερόμενοι ἐλάλησαν ἀπὸ θεοῦ ἄνθρωποι'.

The author of 2 Peter goes further and not only claims divine inspiration for the O.T.; he asserts that its interpretation equally requires divine illumination. Therefore, he warns his readers against private and erroneous interpretations of scripture. Here it is clear that the Christian church no longer accepts the O.T. as it is expounded by Judaism; it lays claim to the pneumatic inspiration which is necessary for its correct understanding. As the author of the Epistle to the Hebrews puts it:

---

100 G. Johnston, op. cit., pp. 119–126.
101 See pp. 45–51. In its polemic against paganism Diaspora Judaism has used πνεῦμα as the *imprimatur* of its inspiration.
102 Mk 12:36. Cf. 2 Kgdms 23:2 'πνεῦμα κυρίου ἐλάλησεν ἐν ἐμοί'. Lk 20:42f 'αὐτὸς γὰρ Δαυειδ λέγει ἐν βίβλῳ ψαλμῶν', omits any reference to πνεῦμα, although there seems to be no significance in this.
103 Acts 1:16; 4:25; 28:25.

When in former times God spoke to our forefathers, he spoke
in fragmentary and varied fashion through the prophets. But
in this the final age he has spoken to us in the Son.[104]

Part of the prophetic task of the new Israel is the elucidation of the prophets
of the past. For this they too have to possess the prophetic spirit. Hence,
prophecy is one of the gifts of the spirit listed by Paul in 1 Cor 12:9. Although
in Acts prophecy is understood in terms of foretelling,[105] this is by no means
the primary emphasis given it by the N.T. We have seen that even in Lucan
theology the outbreak of prophetic activity which accompanies the birth of
Jesus is not portrayed primarily in terms of foretelling, but as a sign of the
dawning of the new age. In Acts the main prophetic task of the church is to
bear witness to Jesus, rather than to predict the future.

This could be said of all N.T. writers for whom the prophet above all is the
one who bears witness to Christ. 'Testimony is the *raison d'être* of prophecy.'[106]
Rev 19:10 clearly enunciates this: 'ἡ γὰρ μαρτυρία Ἰησοῦ ἐστιν τὸ πνεῦμα τῆς
προφητείας'. T. Holtz has shown the similarities of function between πνεῦμα
in Revelation and παράκλητος in the Fourth Gospel.[107] He points to the fact
that both are personified, both are depicted as leading the church into wisdom
and both do the work of Christ in the church. Yet Holtz does not mention the
one sphere in which the parallels are particularly close, i.e. that both spirit and
paraclete are associated with witnessing to Christ.[108] This is the most distinctive
function attributed by N.T. writers to the prophetic spirit. They believe that
the function of prophecy – both past and present – is to point to Jesus as
Messiah. Only in as far as the O.T. can be made to bear this interpretation is it
accepted as inspired by the divine πνεῦμα. Similarly, only in as far as his
hermeneutic is christocentric is the Christian prophet adjudged to be inspired.

This can be clearly seen in the Epistle to the Hebrews. It would be wrong to
suggest that the author of this work gives much emphasis to the role of
πνεῦμα.[109] However, where he does use the term, it is, as in later rabbinism,
for its inspiration of the O.T. Hence the quotation from Ps 94(95): 7–11 is
introduced with 'καθὼς λέγει τὸ πνεῦμα τὸ ἅγιον'.[110] However, the scriptures

104 Heb 1:1–2.
105 See Acts 11:28; 13:2; 21:11. Cf. Rev 22:6 'καὶ ὁ κύριος ὁ θεὸς τῶν πνευμάτων τῶν
    προφητῶν ἀπέστειλεν τὸν ἄλλελον αὐτοῦ δεῖξαι τοῖς δούλοις αὐτοῦ ἃ δεῖ γενέσθαι ἐν
    τάχει'.
106 H.B. Swete, *The Holy Spirit in the New Testament*, p. 278.
107 T. Holtz, *Die Christologie der Apokalypse des Johannes* (Berlin, 1962), pp.209–211.
108 Cf Jn 14:26; 16:13f.
109 H.B. Swete, *The Holy Spirit in the New Testament*, p. 249, 'In Hebrews there is no
    theology of the Spirit'. So also C. Spicq, op. cit., Vol. I, p. 147 and H. Montefiore,
    op. cit., p. 5.
110 Heb 3:7.

are only regarded as inspired in as far as they witness to Christ. Therefore, the author introduces Ps 109(110):1 and Jer 38(31):33f with '*μαρτυρεῖ δὲ ὑμῖν καὶ τὸ πνεῦμα τὸ ἅγιον*'.[111] Of the regulation in Lev 16:16 which permits only the High Priest to enter the Holy of Holies once a year,[112] Heb 9:8 claims that by this 'the holy spirit signifies (*τοῦτο δηλοῦντος τοῦ πνεύματος τοῦ ἁγίου*) that so long as the earlier tent stands, the way into the sanctuary remains unrevealed'. Here the author of Hebrews is exercizing his own 'prophetic' function in perceiving the inner meaning of the O.T.

In this intention he has considerable affinity with Philo. Both authors regard the Jewish scriptures as inspired by the spirit of God; both attempt to interpret the O.T. in terms of their respective theologies. In the case of Philo this is, where possible, to see in the scriptures the basic tenets of Hellenistic philosophy and especially Platonism. With the author of Hebrews it is the attempt to substantiate the church's claim that in Jesus God's Messiah had come. Philo adopts allegory as his chief exegetical tool, i.e. he takes each term as a symbol of an idea, whereas in Hebrews we find the working out of a typological exegesis, i.e. viewing the past as an anticipation of the present.[113] The difference between these two approaches is aptly illustrated by their respective treatments of the figure of Melchizedek. Philo allegorizes him so that he becomes a symbol of right reason.[114] However, in Hebrews Melchizedek is not de-historicized but seen as a prefiguration of Christ.[115] Even Spicq,[116] who is usually more than ready to point to similarities between Philo and Hebrews, has to admit that these two types of exegesis are far removed from one another.

In spite of these real exegetical differences, however, both Philo and the author of Hebrews represent attempts to find some correspondence between their own beliefs and those recorded in the Jewish scriptures. Indeed typology would not be possible unless some symmetry between the two dispensations were assumed. Images of pilgrimage, promised inheritance and rest, the exodus under a new leader, the tests which preceded the final entry into the promised land,[117] all

---

111 Heb 10:15. Cf. Jn 15:26 where the comforter witnesses to Christ.
112 Cf. Philo's account of the place of the High Priest in the Day of Atonement ceremonies in Spec.Leg. I, 72; Ebr. 136. In Gig. 52 he allegorizes the High Priest to signify reason (*λόγος*) which can only approach the Holy of Holies once a year because man is mixed in his nature, possessing passions as well as reason.
113 See S.G. Sowers, *The Hermeneutics of Philo and Hebrews* (Zürich, 1965), pp.89–126, R. Williamson, *Philo and the Epistle to the Hebrews* (Leiden, 1970), pp. 519–38.
114 Leg. Alleg. III, 79.
115 Heb 5:5–10.
116 C. Spicq, op. cit., pp. 63ff. S.G. Sowers, op. cit., pp. 137f, thinks that the author of Hebrews was aware of the conclusions reached by the Alexandrian allegorist, although he himself did not adopt allegory as a method of exegesis.
117 Heb 3:1–4:9.

presuppose a correspondence between the old and new covenants. The same can be said of the working out of the ideas of Christ as superior guide and priest.

Yet whereas for Philo it would be unthinkable for Greek philosophical speculations to supersede biblical revelation, since for all his attempts to reconcile the two he was in no doubt as to the supremacy of the latter, for the author of Hebrews Christian beliefs are superior to the O.T. His whole typological exegesis relies upon the argument *a minori ad maius.*[118] The tabernacle,[119] although not unlike the original, is still only a copy. 'οἵτινες ὑποδείγματι καὶ σκιᾷ λατρεύουσιν τῶν ἐπουρανίων.'[120] The Mosaic covenant was the mere shadow, as opposed to Christ, 'ὃς ὢν ἀπαύγασμα τῆς δόξης καὶ χαρακτὴρ τῆς ὑποστάσεως αὐτοῦ'.[121] Philo had already interpreted Ex 25:40 in terms of Platonic Idealism, identifying the logos as the ἀρχέτυπος of creation, the immaterial plan in the mind of the Maker in accordance with which the material world was created.[122] For Philo as well as for Plato the archetypal Idea is superior to the form which it takes in creation. Hence, in claiming that Moses alone had a vision of the immaterial pattern of the sanctuary,[123] Philo is once more using pagan philosophy in the service of his Jewish theology. He claims for Mosaic revelation an ultimacy denied to all others.

A similar apologetic motive can be detected in the hermeneutic of the author of Hebrews. Like Philo he accepts the Mosaic dispensation, but unlike Philo, he does not accept its supremacy. He, too, uses Platonic language of 'copy' and 'archetype', but unlike Philo he does not locate that archetype in the law of Moses but in Christ. The O.T. is thus only of value in as far as it foretells or reflects the Christ. Inasmuch as the scriptures witness to Jesus, they are valued by Christian exegetes, but they are no longer regarded as the norm by which events are to be judged. That norm has been resited; it now has its *locus* in Christ. Whereas for Philo Hellenistic philosophy was the handmaid of theological exposition, for Christian hermeneutics the scriptures are the handmaid of christology. The prophetic spirit, believed to have inspired those scriptures, is now located exclusively in the person of Jesus and in the disciples who bear witness to him.

118 See S.G. Sowers, op. cit., pp. 127–136.
119 Ex 25:40 LXX where the tabernacle and its furnishings are made 'κατὰν τὸν τύπον' revealed on the mount.
120 Heb 8:5.
121 Heb 1:3.
122 Leg. Alleg. III, 96–103. Cf. Spec. Leg. III, 207 where man's νοῦς is patterned upon the logos which is the ἀρχέτυπος.
123 V. Mos. II, 74–76.

The second Moses and the new Torah

The figure of Moses looms large in those apologetic works of Judaism which have come down to us in fragments preserved by Alexander Polyhistor and quoted by Eusebius. Here Moses is depicted as the fount of all learning and culture. As the inventor of the art of writing[124] it is he who instructed the Egyptian priests in hieroglyphics.[125] His supreme worth was acknowledged by the Egyptians, among whom he was not only a prince,[126] but given the title of Hermes.[127] According to Aristobulus Moses was the true father of Greek as well as Egyptian culture.[128]

The pre-eminence of Moses is stressed even more in the writings of Philo and Josephus. Although Josephus is in some ways more restrained in the claims he makes for the great lawgiver,[129] he, no less than Philo, portrays Moses in terms of the typical Hellenistic θεῖος ἀνήρ. 'For grandeur of intellect and contempt of toils he was the noblest Hebrew of them all.'[130] His birth was predicted by priests,[131] the future course of his life was revealed to Amran in a dream,[132] and the birth itself was miraculously free from labour pains.[133] Even from his youth he displayed superhuman virtues.[134]

It is upon Moses that Philo projects all his claims for the supremacy of Judaism. The two treatises *On the Life of Moses* are solely concerned with the glorification of its founder, in a thinly disguised attempt to magnify Judaism itself. Hence, Moses is the true philosopher;[135] he is the friend of God,[136] who alone attains the beatific vision.[137] Legislator, priest, king, and above all prophet,[138] it is Moses who has supreme revelation. We have seen[139] that the Diaspora authors were making these unique claims when they associated πνεῦμα with the prophetic process in general and with Moses 'the purest of spirits'[140] in particular.

---

124 Eupolemus in Praep.Ev. IX, 26.
125 Artapanus in Praep.Ev. IX, 27; Strom. I, 23, 154.
126 Cf. Ezekiel the Tragedian, 'The Exodus', in Praep. Ev. IX, 29; Strom. I, 23, 155.
127 Artapanus, Praep. Ev. IX, 27.
128 Aristobulus, Praep. Ev. VII, 12; XIII, 12.
129 E.g. Ant. IV, 326 where Josephus denies that Moses did not die, *contra* Philo, V.Mos. II, 288–291 where Moses is included with those such as Enoch and Elijah who did not die but were translated into the very presence of God. See also Qu.Ex. II, 29.
130 Ant. II, 229.   131 Ant. II, 205.
132 Ant. II, 210–216.   133 Ant. II, 218.
134 Ant. II, 230f.   135 Heres. 301; Conf. 1.
136 V. Mos. I, 156–158.
137 Post. C. 388; Mut. 2; Qu. Ex. II, 29.
138 Mut. 2103, 135; Som. II, 189. Cf. Leg. Alleg. III, 43 and Migr. 151 where Moses is προφητικὸς λόγος.
139 Pp. 45–51.
140 Cf. V. Mos. II, 40; Gig. 47.

It is evident that for the Jews of the Dispersion Moses had become not only a cult figure, but the very epitome of their claims for Judaism.[141] In the Dead Sea Scrolls there is reference to an eschatological figure – the prophet – who alongside the two Messiahs of Aaron and Israel will play a part in ushering in the new age.[142] This may reflect a belief in the return of Moses, either as a forerunner of the Messiah or as a Messianic figure himself. Certainly among the biblical material found in Cave IV at Qumran is Deut 18:18f, a passage which was interpreted in terms of a Messiah who would be 'a prophet like Moses'. Josephus, in recording the uprisings of two Messianic pretenders, may also reflect a belief in Moses *redivivus*. In Ant. XX, 97 he mentions the false prophet Theudas, who claimed to be able to divide the waters. 'The Egyptian' pretender put down by Felix[143] may also echo Mosaic claims. On the basis of such little evidence it is difficult to be sure just how developed were any ideas of a Moses-like Messiah. However, it would seem to be a natural outcome of the work of Hellenistic Judaism, that the figure whom it did so much to extol should have taken on an eschatological orientation once it was transferred to a Palestinian *milieu*. In which case the representation of Christ as the second Moses, which we find in the N.T., is considerably indebted to the work of the Jewish apologists of the Diaspora.

This is evident in the Epistle to the Hebrews where Jesus is depicted in terms of a second and better Moses, mediating an authentic covenant and exercizing a priesthood which is truly efficacious:

> Moses also was faithful in God's household; and Jesus, of whom I speak, has been deemed worthy of a greater honour than Moses, as the founder of a house enjoys more honour than his household. For every house has its founder; and the founder of all is God. Moses, then, was faithful as a servitor in God's whole household; his task was to bear witness to the words that God would speak; but Christ is faithful as a son, set over his household.[144]

The covenant of Christ is thus presented as superior to that of Moses;[145] the new law is the true image (εἰκών) rather than the mere copy or shadow (σκιά) of the good things to come.[146]

Unlike that given on Sinai, which was mediated through angels,[147] this word of God is spoken directly. As Spicq has expressed it, 'L'Evangile est à la Loi, ce que le Christ est aux anges'.[148] An unequivocal statement of a belief in the angelic mediation of the law is only found in the N.T. Apart from Hebrews

---

141 For a discussion of the place of Moses in these non-rabbinic sources see W.A. Meeks, *The Prophet-King* (Leiden, 1967), pp. 100–163.

142 1 QS IX, 8–11.

143 B.J. II, 259–263.

144 Heb 3:3–6.

145 Heb 8:6.

146 Heb 10:1.

147 Heb 2:2 'ὁ δι' ἀγγέλων λαληθεὶς λόγος'.

148 Spicq, op. cit., Vol. II, p. 55.

it is mentioned in Acts 7:35, 38 and by Paul in Gal 3:19. No doubt it arose from the mention in Deut 33:2 of the ἄγγελοι who were present at God's right hand when He gave the law to Moses.[149] Josephus, in Ant. XV, 136, also mentions that the law was given through ἄγγελοι. However, R.Marcus[150] has questioned an interpretation which is based upon an assumption that ἄγγελοι here means 'angels'. Marcus, citing evidence of ἄγγελος being used as a designation of a priest or prophet,[151] suggests that this is the more likely meaning in Josephus. The only other place outside the N.T. where there is a possible reference to an angelic agency in the communication of the scriptures is Jub. 1:27: 'And He said to the angel of the presence: "Write for Moses from the beginning of creation till my sanctuary has been built among them for all eternity".' Yet here it should be noticed that it is a history up to the coming of the Messiah which is indicated, and not the Pentateuch. For this, rather than for the Torah, the apocalyptist is claiming angelic mediation.

No evidence of a belief in the angelic mediation of the law is to be found in Philo. In keeping with the general trend in post-exilic Judaism, angels do play a part in his theology. They are disembodied souls (ψυχαὶ ἀσώματοι),[152] called by the Greeks heroes,[153] δαίμονες or πνεύματα.[154] Sometimes Philo refers to the λόγος as an angel.[155] He claims that God can Himself take the form of an angel.[156] But, as we have already maintained,[157] Philo saw no inner necessity for angelic mediation between God and man. Therefore, he obviously felt no need to postulate an angelic mediator in the giving of the law. For Philo it is the figure of Moses as the mediator of the law who is given prominence. By and large the same can be said of N.T. writers – that their emphasis is upon Moses and it is in terms of his successor and superior that Jesus is presented.

In his portrayal of Jesus in the temple, debating with learned rabbis even from an early age,[158] Luke is depicting his hero in terms with which Hellenistic Judaism was familiar. Philo had already so described the young Moses, teaching the learned teachers of Egypt and Greece and, even from his youth, confounding them with his wisdom.[159] In the Lucan narrative of the commissioning of the 70[160] a further parallel is drawn between Jesus and Moses. Obviously the author intended to call to mind the Mosaic commissioning of the 70 Elders in Num 11:25. The motif of the new Sinai is also to be seen in the Pentecost narrative in Acts 2. *Jubilees* 6:21 is the first clear evidence of the Feast of Weeks

149 Deut 33:2 (LXX), 'ἐκ δεξιῶν αὐτοῦ ἄγγελοι μετ' αὐτοῦ'.
150 R. Marcus, *Josephus* (Loeb Edition), Vol. VIII, p. 66, n.a.
151 E.g. Mal 2:7 LXX.   152 Conf. 174; Spec. Leg. I, 66.
153 Plant. 14.   154 Gig. 6; Som. I, 141.
155 Spec. Leg. III, 177–179; Cher. 35.   156 Som. I, 232.
157 Pp. 51–58.   158 Lk 2:41–52.
159 V. Mos. I, 21.   160 Lk 10:1.

being associated with a commemoration of the Sinai covenant. However, this was not accepted by orthodox rabbinic circles until the 2nd century A.D.[161] It does not occur in Philo or Josephus. However, Philo does reflect a tradition concerning the giving of the law which has echoes in the Lucan account of the outpouring of the spirit. In Decal. 32–35 Philo explains that on Sinai God, whose 'voice' is inaudible, gave His own utterance the form of a flaming fire, which sounded like the breath ($\pi\nu\epsilon\hat{\nu}\mu\alpha$) in a trumpet. Unlike normal sound this did not fade with distance:

> The new miraculous voice was set in action and kept in flame by the power of God, which breathed upon it and spread it abroad on every side and made it more illuminating in its ending than in its beginning, by creating in the souls of each and all another kind of hearing, far superior to the hearing of the ears.[162]

Flames of fire, universal miraculous 'hearing' – all these occur in Acts 2. It can be argued, therefore, that Luke is intentionally portraying the Christian Pentecost as a new and better Sinai.[163] The giving of the spirit represents the new and better Torah, mediated by one who is superior to Moses – Jesus of Nazareth. In Stephen's speech before the Sanhedrin[164] this theme is once more taken up. Here the exploits of Moses are outlined and his rejection by Israel is stressed.[165] In the light of this, the rejection of Jesus, the second and greater Moses, is seen as the nation's greatest act of apostasy.

It is apparent that in John's Gospel also Jesus is portrayed in terms of a second Moses and the fulfilment of the Messianic hope of Moses's return.[166] Having fed the 5,000 he is so acclaimed by the crowd: 'Surely this must be the prophet that was to come into the world'.[167] What is more, Jesus is depicted not merely as another Moses, but as a greater than Moses: 'For while the Law was given through Moses, grace and truth came through Jesus Christ. No one has ever seen God, but God's only Son, he who is nearest to the Father's heart, he has made him known'.[168] Hence we find both elements of comparison and contrast in the picture of Jesus as another Moses.

---

161 See H-J. Kraus, *Worship in Israel* (Oxford, 1966), pp. 58–61.
162 Decal. 35. Cf. also *Midrash Tanhuma* 26c where this legend also occurs.
163 See J. Dupont, 'Ascension du Christ et don de l'Esprit d'après Actes 2:33', *Christ and Spirit*, ed. B. Lindars and S. Smalley (Cambridge, 1973), pp. 219–228, who thinks that in Acts 2:33 there is an intentional allusion to Ps 68:19 – a psalm, which in Jewish midrashic tradition, had been interpreted of the promulgation of the law at Sinai. Dupont argues that Luke is here claiming that the gift of the law through Moses at Sinai has now been replaced by the gift of the Spirit.
164 Acts 7:12–53.   165 Acts 7:17–43.
166 See T.F. Glasson, *Moses in the Fourth Gospel* (London, 1963), and W.A. Meeks, *The Prophet-King* (Leiden, 1967).
167 Jn 6:14.   168 Jn 1:17f.

He is not merely the supreme lawgiver, whose words unlike those of Moses have the life-giving property of spirit;[169] he is himself the new Torah:

> 'The truth is, not that Moses gave you bread from heaven, but that my Father gives you the real bread from heaven. The bread that God gives comes down from heaven and brings life to the world.' . . . Jesus said to them, 'I am the bread of life. Whoever comes to me shall never be hungry, and whoever believes in me shall never be thirsty'.[170]

Just as John has portrayed Jesus in his discourse with the Samaritan woman as the new temple, the true sphere of worship,[171] so here he is described as the better manna.[172] We know that in Jewish thinking the bread given by Moses in the wilderness was identified with the law.[173] It was also part of the eschatological hope that the manna would once more be given in the Messianic Age:

> And it shall come to pass at that self same time that the treasury of manna shall again descend from on high, and they will eat of it in those years, because these are they who have come to the consummation of time.[174]

This corresponds to the prophetic hope of a new covenant, which would be written on men's hearts rather than on tablets of stone.[175] According to the author of the Fourth Gospel this promise has been fulfilled in Jesus, himself the new temple, the second Moses, the true manna and the eternal Torah. Hence ascriptions such as life, light, bread and water, which were previously applied to the Torah, are transferred to Jesus. But, as in Paul, only of the law which is Jesus can it be said that it is $\pi\nu\epsilon\hat{\upsilon}\mu\alpha$. The Mosaic dispensation, in the last resort, can only be characterized as $\sigma\acute{\alpha}\rho\xi$.[176] In this way John transfers $\pi\nu\epsilon\hat{\upsilon}\mu\alpha$ – the *imprimatur* of unique revelation – from Judaism to Christianity.

Furthermore, it is not only as lawgiver that Jesus is portrayed as Moses's successor. The intercessory function of the paraclete in John's Gospel also has Mosaic overtones. N. Johannson[177] has pointed to the idea of the intercessory activity of the patriarchs in general, which came to the fore in post-exilic Judaism, as the origin of the figure of the paraclete in the Fourth Gospel. Philo himself speaks of the holiness of the patriarchs as one of the three $\pi\alpha\rho\acute{\alpha}\kappa\lambda\eta\tau\omicron\iota$ who plead before God.[178] But once more we see that it is the person of Moses who is put forward by the Alexandrian as the intercessor *par excellence*. On discovering the Israelites worshipping the golden calf, it is Moses who 'took the part of mediator and reconciler . . . begging that their sins might be forgiven'.[179]

---

169 Jn 6:63.   170 Jn 6:32–35.
171 Jn 4:23f.
172 For a comparison of the concept of manna in John and Philo see P. Borgen, *Bread from Heaven* (Leiden, 1965).
173 E.g. Philo, Congr. 170, 173f.   174 2 Bar. 29:8.
175 See Jer 38(31):31–34.   176 Jn 6:63.
177 N. Johannson, *Parakletoi* (Lund, 1940).
178 Praem. 166–167.   179 V. Mos. II, 166.

The theme of Mosaic intercession in heaven is taken up by the *Assumption of Moses*:[180]

> Moses the great messenger, who every hour day and night had his knees fixed to the earth, praying and looking for help to Him that ruleth all the world with compassion and righteousness.[181]

Similarly Jesus is depicted as praying on behalf of the disciples that the spirit might rest upon them.[182] Just as Hellenistic Judaism regarded Moses as the recipient of the spirit *par excellence,* so John shows Jesus as alone having the 'abiding' spirit. And as Moses bestowed his spirit to Joshua,[183] so Jesus handed it on to his disciples.[184]

G. Bornkamm[185] has maintained that behind the Johannine concept of the paraclete lie Jewish ideas of the Messiah as the second Moses. These, he thinks, have been combined with the figure of the Son of Man who in *Ethiopic Enoch* is thought to be the bearer of the spirit and judge of the world. Bornkamm suggests that John has de-mythologized this apocalyptic tradition, making the paraclete serve Jesus in much the same way as Joshua, although succeeding Moses, served him. It is debatable whether the figure of the Son of Man, at least as it occurs in *Enoch*, has influenced John. However, Bornkamm has rightly emphasized the importance of the figure of Moses for an understanding of both the christology and pneumatology of the Fourth Gospel.

It is in the Pauline Epistles that the relationship between Christ and the Mosaic law is discussed in most detail. Furthermore, it is here that we can see clearly the connection between πνεῦμα and the person of Christ. For the apostle the relationship between the old and new covenants is essentially one of contrast. In 2 Cor 3:7–18 he alludes to Moses, who, having been given the ten commandments, had to veil his face from the people because it reflected the glory of God.[186] Paul goes on to argue *a fortiori* for the greater glory of the Christian revelation: 'Πῶς οὐχὶ μᾶλλον ἡ διακονία τοῦ πνεύματος ἔσται ἐν δόξῃ'.[187] In other words the dispensation of πνεῦμα is seen as superior to the glory of Moses. The way of Christ is characterized by life-giving spirit, and is therefore

---

180 The *Assumption of Moses* is generally believed to be a Palestinian work, dated sometime between A.D. 6 and A.D. 30.
181 Ass. Mos. 11:17.
182 Jn 14:16.
183 Deut 34:9.
184 Jn 20:22.
185 G. Bornkamm, 'Der Paraklet im Johannesevangelium', in *Festschrift Rudolph Bultmann zum 65 Geburtstag überreicht* (Stuttgart, 1949), pp. 12–35.
186 See Ex 34:27–35.
187 2 Cor 3:8.

contrasted with the way of Moses, which only leads to death.[188] This is the main argument of Rom 8: 'In Christ Jesus the life-giving law of the spirit (νόμος τοῦ πνεύματος τῆς ζωῆς) has set you free from the law of sin and death (νόμος τῆς ἁμαρτίας καὶ θανατοῦ)'.[189] Herein lies the key to understanding the Pauline antithesis between πνεῦμα and σάρξ. The apostle characterizes Judaism as σάρξ, of itself unable to give life, powerless, inferior. Christianity, however, is characterized by πνεῦμα, life-giving and radiating the very power and presence of God. The Mosaic religion is the φρόνημα τῆς σαρκός which inevitably leads to death, whereas that of Christ is the φρόνημα τοῦ πνεύματος which results in life and peace.[190] It is only when one is living κατὰ πνεῦμα as opposed to κατὰ σάρκα that the fulfilment of God's commands is possible.[191] Hence Paul goes on to say, 'Τὸ μὲν σῶμα νεκρὸν διὰ ἁμαρτίαν, τὸ δὲ πνεῦμα ζωὴ διὰ δικαιοσύνην'.[192]

In expressing the antithesis between Christian and Jew, Paul not only juxtaposes πνεῦμα and σάρξ or σῶμα; he also contrasts πνεῦμα with γράμμα. In 2 Cor 3:6 the Mosaic law (τὸ γράμμα) written on tablets of stone, is portrayed as inferior to the new covenant of the spirit (πνεῦμα), inscribed on men's hearts, promised in Jer 38(31):31–34 and Ezek 32:26 and fulfilled in Christ. This is no reference to a literal over against a spiritual interpretation of the law,[193] but a claim for the superiority of Christianity over against Judaism. Paul asserts that the church is Israel's successor, and therefore, the disciple of Christ is the inheritor of the promises of God, since the true Jew 'is such inwardly and the true circumcision is of the heart,[194] directed not by written precepts (γράμμα) but by the spirit (πνεῦμα)'.[195] It is true that in Rom 7:14 Paul describes the Torah as πνευματικός,[196] i.e. that it had its origin in God. However, usually Paul retains πνεῦμα and its cognates for the Christian dispensation, against which the γράμμα of the Mosaic law is no match.

---

188 For the Mosaic law's inability to bestow life see also Rom 3:22. A similar emphasis upon the life-giving nature of the spirit is to be found in Tit 3:3, where terms of regeneration (παλινγενέσια) and renewal (ἀνακαίνωσις) are used. Cf. Jn 3:3–8.
189 Rom 8:2. Νόμος here can hardly refer to the Torah, since the new dispensation is also described as νόμος. Therefore, with C.K. Barrett, F.J. Leenhardt, W. Sanday and A.C. Headlam, and C.H. Dodd, it is better to interpret it in terms of a religious dispensation, outlook or attitude.
190 Rom 8:5 f.   191 Rom 8:4.
192 Rom 8:10.
193 Cf. the metaphorical use in 2 Cor 3:3 where Paul describes his Corinthian converts as letters, written not with ink but πνεύματι θεοῦ ζῶτος.
194 Cf. Deut 10:16, Jer 4:4. Circumcision of the heart is associated with the spirit in the *Odes of Solomon* 11:1–3.
195 Rom 2:29. Cf. Rom 7:6 where ἐν καινότητι πνεύματος is contrasted with παλαιότητι γράμματος.
196 Rom 7:14 'ὁ νόμος πνευματικός ἐστιν'.

Jewish claims to supreme revelation mediated through their cult hero, Moses, have been taken by Paul and applied to the Christian church and her Lord. Furthermore, the term πνεῦμα, which had been honed by Diaspora Jews for the purposes of polemic, and used by them as a weapon against the pagan world, has been adopted by Paul in his debate against Judaism to make those self same assertions for the supremacy of Christianity. Thus, the very term πνεῦμα, which had been claimed by Judaism as her own, is taken over by Paul and used by him against his erstwhile co-religionists.

Πνεῦμα and the wisdom of God

It is generally accepted[197] that one of the sources of the logos christology of the N.T. is the figure of wisdom, as developed in later Judaism. Over fifty years ago Rendel Harris pointed out that everything that was said of λόγος in the Prologue of John's Gospel had previously been said of wisdom in earlier Jewish Wisdom literature.[198] Everything, that is, except the last verse, 'And the Word became flesh'.

The figure of *hokmah* began to play an important role during the post-exilic period. Job 28:23–28, Prov 1–9 (especially 8:1–31), Ecclus 24:3–22 – all reflect this tendency, whereby wisdom is personified, not only as God's agent in revelation, but also with Him prior to and at the time of the creation of the world. In Ecclus wisdom, the supreme revelation of God, is to be identified with the sacred scriptures. The identification of wisdom with the pre-existent Torah is quite explicit by the time we reach the rabbinic writings.[199]

But it is particularly to Hellenistic Judaism that we must look for the development of the figure of wisdom (σοφία). We have already seen that both in Sap Sol[200] and in Philo[201] σοφία is closely connected with λόγος. Frequently the two are synonymous.[202] Hence, the λόγος which in Philo is the agent of creation[203] is no different from the σοφία of Sap Sol,[204] present beside the throne of God when the world was made. Created before the world, the Philonic λόγος is described as πρωτόγονος, πρεσβύτατος, ἀρχὴ and εἰκών,[205]

---

197 So R.H. Fuller, *The Foundation of New Testament Christology* (London, 1965), pp.72–75, and O. Cullmann, *The Christology of the New Testament* (London, 1959), pp. 256–258.
198 J.R. Harris, *The Origin of the Prologue to St. John's Gospel* (Cambridge, 1917), p.43.
199 See Strack-Billerbeck, op. cit., Vol. II, pp. 353–355.
200 See pp. 20–24.   201 See pp. 45–51.
202 E.g. Leg. Alleg. I, 65.
203 Cher. 35; Post. C. 8; Immut. 58.
204 Sap Sol 9:4, 9.
205 Conf. 146f; Heres. 205f.

whilst in Sap Sol 7:26 σοφία is the 'flawless mirror of the active power of God and the image of His goodness'. The archetype of divine light can be λόγος[206] or σοφία;[207] in Philo's mind there is such little distinction between the two. He identifies the manna with the gift of heavenly σοφία,[208] the true food which is the words of God.[209] This no doubt reflects the tradition which identifies wisdom with the Torah.

So evident are the parallels between the descriptions of σοφία/λόγος in Sap Sol and Philo, and the λόγος in the Fourth Gospel, that Sidebottom concludes that Wisdom Literature was 'an actual source from which he (John) borrowed'.[210] Of course, it is always difficult to substantiate any claim for direct borrowing. What is clear is that John has drawn upon Jewish wisdom tradition in general and that this has influenced his conception of the λόγος.

What is not usually recognized, however, is that Johannine pneumatology also owes something to the figure of wisdom. It is true that in his study of John's Prologue Rendel Harris stated, 'The Holy Spirit came into Christian theology through the bifurcation of the doctrine of Divine Wisdom, which on the one side, became the Logos, and on the other the Holy Ghost'.[211] However, he did not go on to substantiate or develop this claim. It is evident that Harris was right to see the figure of wisdom behind both πνεῦμα and λόγος, although it is an over-simplification to talk of a 'bifurcation'. Whatever was to take place in later theology, no such development has taken place in the Fourth Gospel. We have already seen[212] that John keeps Jesus and the spirit-paraclete in the closest possible relationship. In fact it could be argued that, far from reflecting any division, John drew upon wisdom concepts precisely in order to emphasize a continuity between the ministry of Jesus and that of the spirit.

We have already discussed certain similarities between the Johannine concept of πνεῦμα and that found in the Dead Sea Scrolls.[213] Nötscher has concluded from his studies of the respective texts that the holy spirit of Qumran is none other than the spirit of wisdom.[214] Thus, it is not forwards to the rabbinic *yeser* doctrine that we must look for an understanding of 'the spirit of truth',

---

206 Som. I, 75.
207 Abr. 40. Cf. Sap Sol 7:29.
208 Mut. 258–260. Cf. Leg. Alleg. III, 162–163, 168.
209 Cong. 170, 173f.
210 E.M. Sidebottom, *The Christ of the Fourth Gospel* (London, 1961), p. 207. See also A.W. Argyle, 'Philo and the Fourth Gospel', Exp.T. 63 (1963), pp. 385–386, who believes that John is directly dependent upon Philo for his λόγος doctrine.
211 J.R. Harris, op. cit., p. 38.
212 See pp. 122ff.
213 See pp. 94, 106ff.
214 F. Nötscher, 'Geist und Geister in den Texten von Qumran', *L'Evangile de Jean*, p. 307.

but back to the figure of wisdom. Nötscher believes that it is the role of wisdom which offers the most parallels to the part played by the holy spirit in Qumran.[215] Equally we can claim a correspondence between the spirit-paraclete of the Fourth Gospel and the figure of σοφία as developed in Hellenistic Judaism. In both traditions wisdom/spirit is personified. She is sent from God[216] to the elect[217] in answer to prayer,[218] making men friends of God and turning them into prophets.[219] Her supreme function is to initiate her followers into divine knowledge.[220] Therefore, the similarities between the pneumatology of John and that of the Qumran community may be due to the fact that both have drawn independently upon Jewish wisdom traditions.

Elements of Jewish wisdom tradition are also discernible in Pauline christology. Writing to the Corinthians, the apostle develops the theme of wisdom, contrasting that which has its origin in man with that which comes from God.[221] He claims that the crucified Christ is the power (δύναμις) and wisdom (σοφία) of God.[222] It is Jesus 'ὃς ἐγενήθη σοφία ἡμῖν ἀπὸ θεοῦ'.[223] A similar identification of Christ with wisdom can be seen in the first chapter of Colossians,[224] where Paul applies to Christ terms which have previously been used of the figure of wisdom in Jewish sapiential literature. Thus Christ is described as the image (εἰκών) of the invisible God;[225] the firstborn (πρωτότοκος) of all creation,[226] which came into being through him.[227] As the pre-existent consort of God,[228] it is he who continues to sustain the creation.

It is evident that in these passages Paul has drawn upon the figure of wisdom for his christological model. However, the apostle normally uses σοφία of divine revelation in general[229] and not simply as a christological title. Above all it is the knowledge of man's relationship to God – that of sonship[230] – which is the possession of all Christians who are ἐν πνεύματι. That revelation has, of course, been mediated through the person of Christ, and therefore, in Pauline thought we are always brought back to christology. However, unlike the portrayal of the spirit-paraclete in the Fourth Gospel, the element of personification is not retained in Paul's use of the wisdom motif.

COPPENS

215 F. Nötscher, op. cit., p. 220.
216 Sap Sol 9:17; Jn 14:26; 15:26.
217 Jn 14:17.   218 Sap Sol 7:7; Jn 14:16.   219 Sap Sol 7:27.
220 Sap Sol 9:11; 10:10, 17; Jn 14:17; 14:26; 15:26; 16:13.
221 I Cor 1:18–31.   222 1 Cor 1:24.   223 1 Cor 1:30.
224 Col 1:15–20.   225 Col 1:15.   226 Col 1:16.
227 Cf. also 1 Cor 8:6.
228 Col 1:17. Cf. Phil 2:6–11.
229 Cf. 1 Cor 2:10; 7:40; 2 Cor 11:4; Col 1:9. Cf. Eph 1:17.
230 Rom 8:16.

The doctrine of Christ's pre-existence[231] obviously owes much to Jewish wisdom ideas, and probably arose from the identification of Christ with wisdom. A. Deissmann believed that the doctrine of pre-existence arose from the identification of Christ with the spirit.[232] However, we would maintain that behind both the idea of Christ's pre-existence and his identification with the spirit lies the figure of wisdom. We have already seen that in Hellenistic Judaism πνεῦμα and σοφία were closely associated, and could be used synonymously.[233] Therefore in view of the fact that Paul overtly drew upon the figure of wisdom in his presentation of Christ, the occasions upon which he makes little or no distinction between Christ and the spirit become explicable. The connection between pre-existence, wisdom, and spirit can be seen if we compare Paul's treatment of the rock in Ex 17:1−6 and Num 20:2−11 with the way Philo deals with it. In 1 Cor 10:2f Paul identifies Christ with the rock from which Moses produced water in the wilderness. Philo, on the other hand, interprets the rock as the wisdom of God.[234] As H. Conzelmann has suggested,[235] both Paul and Philo may be drawing upon a common allegorical tradition. Be that as it may, their respective treatments of the rock aptly demonstrate the connection between pre-existence, Christ and wisdom. The fact that in Hellenistic Judaism πνεῦμα and σοφία could be used synonymously, may well explain the process whereby Christ and the spirit became identified in Pauline thought.[236] The apostle's dominant concern was to deal with Jewish claims which would equate God's wisdom with the Mosaic Torah. In locating πνεῦμα exclusively in Christ and his church, Paul is asserting that they alone have the wisdom of God.

For both John and Paul therefore, pneumatology and christology are essentially connected, since both draw upon the Hellenistic Jewish wisdom tradition, in which σοφία, λόγος and πνεῦμα are inter-related concepts.

---

231 See also 1 Pet 1:11 where τὸ ἐν αὐτοῖς πνεῦμα Χριστοῦ could be a reference to Christ's pre-existence, if, with A.R.C. Leaney, *The Letters of Peter and Jude* (Cambridge, 1967), p. 22, C.E.B. Cranfield, *1 and 2 Peter* (London, 1960), p. 43, and E. Best, *1 Peter* (London, 1967), p. 60 we take the subject to be the O.T. prophets who foretold the coming passion and glory of Christ. F.W. Beare, *The First Epistle of Peter* (2nd ed. Oxford, 1958), pp. 65−66 interprets πνεῦμα Χριστοῦ as the pre-existent Christ who is himself the spirit. However, E.G. Selwyn, op. cit., p. 249, translates it as 'spirit who derived its mission to the church from Christ'. Should, as Selwyn also believes (op. cit., pp. 135, 259−261), the prophets be those of the Christian community who predict the sufferings which lie in store for their fellow believers, then a doctrine of pre-existence would not be implied in this passage.
232 A. Deissmann, *Paul*, p. 195.   233 See pp. 38−41, 45.
234 Philo, Det. 115; Leg. Alleg. II, 86.
235 H. Conzelmann, *Der erste Briefe an die Korinther* (Göttingen, 1969), p. 197.
236 Cf. Phil 1:19; Gal 4:6.

Πνεῦμα and the historical Jesus

Considering the important role played by the spirit in Paul and Acts, the paucity of references to πνεῦμα in the Synoptic Gospels is particularly noticeable. Is this discrepancy due to the fact that 'spirit' was a category used by the early church but absent from the original teaching of Jesus?

Few scholars today would pronounce so unequivocally as Foakes Jackson and Kirsopp Lake that, 'It is certain that he (Jesus) claimed to act and speak in the power of the spirit of God'.[237] All six pericopae which refer to πνεῦμα in the Synoptics have come under fire from some quarter or other as stemming from the church rather than from the *ipsissima verba* of Jesus. However, few scholars agree as to which, if any are genuine. For example, Schweizer claims that only Mk 13:11 and parallels goes back to the ministry.[238] Scott, on the other hand, regards Mk 3:28—30 as the only incontestable logion.[239] No one doubts that πνεῦμα was a concept which played a large part in the thinking of the early church. What is more difficult to determine is whether the Synoptic writers have read back their later experience into the life of Jesus.

H. Windisch in his study of the spirit in the Synoptics[240] concluded that this in fact has occurred. Yet he also asserts that in the earliest tradition Jesus was seen as a *'Pneumatiker'*.[241] Windisch postulates a pre-literary stage in the transmission of the tradition in which there had been a tendency to suppress the pneumatic element, to account for the comparative silence in the Gospels on the pneumatic inspiration of Jesus. This suppression had been motivated by a desire to portray Jesus as unique. An ecstatic, wonder-working, spirit-filled prophet could all too easily have been paralleled. Therefore, in order to avoid any suggestion of Jesus's subordination to the spirit, the pneumatic element of the prophet had been omitted and replaced by a Son of God christology. The paucity of references to πνεῦμα in the Synoptics is due to this pre-literary 'censorship'. However, Windisch also maintains that in the Synoptic Gospels we have evidence of another tendency at work, i.e. the re-introduction of a pneumatic element.[242] The evangelists' motive is not so much to reassert the previous primitive pneumatology, but to replace it with another which would serve a 'higher' christology. Windisch's thesis maintains both the originality of the concept of spirit to the ministry of Jesus, and its modification by the church.

---

237 F.J. Foakes Jackson and K. Lake, *The Beginnings of Christianity* (London, 1920), Vol. I, p. 288.
238 E. Schweizer, *Spirit of God*, p. 33.
239 E.F. Scott, *The Holy Spirit in the New Testament*, p. 76.
240 H. Windisch, 'Jesus und der Geist nach synoptische Überlieferung', in *Studies in Early Christianity,* ed. S.J. Case (London and New York, 1928), pp. 209—236.
241 H. Windisch, op. cit., p. 230.
242 E.g. at Jesus's birth and baptism.

C.K. Barrett,[243] unlike Windisch, sees no place for the concept of spirit in the life of the historical Jesus. Where πνεῦμα does occur in the Gospels he sees not only the church's christological motives at work, but also an attempt to reorientate her eschatology. Barrett claims that the paucity of references to πνεῦμα is a reflection of the fact that Jesus did not speak of himself in terms of spirit; it was not a primary category in his Messianic thinking.[244] Furthermore, as it is presented by Mark, Jesus's pneumatic endowment is part of the Messianic secret.[245] Like the kingdom, the spirit was present with Jesus, but, as with the kingdom, it was not fully consummated in his earthly life.[246] Barrett believes that Jesus did not foresee the existence of a spirit-filled community, and therefore could not have promised the outpouring of the spirit on his disciples. Since, according to Barrett, Jesus did not envisage an interval between his humiliation and final glorification, there was no role for the spirit to play.[247] It is only because as it happened there was a gap between the resurrection and the parousia that the need for Pentecost arose. Barrett believes that the early church read back into their accounts of the life of Jesus references to the spirit, which would provide for the church living between the 'now' and the 'not yet'.

The major weakness of Barrett's thesis is that it assumes that the spirit had no place in Jesus's thinking about the final consummation. Even if we accept that Jesus did not envisage an interval between his humiliation and glorification,[248] this does not mean that he could not have spoken of that consummation in terms of an outpouring of the spirit. Joel 2:28ff certainly associates the spirit with the eschaton. There is no *a priori* reason why Jesus could not have had a similar hope. Undoubtedly the delay of the parousia led to the early church modifying that promise, so that the spirit now becomes the ἀρραβών which

243 C.K. Barrett, *The Holy Spirit and the Gospel Tradition* (2nd ed. London, 1965), especially pp. 160–162 and idem, 'Important Hypotheses Reconsidered. V The Holy Spirit and the Gospel Tradition', Exp.T. 67 (1955–1956), pp. 142–145.
244 C.K. Barrett, Gospel Tradition, pp.113–121.
245 Cf. R.N. Flew, *Jesus and His Church* (2nd ed. London, 1943), pp. 70–71, who claims that 'spirit', like the title 'Messiah' was repudiated by Jesus because of the dangers of it being misunderstood.
246 C.K. Barrett, Gospel Tradition, pp. 157–159. Cf. J.D.G. Dunn 'Spirit and Kingdom', Exp.T. 82 (Nov. 1970), pp. 36–40, who argues that πνεῦμα displays the same present/ future duality as βασιλεία. It is therefore to be understood in the light of the tension between 'realized' and 'future' eschatology. Dunn claims that it would have been inappropriate to use πνεῦμα before Pentecost, since not until then does the kingdom come for the disciples. Even then, like the kingdom, spirit is only the ἀρραβών.
247 Barrett, Gospel Tradition, pp. 135–139.
248 *Contra* G. Beasley Murray, *Jesus and the Future* (London, 1954), pp. 183–199 who claims that Jesus expected a gap between his resurrection and parousia.

anticipates and looks forward to the final eschaton. But such a process of re-
fashioning does not necessarily imply that the promise of the spirit had no
place in the teaching of the historical Jesus.

Hans Leisegang[249] was also one who did not accept that the concept of spirit
played any part in the historical life of Jesus. He, however, unlike Barrett,
looked to paganism rather than to Judaism for the origin of πνεῦμα as it occurs
in the Synoptic Gospels. Leisegang put forward the thesis that all references to
πνεῦμα have their origin, not in a Palestinian *milieu*, but in the church which
looked back upon the ministry of Jesus through the eyes of Greek mysticism.[250]
Behind the birth narratives he detects Hellenistic myths of the union of the
soul with God, issuing in the birth of prophecy.[251] Similarly, the story of Jesus's
reception of the spirit at his baptism reflects pagan ideas of the birth of his
pneumatic soul.[252] He conjectures that the logion of the sin against the holy
spirit in Mk 3:28–30 (and parallels) was originally a reference to blasphemy
against God Himself.[253] In an attempt to support this he claims that the power
with which Jesus said that he cast out demons,[254] was that of the name of God.
Leisegang would therefore read ἐν ὀνόματι θεοῦ[255] in place of the Matthean ἐν
πνεύματι θεοῦ or the Lucan ἐν δακτύλῳ θεοῦ. He concludes that the concept
of πνεῦμα originated in the mystical, ecstatic experience of the early church,
which had been influenced by pagan Hellenistic ideas both of mysticism and
ethics.[256] Therefore, 'Der Geist begriff und die Wirkungen des Geistes mit dem
Leben und Prediген Jesu ursprünglich nichts zu tun hatten'.[257]

In our study of πνεῦμα in Hellenistic Judaism we have criticized Leisegang for
overestimating the extent of pagan influence on Philo of Alexandria, and underestimating the influence of the Jewish concept of *ruach* upon Greek ideas of
πνεῦμα. From our examination of the evidence it would seem that this criticism
could apply equally to Leisegang's work on spirit in the Synoptic Gospels. He
has overestimated the extent of pagan notions of πνεῦμα, whilst underestimating
the 'Judaizing' of the concept by the authors of the Diaspora. Any pagan
Hellenistic ideas of spirit had been already sifted by Hellenistic Judaism before
they reached Christianity. Furthermore, only Greek notions which they believed
to accord with the O.T. had been retained. It is therefore to the writers of the

---

249 H. Leisegang, *Hagion Pneuma* (Leipzig, 1922).
250 H. Leisegang, op. cit., p. 5.
251 H. Leisegang, op. cit., pp.14–71.
252 H. Leisegang, op. cit., pp. 80–95.
253 Cf. Lev. 24:15–16.
254 Mt 12:27f; Lk 11:19f.
255 H. Leisegang, op. cit., pp. 98–105.
256 H. Leisegang, op. cit., p. 143. See also idem, *Der Heilige Geist*, p. 240.
257 H. Leisegang, *Hagion Pneuma*, p.142.

Dispersion and especially to the LXX that we must look for the pre-Christian history of the concept of πνεῦμα, and it is our contention that a study of such writings does not uphold Leisegang's thesis of extensive pagan borrowing.

We have seen that as it is used in the N.T. πνεῦμα is predominantly an eschatological and christological term. Furthermore it is applied far more to the life of the church and its beliefs about the risen Christ than to the earthly ministry of Jesus. This does not necessarily mean, however, that the concept of spirit was the product of the early church or that Jesus never thought in such terms. We have noted that 'spirit' as a referent of the divine did not play a dominant part in contemporary thinking, be it Jewish or pagan. In popular belief spirit was more usually associated with demonology than with theology, as can be seen in the Marcan exorcisms. It is therefore quite probable that Jesus himself spoke very little of the spirit of God.[258] In which case the paucity of references to the spirit in the Synoptic Gospels[259] may be a true reflection of the historical situation. But because Jesus rarely spoke of his ministry in terms of 'spirit', it does not necessarily follow that all such references are the product of the early church. Each pericope has to be judged on its own merits, rather than its authenticity being doubted as an axiom. There is little reason to doubt that Jesus saw himself in some prophetic role. In which case he could well have attributed his calling and prophetic powers to the spirit of God. He could also have seen himself engaged in an eschatological conflict with the powers of evil and it may well be that he expressed this in terms of the holy spirit of God versus the unclean spirits of Satan.

Obviously the concept of spirit has undergone considerable adaptation within the life of the early church. Here, as a category of thought it comes to the fore, and is used to express the church's beliefs about her own identity and that of her Lord. The *Sitz im Leben* which brought this about was the church's need for ammunition in its polemic against Judaism.

---

258 So E. Schweizer, *Spirit of God,* p. 35, 'Therefore it may be taken as a historical fact that Jesus himself said hardly anything about the spirit'.

259 J.E. Yates, *The Spirit and the Kingdom* (London, 1963), p. 37, sees no more significance in the paucity of references to the spirit in the Synoptics than the fact that they also rarely use the divine name itself. Yet this does not account for its abundant use in other parts of the N.T.

11
CONCLUSIONS

Πνεῦμα is predominantly a theological concept

We have seen that the authors of the LXX, in choosing to translate *ruach* in terms of πνεῦμα, have introduced Jewish theological ideas into pagan Greek concepts of πνεῦμα. In so doing they began a process, which was continued by other writers of Hellenistic Judaism, whereby πνεῦμα became predominantly πνεῦμα θεοῦ, infused with Jewish ideas of the nature of God and His dealings with His chosen people. Only in Stoicism was πνεῦμα important as a signification of the divine. In an attempt to refute certain Stoic notions of πνεῦμα, and in an effort to introduce biblical ideas of God, Diaspora writers such as Philo brought πνεῦμα to the fore as a theological concept.

Early Christian writers are indebted to their Hellenistic Jewish predecessors for this preliminary work, since it is pre-eminently as a theological concept that πνεῦμα occurs in the N.T., so much so that it is often difficult to determine whether the spirit of man or the spirit of God is meant. This is understandable in the light of the way in which Philo uses πνεῦμα as a term of kinship; as the image of God in man. As such it is never wholly free from its divine signification, even when it is treated as a constituent part of human nature. In the N.T. this is even more evident, for writers such as Paul view πνεῦμα primarily as an eschatological gift rather than as a term of anthropology.

It is usual to deny that Hellenistic Judaism contributed anything to the eschatology of the N.T. Thus R.H. Fuller says, 'Hellenistic Judaism yields nothing creative for the eschatological interpretation of Jesus'.[1] Such a statement needs modification, however. As we have seen, Diaspora Judaism developed traditions concerning the figure of Moses which were to be taken up and given an eschatological orientation by N.T. writers. Furthermore, the way in which Hellenistic Jewish authors retain the word πνεῦμα for the one, good and holy Deity of Judaism, refusing to allow its use for the demonic, may have exercized an influence upon N.T. eschatological vocabulary. Unlike *ruach* which was part of the terminology of demonology, πνεῦμα was not. The LXX translators and their Diaspora successors preferred to use δαίμων and its cognates when they wished

---

1   R.H. Fuller, *The Foundation of New Testament Christology* (London, 1965), p. 67.

to signify evil spirits. With the notable exception of Mark, this tendency can be observed in the N.T. and may be attributable to the influence of Hellenistic Judaism.

Πνεῦμα is a term used in anti-Jewish polemic

The ways in which the writers of Hellenistic Judaism used the term πνεῦμα reflect the claims made by the Jews for their faith over against the claims made by paganism. Not only do they use πνεῦμα as a designation of their God, Jahweh, they claim the inspiration of πνεῦμα for the Jewish scriptures, for their great law-giver Moses, and they assert that it is the possession of the Jewish community, in whom it engenders superior wisdom. Inevitably, therefore, πνεῦμα carries with it claims to a unique and superior revelation. Even in the apologetic works of Philo this is true, for although the Alexandrian philosopher occasionally used πνεῦμα as the divinely implanted principle of reason in all men, his predominant use of the term is in the interests of maintaining the superiority of the revelation granted to Judaism. In this sense πνεῦμα may be described as part of the vocabulary of Jewish particularism.

Samuel Sandmel has written, 'In my view Christianity emerged not as a pure universalism but as a new particularism'.[2] Our study of πνεῦμα would lend support to this judgement, since N.T. writers, even more than those of Hellenistic Judaism, use the concept in order to stress their exclusive claims to a final revelation. J.C. O'Neill has pointed out that in a number of respects the author of Acts is indebted to the missionaries of Hellenistic Judaism. He classifies Acts as apologetic in *genre* and claims that Luke, in common with his Diaspora predecessors, adopts similar techniques, e.g. commending heroes of the faith, appealing to the state, and using philosophical arguments.[3] We would maintain that it is against such a background that the N.T. understanding of πνεῦμα can be understood. Just as Hellenistic Judaism used the concept of πνεῦμα to press the superiority of its claims, so Christian writers adopted the self-same usages in order to assert the supremacy of their faith over against Judaism.

As the Diaspora Jews located πνεῦμα in Israel, so N.T. writers asserted that the church, the new Israel, was the only true place of faith and home of the spirit, and as such, was the eschatological community which had superseded Judaism. As Hellenistic Judaism had claimed that their scriptures had been inspired by the prophetic πνεῦμα, so the early church now laid claim to pneumatic inspiration which granted them alone true insight into the inner meaning of those

---

2 S. Sandmel, *The First Christian Century in Judaism and Christianity: Certainties and Uncertainties* (Oxford, 1969), p. 81.
3 J.C. O'Neill, *The Theology of Acts in its Historical Setting* (2nd ed. London, 1970), pp. 139–159.

scriptures. Only in as far as the O.T. witnessed to Christ could it be said to have the inspiration of the spirit; the supreme task of the prophet within the church was to bear witness to Jesus, the Christ. The old dispensation which had asserted that it was inspired by πνεῦμα is in fact, according to Paul, mere γράμμα or σάρξ; the true πνεῦμα resides in Christ and his church. As Hellenistic Judaism had claimed superior revelation for Moses and attributed him with a greater portion of the divine πνεῦμα, so N.T. writers make similar claims for Jesus. Hence he is depicted as being endowed with an inspiration which is superior to that of Moses and his revelation is seen as superseding the Mosaic Torah. Thus the power and presence of God signified by πνεῦμα, which had previously been claimed for their faith by Hellenistic Jews in their polemic against Gentile pretentions to revelation, have been taken up by N.T. writers in their debate with Judaism, and located exclusively in Christ and the Christian community. The use of πνεῦμα in the N.T., notably in the Epistle to the Hebrews, Luke–Acts, John and especially the Pauline Epistles, may therefore be seen within the context of the church's polemic against Jewish claims to supreme revelation.[4]

The pneumatology of the N.T. is indebted to the figure of wisdom in Hellenistic Judaism

The figure of wisdom as developed in Hellenistic Judaism has not only influenced the christology of the N.T., but also its pneumatology. In the literature of the Diaspora σοφία, λόγος and πνεῦμα were inter-related concepts, and this may throw light on the relationship between pneumatology and christology, since in both areas of thought wisdom ideas are utilized.

We have seen that the figure of wisdom may well lie behind the Johannine 'spirit of truth' and 'spirit-paraclete'. Furthermore, not only the doctrine of the pre-existence of Christ, but also the close association (and possible identification) of Christ with the spirit which we find in Johannine and Pauline writings, may have arisen out of an identification of Christ with the wisdom figure of Hellenistic Judaism. If this hypothesis is correct then it would help to explain the close connection between the doctrine of the person of Christ and the doctrine of the spirit which we find in the N.T.

---

4 E.J. Epp, *The Theological Tendency of Codex Bezae Cantabrigiensis in Acts* (Cambridge, 1966), has noted anti-Judaic tendencies in Codex Bezae. A number of additional references to πνεῦμα are to be found in this text (see Appendix E, p. 157). According to Epp, op. cit., p. 118 these reflect a similar tendency, in which case they demonstrate a development of the same anti-Jewish use of πνεῦμα as we have in our text.

APPENDICES

APPENDIX A
The Literature of Hellenistic Judaism
which has survived in whole or part

I – Translation of the Scriptures

The LXX (K):

The Law	3rd Century B.C.
The Prophets	2nd Century B.C.
The Writings	1st Century B.C. – 1st Century A.D.

Judaistic Revisers:[1]

i) Aquila	Early 2nd Century A.D.
ii) Theodotion	Late 2nd Century A.D.
iii) Symmachus	Early 3rd Century A.D.

II – Revision and Completion of Scriptural Literature

(a) *Books canonical in Palestine:*
   i) *1 Esdras*   c. 150 B.C.
      (all but 3:1–5:6 probably had a Semitic original)

   ii) Additions to *Esther* –   c. 100 B.C.
       i.e. 11:2–12:6; 13:1–7; 13:8–18; 14:1–19; 15:1–16; 16:1–24

   iii) Additions to *Daniel*[2] –   c. 100 B.C.
        (behind which possibly lie Semitic originals)
        i.e. *Prayer of Azariah, Song of the Three Holy Children,
           History of Susanna, Bel and the Dragon*

   iv) *Prayer of Manasseh*   1st Century B.C. – 3rd Century A.D.
       (possibly having a Semitic original)

(b) *Additional works accepted as canonical by Hellenistic Judaism:*
   i) *Baruch*   c. 100 B.C.?
      (possibly all but 4:5–5:9 had a Semitic original)

   ii) *Epistle of Jeremiah*   323 – 100 B.C.
       (possibly having a Semitic original)

---

1 Whilst all three Judaistic revisers present students of the LXX with the problem of the appearance of characteristic readings before their time (see S. Jellicoe, op. cit., pp. 74–99), these revisions as we now have them date from the 2nd century A.D. onwards and therefore cannot be used as evidence of the pre-Christian usage of πνεῦμα.
2 By the late 3rd century A.D. the Theodotionic version of *Daniel* had supplanted the Alexandrian version.

III — Historical Literature

i)	Demetrius	Late 3rd Century B.C.
ii)	Eupolemus	Mid 2nd Century B.C.
iii)	Artapanus	c. 100 B.C.
iv)	Aristeas	c. 100 B.C.
v)	Cleodemus or Malchus	c. 100 B.C.
vi)	An anonymous work[3]	c. 100 B.C.
vii)	Jason of Cyrene and 2 *Maccabees*	c. 160 B.C.
viii)	Pseudo-Hecataeus	c. 200 — 150 B.C.
ix)	*3 Maccabees*	1st Century B.C. — 1st Century A.D.
x)	Historical works of Philo Judaeus:	Early 1st Century A.D.

De Vita Mosis, De Vita Contemplativa, Legatione ad Gaium, In Flaccum

xi) The historical works of Flavius Josephus:

Vita	c. A.D. 100
Bellum Judaicum	A.D. 75–79
Antiquitates Judaicae	A.D. 93–94

xii) Justus Tiberius   1st Century A.D.

IV — Epic Poetry and Drama

i)	Philo the Epic Writer[4]	2nd Century B.C.
ii)	Theodotus[5]	2nd Century B.C.
iii)	Ezekiel the Tragedian[6]	2nd Century B.C.

V — Wisdom Literature and Philosophy

i)	*The Wisdom of Solomon*	c. 150 B.C.
ii)	Aristobulus[7]	181 — 145 B.C.
iii)	*4 Maccabees*	Early 1st Century A.D.
iv)	Philo Judaeus[8] :	Early 1st Century A.D.

Allegorical commentaries on the Pentateuch:

Quastiones in Exodum (Extant in Armenian), *Quastiones in Genesin* (Extant in Armenian), *Legum Allegoriae, De Cherubim, Quod Deterius Potiori Insidiari Soleat, Quod Deus Sit Immutabilis,*

---

3   Authors i) to vi) are quoted from Polyhistor in Strom. I, 21–23 and Praep.Ev. IX, 17–39. See Müller, Fr. III, 207ff.
4   See Praep.Ev. IX, 20, 24, 37; Strom. I, 21, 141.
5   See Praep.Ev. IX, 22.
6   See Praep.Ev. IX, 28, 19; Strom. I, 23, 155.
7   See Praep.Ev. VII, 12; XIII, 12; Hist. Eccl. VII, 32, 17–18.
8   Most of these works could also be classified as Apologetic.

Allegorical commentaries on the Pentateuch (continued):
De Agricultura, De Plantatione, De Sacrificiis Abelis et Caini,
De Ebrietate, De Sobrietate, De Gigantibus, De Posteritate Caini,
De Confusione Linguarum, De Migratione Abrahae,
Quis Rerum Divinarum Heres Sit, De Congressu Eruditionis Gratia,
De Fuga et Inventione, De Mutatione Nominum, De Somniis

Other works:
De Aeternitate Mundi, Quod Omnis Probus Liber Sit,
De Providentia (Fragments), *De Opificio Mundi, De Decalogo,*
De Abrahamo, De Josepho, De Specialibus Legibus,
De Praemis et Poenis, De Virtutibus, Alexander

VI – Apologetics
   i) Philo   1st Century A.D.
     See above (V).
     Hypothetica (Armenian fragments of Apologia[9] no longer extant)
  ii) Josephus
     Contra Apionem   c. 100 A.D.

VII– Jewish Propaganda in the Guise of Pagan Authorship
   i) *Sibylline Oracles*   1st Century A.D.
     Bk. III, 98–808[10]
  ii) Pseudo-Hecataeus[11]   3rd Century B.C.
 iii) *The Letter of Aristeas*   c. 100 B.C.
 iv) Pseudo-Phocylides   1st Century B.C.

VIII Apocalyptic Writings
   i) *2 Enoch*   1st Century A.D.
     (extant only in Slavonic)
  ii) *3 Baruch*   2nd – 3rd Centuries A.D.?

IX Liturgy
   i) Prayers embodied in   2nd Century A.D.
     Const. Apost. VII, 33–38

---

9 See Praep. Ev. VIII, 1–11.
10 Some of Books IV and V are also probably Jewish in part, dating from the 1st Century A.D.
11 See C. Ap. I, 183–204.

APPENDIX B
A Classification of the various occurrences of πνεῦμα
in the Literature of Hellenistic Judaism

(For the occurrence of πνεῦμα in the LXX cf. E. Hatch and H.A. Redpath,
A Concordance to the Septuagint and other Greek versions of the O.T.
Vol. II, pp. 1151–1153)

I – Πνεῦμα as wind
Sap Sol 5:23; 7:20; 13:2(?); 17:18;
Song of the Three Holy Children 26 (Dan 3:50 LXX); 42 (Dan 3:65 LXX);
Epistle of Jeremiah; 2 Enoch 21:5 (extant only in Slavonic); Sib. Or. III, 102;
Philo: Abr.43; 92; 160; Aet.11; 139; Agr. 174; Cher. 13; 37f; Congr. 133;
    Flacc. 155; Immut. 26; 60; 98; 175; Jos. 32; Leg. ad Gaium 177;
    Leg. Alleg. III, 53; 223; Migr. 148, 217; Opif. 41; 58; 80; Post. C. 22;
    Prob. 26(?); Prov. 2.45; Qu. Ex. II, 55; Som. II, 13; 67; Som. II, 85; 86;
    143; 166; Spec. Leg. I, 26; 92; 301; Spec. Leg. II, 71; 191;
    Spec. Leg. IV, 27; V. Mos. I, 41; 179; V. Mos. II, 104.
Josephus: Ant. II, 343; 349; VIII, 346; IX, 36; 210; X, 279; XII, 75; XIV, 28;
    XVI, 17; 20; 62.

II – Πνεῦμα as air
(a) *Used as synonymous with ἀήρ*
Sap Sol 5:11; Philo: Gig.10; Praem. 41; Spec. Leg. II, 153; Virt. 135;
Josephus: B.J. IV, 477.
(b) *One of the elements*
Philo: Aet. 111; Cher. 111; Ebr. 106; Gig. 22; Leg. Alleg. I, 91; Opif. 29;
Sacr. 97.
(c) *As a cohesive force (ἕξις)*
Philo: Aet. 86; 125; Heres. 242; Immut. 35; Opif. 131; Praem. 48; Prob.26(?).

III – Πνεῦμα as breath
(a) *Respiration*
Bel and the Dragon 36 (Th.); 4 Macc. 11:11; Sap Sol 11:20; Philo: Decal.33;
Immut. 84; Leg. ad Gaium 125; 188; 243; Leg. Alleg. III, 14; Som. I, 20;
Spec. Leg. I, 338; Josephus: Ant. I, 27; III, 291; XVII, 169.
– *essential for life:* Baruch 2:17; 2 Macc 7:22f; 14:46; Sap Sol 2:3.

(b) *Principle upon which life depends*
2 Enoch 30:7(A); Esther 16:12 (LXX 8:13); Epistle of Jeremiah 25;
3 Macc.6:24; Sap Sol 15:11; 16:14; Philo: Det.80; Leg. ad Gaium 63 (cf.
3 Macc.6:24); Opif. 30; Spec. Leg. IV, 217; Qu. Gen. I, 4; II, 8:15; III, 3;
Josephus: Ant. XI, 240.

IV – Πνεῦμα as the spirit of man
(a) *One of the components of man*
Sap Sol 15:16; 2 Enoch 30:8; Philo: Opif. 135; 144; Qu. Gen. I, 51;
Josephus: Ant. I, 34; III, 260.
(i) *equated with* ψυχή: Baruch 3:1; Song of the Three Holy Children 63
(LXX Dan 3:86); Sap Sol 15:11; Philo: Plant 18; Josephus: Ant. XI, 240.
(ii) *given to the* ψυχή: Philo: Opif. 67.
(iii) *the essence of the* ψυχή: Philo: Det. 80; Heres. 55; Spec. Leg. IV, 123;
Qu. Gen. II, 59.
(iv) *equated or closely associated with the rational side of man:* Philo: Det.83;
Fug. 182; Leg. Alleg. I, 6; Qu. Ex. I, 5. – *equated with* νοῦς: Philo: Fug. 133;
Leg. Alleg. I, 33; 37; 42. – *equated with* λογισμός: Philo: Heres. 57; cf.
4 Macc. 7:13. – Λογικόν πνεῦμα *the dominant part of man:* Philo: Spec. Leg. I,
171; 277.
(v) *interior, moral guide:* Sib. Or., III, 5f. Philo: Som. II, 252.
(b) *Denoting human emotion, disposition*
– *frenzy:* Sib. Or. III, 40; Josephus: B.J. III, 92 – *anguish:* Sap Sol 5:3
– *humility:* Song of the Three Holy Children 15 (LXX Dan 3.39)
– *steadfastness:* Philo: Det. 17 – *mood, inclination:* Esther 15:8 (LXX 5:1)
– *essential character, personality:* Philo: V. Mos. II, 40.

V – The Spirit of God (πνεῦμα θεῖον or πνεῦμα θεοῦ)
(a) *Expressing the nature of God*
(i) *powerful, one, holy etc:* Sap Sol 1:5; 7:22f; 9:17; 11:20; Sib. Or. III, 701;
Philo: Det. 83; Plant. 18; Josephus: B.J. II, 138f (Slav. add.).
(ii) *the presence of God:* Josephus: Ant. VIII, 114; Philo: Spec. Leg. IV, 123.
(iii) *transient:* Philo: Gig. 19; 28; 53; Immut. 2.
(b) *The source of life*[1]
(i) *in creation:* Philo: Leg. Alleg. I, 33; Qu. Gen. IV, 5; Qu. Gen. II, 28 *(brought
about the cessation of the flood).*
(ii) *all pervading:* Sap Sol 12:1; 1:7; Philo: Gig. 26f.
(iii) *given to the righteous after Judgement:* Sib. Or. IV, 46; 189.

---

1 Cf. III(b). Πνεῦμα as breath, the principle upon which life depends.

(c) *One of the components of man*[2]
Philo: Opif. 135; Qu. Gen. I, 51; II, 59 — *given in full strength to archetypal man:* Philo: Opif. 144 — *the dominant part of the* ψυχή: Philo: Heres. 53; Spec. Leg. IV, 123; Virt. 217.
(d) *Inspirational*
Philo: Qu. Ex. II, 33
(i) *source of understanding, wisdom etc:* Sap Sol 1:5f; 7:7; 9:17; Susanna 42; 64 (LXX); 4 Macc. 7:13; Philo: Gig. 23f; 47; Heres. 57; Jos. 116; Leg.Alleg. I, 36; Plant. 24; Qu. Gen. I, 90; Qu. Ex. II, 7; V. Mos. II, 265; Josephus: Ant.X, 239.
(ii) *source of prophecy:* Philo: Decal. 175; Fug. 186; Qu. Ex. I, 4; II, 29; V.Mos. I, 175; 277; Josephus: Ant. IV, 108; 118; 119f; VI, 166; 222f; VIII, 408 — *evicts the* νοῦς: Philo: Heres. 265; Qu. Gen. III, 9; Qu. Ex. II, 105; Spec. Leg. IV, 49.

VI — Denoting supernatural beings

(a) *Disembodied, supernatural beings in general*
2 Macc 3:24 (variant reading); Philo: Agr. 44; Post. C. 67; Virt. 58; Qu. Gen. II, 8.
(b) *Angels*
2 Enoch 12:1; (B); 16:7; Philo: Qu. Gen. I, 92; Abr. 113; Josephus: Ant. IV, 108.
(c) *Demons, evil spirits*
2 Enoch 31:4 (A); Josephus: Ant. VI, 211; 214.
(d) *Disembodied spirits of the wicked*
Josephus: B.J. VII, 185.

---

2 Cf. IV(a). In certain respects there is no clear distinction between the spirit of man and the Spirit of God.

APPENDIX C
The Distribution of Πνεῦμα and Cognates in the N.T.

	πνεῦμα	πνευματικός	πνευματικῶς
Matthew	19	0	0
Mark	22	0	0
Luke[1]	36	0	0
John	23	0	0
Acts[2]	71	0	0
Romans	34	3	0
1 Corinthians	39	16	2
2 Corinthians	17	0	0
Galatians	18	1	0
Ephesians	14	3	0
Philippians	5	0	0
Colossians	2	2	0
1 Thessalonians	5	0	0
2 Thessalonians	3	0	0
1 Timothy	3	0	0
2 Timothy	3	0	0
Titus	3	0	0
Philemon	1	0	0
Hebrews	12	0	0
James	2	0	0
1 Peter	8	2	0
2 Peter	1	0	0
1 John	12	0	0
2 John	0	0	0
3 John	0	0	0
Jude	2	0	0
Revelation	24	0	1
Total = 409	379	27	3

1 Taking Lk 9:55 as a textual addition and therefore not included in the total.
See J.M. Creed, Luke, p. 141.
2 Not including the 7 additional references to πνεῦμα in Codex Bezae.
See Appendix E, p. 157.

APPENDIX D
A Classification of the various occurrences of Πνεῦμα
in the New Testament

I – Πνεῦμα as wind
John 3:8.

II – Πνεῦμα as breath
(a) *Respiration*
Jas 2:26; Rev 13:15; 2 Thes 2:8 (LXX Ps 32:6, MT 33:6).
(b) *Principle upon which life depends*
Mt 27:50; Lk 8:55; 23:46 (LXX Ps 31:5); Jn 19:30; Acts 7:59; Rev 11:11.

III – The spirit of man
(a) *One of the components of man*
1 Cor 2:11; 5:3, 5; 7:34; 14:14; 2 Cor 7:1; 1 Thes 5:23; Col 2:5; Heb 4:12(?);
Jas 4:5(?); Rev 22:6(?).
(i) *the will:* Mk 14:38; Mt 26:41.
(ii) *the ψυχή or self:* Mk 2:8; 8:12; Lk 1:47; Rom 1:9; 8:16; 1 Cor 5:4; 16:18;
2 Cor 2:13; 7:13; Gal 6:18; Phil 1:27; 4:23; 2 Tim 4:22; Philem 25:
Heb 9:14(?).
(iii) *νοῦς:* Eph 4:23.
(b) *Human emotion, disposition*
John 11:33 – *humility:* Mt 5:3 – *exasperation:* Acts 17:16
– *enthusiasm:* Acts 18:25; Rom 12:11 – *agitation:* Jn 13:21
– *gentleness, meekness:* Gal 6:1; 1 Cor 4:21; 1 Pet 3:4 – *stupor:* Rom 11:8
– *fear:* 2 Tim 1:7 – *prophecy:* 1 Jn 4:1, 2, 3(?); 2 Thes 2:2(?) (Cf. 1 Cor
14:37 where πνευματικός = a prophet.)

IV – The Spirit of God
(a) *Expressing the nature of God*
Jn 4:24; 1 Cor 2:12; 12:4, 8–11 (cf Eph 2:18); 2 Cor 3:3, 8, 17, 18;
1 Pet 4:14; 7 spirits = the fulness of the godhead: Rev 1:4; 3:1; 4:5; 5:6.
(b) *An eschatological gift*
expressed in terms of – *grace:* 2 Cor 13:13; Heb 10:29 – *joy:* Acts 13:52
(cf Lk 10:21); Rom 14:17; 15:13; 1 Thes 1:6 – *new life:* Rom 8:10, 11;
1 Cor 15:45 – *rebirth:* Jn 3:5, 8; Tit 3:5.

(i) *located in Christ:* Mk 1:10, 12; 3:29; Mt 1:18, 20; 3:16; 4:1; 12:18, 28, 31f; Lk 1:15, 17, 35, 80; 3:22; 4:1, 14, 18 (LXX Isa 61:1f); 12:10; Jn 1:32, 33; 3:34; Acts 2:33; 1 Cor 15:45; 1 Cor 6:17 (cf. Eph 2:18) – *the spirit of Christ:* Rom 8:9f; Phil 1:19; 1 Pet 1:11 – *the spirit of His son:* Gal 4:6 – *the spirit of Jesus:* Acts 16:7.

(ii) *located in the church* – *compulsive force:* Acts 8:39; Rev 1:10; 4:2; 17:3; 21:10 – *associated with power:* Acts 1:8; 10:38; Rom 15:13, 19; I Cor 2:4; 1 Thes 1:5; Eph 3:16; 2 Tim 1:7; Heb 2:4; cf. Gal 3:5. *For the power of* πνευματικόν Χάρισμα – see Rom 1:11. – *a gift:* 1 Cor 12:7, 8–11; 2 Cor 6:6; 11:4; 1 Thes 4:8; Heb 6:4 (cf. πνευματικός in 1 Cor 2:13; 12:1; 14:1; Eph 1:3) – *given to disciples:* Jn 20:22; Acts 10:44, 45; 11:15; Acts 5:8; Rom 5:5 – *sign of sonship:* Rom 8:14, 15, 16; Gal 4:6 – *first fruit:* Rom 8:23 – *'earnest':* 2 Cor 1:22; 5:5: Eph 1:13 – *associated with faith, obedience:* Jn 7:39; 14:17; Acts 5:32; 6:5; 9:17; 11:24; 14:17; 2 Cor 4:13; Gal 3:2; 3:14; 5:5 – *indwelling:* Rom 8:9, 11; 1 Cor 3:16; 2 Tim 4:22; 1 Jn 3:24; 4:13 – *connected with the church's rites:*– *baptism:* Mk 1:8; Mt 3:11; 28:19; Lk 3:16; Acts 1:5; 11:16; 1 Cor 6:11; 12:13; Eph 4:30(?) (*preceding baptism:* Acts 10:47, *following baptism:* Acts 2:38) – *laying on of hands:* Acts 8:17, 18, 19; 19:2, 6 – *prayer:* Lk 11:13; Acts 8:15; Rom 8:26, 27; Eph 6:18; Jude 20 – *the sphere of true worship:* Jn 4:23, 24; Phil 3:3 – *the principle of unity:* Phil 2:1; Eph 3:4 – *the church's guide and helper:* Mk 13:11; Mt 10:20; Lk 12:12 (*paraclete:* Jn 14:17; 14:26; 16:13); Acts 1:2; 5:3, 9; 7:51; 8:29; 9:31; 10:19; 11:12; 13:4; 15:28; 16:6, 7; 20:22, 23, 28; 21:4; 1 Tim 4:1; Rev 2:7, 11, 17, 29; Rev 3:6, 13, 22; 14:13; 22:17 – *empowers the church's preaching:* Acts 2:4; 4:8; 4:31; 7:55; Acts 13:9; 1 Pet 1:12; cf Eph 6:17 – *associated with the work of sanctification:* Rom 15:16, 30; (cf. Rom 9:1); 1 Cor 6:19 (cf. Eph 2:22); Gal 5:16, 22, 25; 6:8; 2 Thes 2:13; Col 1:8; Eph 5:18; 1 Pet 1:2.

(iii) *inspirational* – *inspired the Scriptures:* Heb 3:7; 9:8; 10:15; 2 Pet 1:21 – *inspired David:* Mk 12:36; Mt 22:43; Acts 1:16; 4:25 – *inspired Isaiah:* Acts 28:25 – *inspired N.T. prophets:* Lk 1:41, 67; 2:25, 26, 27; Acts 2:17,18; 11:28; 13:2; 21:11; 1 Cor 14:32; 1 Thes 5:19; Eph 3:5; Rev 22:6 – *ecstatic:* 1 Cor 14:2, 15f – *associated with understanding, wisdom:* Acts 6:3, 10; 1 Cor 2:10; 7:40; Eph 1:17 (cf. πνευματικός in Col 1:9) – *spirit of truth:* Jn 14:17; 16:13; 1 Jn 4:6 (cf. 1 Jn 5:6) – *bears witness to Jesus as the Christ:* Jn 15:26; 1 Jn 4:2; 1 Jn 5:6, 8; 1 Cor 12:3; cf. Rev 19:10.

(c) *Characterizing life in Christ and contrasted with:*

(i) Σάρξ: Jn 3:6; 6:63; Rom 8:4, 5, 6, 13; Gal 5:17; 6:8; 4:29; 3:3; 1 Pet 4:6 (for Christians as πνευματικοί see 1 Cor 2:15; Gal 6:1); *a spiritual temple, offering spiritual sacrifices:* 1 Pet 2:5; *who sing spiritual songs:* Eph 5:19; Col 3:16; (for the πνευματικός/ψυχικός contrast see 1 Cor 15:44, 46; for the

πνευματικός/σαρκινός contrast see 1 Cor 3:1; Rom 15:27; 1 Cor 9:11) ;
2 aspects of Christ: Rom 1:4; 1 Tim 3:16; 1 Pet 3:18.
(ii) Γράμμα: Rom 2:29; 7:6 (cf. Rom 8:4); 2 Cor 3:6.
(iii) Νόμος: Gal 5:18; Rom 8:2, although in Rom 7:14 the Law is described
as πνευματικός. (Cf. 1 Cor 10:3f where the manna and the rock are described
as πνευματικός. Πνευματικῶς in Rev 11:8 is used in the sense of inner or
allegorical meaning.)

V – Supernatural beings
(a) *Demons, unclean spirits:*
Mk 1:23, 26, 27; 3:11, 30; 5:2, 8, 13; 6:7; 7:25; 9:17, 20, 25; Mt 8:16; 10:1;
12:43, 45; Lk 4:33, 36; 6:18; 7:21; 8:2, 29; 9:39, 42; (9:55) 10:20; 11:24, 26;
13:11; Acts 5:16; 8:7; 16:16, 18; 19:12, 13, 15, 16; Rev 16:13, 14; 18:2;
Eph 2:2; 1 Tim 4:1(?). Cf. Eph 6:12 τὰ πνεύματα τῆς πονηρίας.
(b) *Disembodied spirits*
Lk 24:37, 39; Heb 12:9(?); Heb 12:23; 1 Pet 3:19(?).
(c) *Angels*
Acts 23:8, 9(?); Heb 1:7, 14; Rev 1:4(?); 3:1(?); 4:5(?); 5:6(?).

APPENDIX E
Additional references to Πνεῦμα
in the Western Text *(Codex Bezae)* of Acts

Acts 11:17   Into Peter's speech on his vision concerning Cornelius, D adds: τοῦ μή δοῦναι αὐτοῖς πνεῦμα ἅγιον πιστεύσασιν ἐπ᾽ αὐτῷ.

Acts 15:7   Peter's speech at the Council of Jerusalem is attributed to the inspiration of the spirit by the addition of: ἀνέστησεν ἐν πνεύματι.

Acts 15:29   To the apostolic letter concerning the admission of Gentiles is added: φερόμενοι ἐν τῷ ἁγίῳ πνεύματι.

Acts 15:32   The bearers of the apostolic letter, Judas and Silas, are: πλήρεις πνεύματος ἁγίου.

Acts 19:1   An explanation as to why Paul did not go to Jerusalem at this point is added by D: Θέλοντες δὲ τοῦ Παύλου κατὰ ἰδίαν βουλήν πορεύεσθαι εἰς Ἱεροσόλυμα εἶπεν αὐτῷ τὸ πνεῦμα ὑποστρέφειν εἰς τὴν Ἀσιαν.

Acts 20:3   The spirit is shown by D to inspire the apostle's choice of route: εἶπεν δὲ τὸ πνεῦμα αὐτῷ.

(Acts 26:1   The Syriac Harklean margin adds a reference to Paul's consolation by the spirit whilst he was before Agrippa: confidens et in spiritu sancto consolationem accipiens.)

BIBLIOGRAPHY

Aalen, S., *Die Befgriffe 'Licht' und 'Finsternis' im Alten Testament im Spätjudentums und im Rabbinismus,* Oslo, 1951.

Abbott, T.K., *The Epistles to the Ephesians and to the Colossians,* ICC, Edinburgh, 1897.

Abelson, J., *The Immanence of God in Rabbinical Literature,* London, 1912.

Abrahams, I., *Studies in Pharisaism and the Gospels,* Cambridge, 1917.

Albright, W.F., 'Recent Discoveries in Palestine and the Gospel of St. John', in *The Background of the N.T. and its Eschatology,* ed. W.D. Davies and D. Daube, Essays in Honour of C.H. Dodd, Cambridge, 1954, pp. 153–171.

Allen, W.C., *The Gospel According to St. Matthew,* ICC, 3rd ed., Edinburgh, 1912.

Allo, E-B., *Saint Paul Seconde Epître aux Corinthiens,* EB, Paris, 1956.

Allo, E-B., *Saint Jean L'Apocalypse,* EB, 4th ed., Paris, 1933.

Argyle, A.W., 'Philo and the Fourth Gospel', Exp.T., 63, 1951, pp. 385–386.

Arnim, H. von, *Stoicorum Veterum Fragmenta,* 4 Vols., Leipzig, 1903–1924.

Bakker, A., 'Christ an Angel?' ZNTW 32, 1933, pp. 255–265.

Bardy, J., ed., *Théophile D'Antioch, Trois Livre à Autolycus,* Paris, 1948.

Barr, J., *Old and New in Interpretation,* London, 1966.

Barr, J., *The Semantics of Biblical Language,* Oxford, 1961.

Barr, J., 'Which language did Jesus speak? Some remarks of a Semitist', BJRL 53, 1970, pp. 9–29.

Barrett, C.K., *The Holy Spirit and the Gospel Tradition,* 2nd ed., London, 1966.

Barrett, C.K., 'Important Hypotheses Reconsidered. V The Holy Spirit and the Gospel Tradition', Exp.T. 67, 1955–1956, pp. 142–145.

Barrett, C.K., 'The Holy Spirit and the Fourth Gospel', JTS 1, 1950, pp. 1–15.

Barrett, C.K., *The Gospel According to St. John,* London, 1955.

Barrett, C.K., *The Epistle to the Romans,* BNTC, London, 1957.

Barrett, C.K., *Luke the Historian in Recent Study,* London, 1961.

Barrett, C.K., 'The Eschatology of the Epistle to the Hebrews', in *The Background of the N.T. and its Eschatology,* ed. W.D. Davies and D. Daube, Cambridge, 1956, pp. 363–393.

Barrett, C.K., *From First Adam to Last,* London, 1962.

Bauer, W., *Griechisch-Deutsches Wörterbuch zu den Schriften des Neuen Testaments und der übrigen ürchristlichen Literatur,* 4th ed., Tübingen, 1952 (ET W.F. Arndt and F.W. Gingrich, *A Greek-English Lexicon of the N.T. and other Early Christian Literature,* Cambridge and Chicago, 1957).

Beare, F.W., *The Epistle to the Philippians,* BNTC, London, 1959.

Beare, F.W., *The First Epistle of Peter,* 2nd ed., Oxford, 1958.

Beare, F.W., *The Earliest Records of Jesus,* Oxford, 1964.

Behm, J., 'Παράκλητος', in TWNTE, Vol. V, pp. 800–814.

Belkin, S., *Philo and the Oral Law. The Philonic Interpretation of Biblical Law in Relation to the Palestinian Halakah,* Cambridge, Mass., 1940.

Bernard, J.H., *The Gospel According to St. John,* ICC, 2 Vols., Edinburgh, 1928.

Best, E., 'The use and non-use of pneuma by Josephus', NT, 3, 1959, pp. 218–225.

Best, E., *One Body in Christ,* London, 1955.

Best, E., *1 Peter,* CB, London, 1971.

Betz, O., *Der Paraklet,* Leiden, 1963.

Bevan, E., *Stoics and Sceptics,* Oxford, 1913.

Bevan, E., *Sibyls and Seers,* London, 1928.

Bevan, E., *Hellenism and Christianity,* London, 1921.

Bickermann, E., *Der Gott der Makkabäer,* Berlin, 1937.
Bicknell, E.J., *The First and Second Epistles to the Thessalonians,* WC, London, 1932.
Bigg, C., *The Epistles of St. Peter and St. Jude,* 2nd ed., ICC, Edinburgh, 1902.
Black, M., *The Scrolls and Christian Origins,* London, 1961.
Blass, F., and Debrunner, A., revised Funk, R.W., *A Greek Grammar of the N.T. and other Early Christian Literature,* 10th ed., Chicago, 1961.
Blau, L., 'Shekinah', in *The Jewish Encyclopaedia* XL, New York and London, 1905, pp. 258–260.
Boman, T., 'Hebraic and Greek Thought-forms in the N.T.', in *Current Issues in N.T. Interpretation,* Essays in Honour of Otto A. Piper, ed. W. Klassen and G.F. Snyder, London, 1962.
Boman, T., *Hebrew Thought Compared with Greek,* London, 1960.
Bonnard, P., *L'Evangile selon Saint Matthieu,* Neuchâtel, 1963.
Bonsirven, J., *Le Judaisme Palestinien temps de Jésus-Christ,* 2 Vols., Paris, 1934–1935.
Borgen, P., *Bread from Heaven,* Leiden, 1965.
Bornkamm, G., 'Der Paraklet im Johannesevangelium', in *Festschrift Rudolph Bultmann zum 65 Geburtstag überreicht,* Stuttgart, 1949, pp. 12–35.
Bousset, W., *Die Offenbarung Johannes,* Göttingen, 1906.
Bousset, W., *Kyrios Christos,* 2nd ed., Göttingen, 1921.
Bousset, W., *Die Religion des Judentums im späthellenistischen Zeitalter,* 3rd ed., Tübingen, 1926.
Bousset, W., 'Eine jüdische Gebetsammlung im siebenten Buch der apostolischen Konstitutionen', *Nachrichten von der K. Gesellschaft der Wissenschaft zu Göttingen* (Philologische-historische Klasses), 1915, pp. 435–485.
Bowman, J.W., *Hebrews, James, 1 and 2 Peter,* London, 1963.
Box, H., *In Flaccum,* Oxford, 1939.
Bréhier, E., *Les idées philosophiques et religieuses de Philon d'Alexandrie,* 3rd ed., 1950.
Briggs, C.A., 'The use of *ruach* in the O.T.', JBL, 19, 1900, pp. 132–145.
Brooke, A.E., *The Johannine Epistles,* ICC, Edinburgh, 1912.
Brown, R.E., *The Gospel According to St. John,* 2 Vols., New York, 1966–1970.
Brown, R.E., 'The Paraclete in the Fourth Gospel', NTS, 13, 1967, pp. 113–132.
Bruce, F.F., ' "To the Hebrews" or "To the Essenes"?' , NTS, 9, 1963, pp. 217–232.
Bruce, F.F., *The Acts of the Apostles,* 2nd ed., London, 1952.
Bruce, F.F., 'The Spirit in the Apocalypse', *Christ and Spirit,* ed. B. Lindars and S.Smalley, Cambridge, 1973, pp. 333–344.
Büchsel, F., *Der Geist Gottes im Neuen Testament,* Gütersloh, 1926.
Bultmann, R., *The History of the Synoptic Tradition,* 2nd ed., Oxford, 1968.
Bultmann, R., *The Gospel of John: A Commentary,* Oxford, 1971.
Bultmann, R., *Theology of the New Testament,* 2 Vols., London, 1952–1955.
Burrows, M., *More Light on the Dead Sea Scrolls,* London, 1958.
Burton, E. de Witt, *The Epistle to the Galatians,* ICC, Edinburgh, 1921.
Burton, E. de Witt, *Spirit, Soul and Flesh,* Chicago, 1918.
Butler, B.C., *The Originality of St. Matthew,* Cambridge, 1951.
Caird, G.B., *The Revelation of St. John the Divine,* BNTC, London, 1966.
Caird, G.B., *St. Luke,* PGC, Harmondsworth, 1963.
Caird, G.B., *Principalities and Powers,* Oxford, 1956.
Carpzov, J.B., *Sacrae exercitationes in S. Pauli epistolam ad Hebraeos ex Philone Alexandrine,* Helmstadt, 1750.
Cerfaux, L., *Christ in the Theology of St. Paul,* New York, 1959.
Chadwick, H., 'St. Paul and Philo of Alexandria', BJRL, 48, 1966, pp. 286–307.
Chadwick, H., *The Early Church,* Harmondsworth, 1967.
Chadwick, H., 'Philo and the Beginnings of Christian Thought', in *The Cambridge History of Later Greek and Early Medieval Philosophy,* ed., A.H. Armstrong, Cambridge, 1967, pp. 137–157.

Charles, R.H., ed., *The Apocrypha and Pseudepigrapha of the O.T. in English,* 2 Vols., Oxford, 1913.
Charles, R.H., *The Revelation of St. John,* ICC, 2 Vols., Edinburgh, 1920.
Clark, A.C., *The Acts of the Apostles,* Oxford, 1933.
Cohn, L., Wendland, P., Reiter, S., ed., *Philonis Alexandrini Opera,* 6 Vols., Berlin, 1896–1930.
Colson, F.H., 'Philo's Quotations from the O.T.', JTS, 41, 1940, pp. 250f.
Colson, F.H., Whitaker, G.H., Earp, J.W., *Philo,* Loeb Classical Library, 10 Vols., London and Cambridge, Mass., 1928–1962.
Conybeare, F.C., 'N.T. Notes. 1. The Holy Spirit as a Dove', Exp.T. 9, 1894, pp. 51–58.
Conzelmann, H., *Der erste Brief an die Korinther,* Göttingen, 1969.
Conzelmann, H., *Die Apostelgeschichte,* Tübingen, 1963.
Conzelmann, H., *The Theology of St. Luke,* London, 1960.
Coppens, J., 'Les Affinités qumraniennes de l'épître aux Hebreux', *Nouvelle Revue Théologique,* 84, 1962, pp. 270f.
Coppens, J., 'Le Don de l'Esprit d'Après Les Textes de Qumrân et Le Quatrième Evangile', in *Mélanges Bibliques rédiges en l'honneur de André Robert,* Paris, 1957, pp.209–223.
Cranfield, C.E.B., *1 and 2 Peter and Jude,* TBC, London, 1960.
Cranfield, C.E.B., *The Gospel According to St. Mark,* Cambridge, 1959.
Creed, J.M., *The Gospel According to St. Luke,* London, 1930.
Cross, F.M. Jr., 'The History of the Biblical Text in the light of discoveries in the Judean desert', HTR 62, 1964, pp. 281–99.
Cross, F.M. Jr., *The Ancient Library of Qumran,* New York, 1961.
Cullmann, O., 'The Significance of the Qumran Texts for Research into the Beginnings of Christianity', in *The Scrolls and the New Testament,* ed. K. Stendahl, London, 1958, pp. 18–32.
Cullmann, O., *The Christology of the New Testament,* London, 1959.
Dalman, G., *The Words of Jesus,* Edinburgh, 1902.
Dalton, W.J., *Christ's Proclamation to the Spirits,* Rome, 1965.
Daniélou, J., *Philon d'Alexandrie,* Paris, 1958.
Daube, D., *The New Testament and Rabbinic Judaism,* London, 1955.
Davies, W.D., *Paul and Rabbinic Judaism,* 2nd ed., London, 1955.
Davies, W.D., 'Paul and the Dead Sea Scrolls: Flesh and Spirit', in *The Scrolls and the N.T.,* ed., K. Stendahl, London, 1958, pp. 157–182.
Davies, W.D., *Christian Origins and Judaism,* London, 1962.
Davies, J.G., 'The Primary Meaning of Παράκλητος', JTS, 4, 1953, pp. 35–38.
Deissmann, A., *Paul: a Study in Social and Religious History,* 2nd ed., New York, 1927.
Delling, G., *Bibliographie zur jüdisch-hellenistischen und intertestamentorischen Literatur, 1900–1965,* Berlin, 1969.
Delling, G., 'Josephus und das Wunderbare', NT, 2, 1957, pp. 291–309.
Denis, A-M., *Introduction aux pseudépigraphes grecs d'Ancien Testament,* Leiden, 1970.
Dibelius, M., *Die urchristliche Überlieferung von Johannes dem Täufer,* Göttingen, 1911.
Dibelius, M., *Der Brief des Jakobus,* 11th ed., Göttingen, 1964.
Diels, H., *Die Fragmente der Vorsokratiker,* 5th ed., Berlin, 3 Vols., 1934–1935.
Dobschütz, E. von, *Die Thessalonischerbriefe,* Leipzig, 1909.
Dodd, C.H., *The Bible and the Greeks,* London, 1935.
Dodd, C.H., *The Epistle of Paul to the Romans,* MNTC, London, 1932.
Dodd, C.H., *The Interpretation of the Fourth Gospel,* Cambridge, 1953.
Dodd, C.H., *Historical Tradition in the Fourth Gospel,* Cambridge, 1965.
Dodd, C.H., *The Johannine Epistles,* MNTC, London, 1946.
Drummond, J., *Philo Judaeus; or the Jewish-Alexandrian Philosophy in its Development and Completion,* 2 Vols., London, 1888.
Duncan, G.S., *The Epistle of Paul to the Galatians,* MNTC, London, 1934.
Dunn, J.D.G., '2 Corinthians III 17 – "The Lord is the Spirit"', JTS, 21, 1970, pp.309–320.

Dunn, J.D.G., *Baptism in the Holy Spirit,* London, 1970.
Dunn, J.D.G., 'Spirit and Kingdom', Exp.T. 82, 1970, pp. 36–40.
Dupont, J., 'Ascension du Christ et don de l'Esprit d'après Actes 2:33', *Christ and Spirit,* ed. B. Lindars and S. Smalley, Cambridge, 1973, pp. 219–228.
Edwards, T.C., *The First Epistle of St. Paul to the Corinthians,* London, 1885.
Eichrodt, W., *Theology of the Old Testament,* 2 Vols., London, 1967.
Eisler, R., *The Messiah Jesus and John the Baptist According to Flavius Josephus' Recently Rediscovered 'Capture of Jerusalem' and Other Jewish and Christian Sources,* London, 1931.
Eissfeldt, O., *The Old Testament, An Introduction,* Oxford, 1965.
Ellicott, C.J., *St. Paul's Epistles to the Thessalonians,* 3rd ed., London, 1866.
Ellis, E.E., *The Gospel of Luke,* CB, London, 1966.
Ellis, E.E., *Paul's Use of the Old Testament,* Edinburgh, 1957.
Epp, E.J., *The Theological Tendency of Codex Bezae Cantabrigiensis in Acts,* Cambridge, 1966.
Evans, C.F., 'The Central Section of St. Luke's Gospel', in *Studies in the Gospels,* Essays in Memory of R.H. Lightfoot, ed. D.E. Nineham, Oxford, 1957.
Evans, E., *The Epistles of Paul to the Corinthians,* London, 1922.
Farrer, A., *A Study in Mark,* London, 1951.
Fascher, E., *Textgeschichtes als hermeneutisches Problem,* Halle, 1953.
Feibleman, J.K., *Religious Platonism: The Influence of Religion on Plato and the Influence of Plato on Religion,* London, 1959.
Feldman, L.H., *Scholarship on Philo and Josephus, 1937–1962,* Studies in Judaica, New York, 1962.
Fenton, J.C., *St. Matthew,* PGC, Harmondsworth, 1963.
Festugière, A.J., *La Révélation d'Hermès Trismégiste, II Le Dieu Cosmique,* Paris, 1949.
Feuillet, A., *L'Apocalypse: Etat de la question,* Paris and Bruges, 1962.
Filson, F.F., *A Commentary on the Gospel According to St. Matthew,* BNTC, London, 1960.
Finkelstein, L., *The Jews, Their History, Culture and Religion,* 2 Vols., London, 1949.
Fitzmyer, J.A., 'Further Light on Melchizedek from Qumran Cave 11', JBL, 86, 1967, pp. 25–41.
Flemington, W.F., *The New Testament Doctrine of Baptism,* London, 1948.
Flew, R.N., *Jesus and His Church, A Study in the Idea of the Ecclesia in the New Testament,* 2nd ed., London, 1943.
Focke, F., *Die Entstehung der Weisheit Salamos,* Göttingen, 1913.
Förster, W., *Palestinian Judaism in New Testament Times,* London, 1964.
Förster, W., 'Der Heilige Geist im Spätjudentum', NTS, 8, 1961–1962, pp. 117–134.
Frame, J.E., *The Epistles of St. Paul to the Thessalonians,* ICC, Edinburgh, 1912.
Freed, E.D., *Old Testament Quotations on the Gospel of John,* Leiden, 1965.
Frey, J.B., *Corpus Inscriptionum Judaicarum,* Rome, 1936.
Friedländer, M., *Die Jüden in der vorchristlichen griechischen Welt,* Vienna, 1897.
Fuller, F.H., *The Foundations of New Testament Christology,* London, 1965.
Gärtner, B.E., 'The Pauline and Johannine Idea of "To Know God" Against the Hellenistic Background', JTS, 14, 1968, pp. 209–231.
Gaster, T.H., *The Scriptures of the Dead Sea Sect,* London, 1957.
Geffcken, J., *Die Oracula Sibyllina,* Leipzig, 1902.
Gelin, A., *The Poor of Jahweh,* Collegeville, Minnesota, 1964.
Gerhardson, B., *The Testing of God's Son,* Lund, 1966.
Ginsberg, L., *The Legends of the Jews,* 7 Vols., Philadelphia, 1901–1938.
Glasson, T.F., *Moses in the Fourth Gospel,* London, 1963.
Glasson, T.F., *Greek Influence in Jewish Eschatology,* London, 1961.
Gnilka, H., *Der Philipperbrief,* Freiburg, 1968.
Goodenough, E.R., *Jewish Symbols in the Graeco-Roman Period,* 13 Vols., New York, 1953–1968.

163

Goodenough, E.R., *An Introduction to Philo Judaeus,* 2nd ed., Oxford, 1962.
Goodenough, E.R., *The Politics of Philo Judaeus with a General Bibliography of Philo* (with H.L. Goodhart), New Haven, 1938.
Goodenough, E.R., *By Light, Light,* New Haven, 1937.
Goodenough, E.R., *De Specialibus Legibus: The Jurisprudence of the Jewish Courts in Egypt,* New Haven, 1929.
Goodenough, E.R., 'John a Primitive Gospel', JBL, 64, 1945, pp. 145–182.
Goodrick, A.T.S., *The Book of Wisdom,* New York, 1913.
Goudge, H.L., *The First Epistle to the Corinthians,* WC, 5th ed., London, 1926.
Gould, E.P., *The Gospel According to St. Mark,* ICC, Edinburgh, 1896.
Grant, R.M., 'Hellenistic Elements in 1 Corinthians', in *Early Christian Origins,* Studies in Honour of H.R. Willoughby, ed. A. Wikgren, Chicago, 1961, pp. 60–66.
Grant, R.M., *Gnosticism and Early Christianity,* New York, 1959.
Grimm, C.L.W., *Das Buch der Weisheit ërklart,* Leipzig, 1860.
Hadas, M., 'Plato in Hellenistic Fusion', *Journal of the History of Ideas* 19, 1958, pp. 3–13.
Haenchen, E., *Die Apostelgeschichte,* 12th ed., Göttingen, 1959.
Hahn, F., *The Titles of Jesus in Christology,* London, 1969.
Hamilton, N.Q., *The Holy Spirit and Eschatology in Paul,* Edinburgh, 1957.
Hanson, A.T., *Jesus Christ in the Old Testament,* London, 1965.
Harris, J.R., *The Origin of the Prologue to St. John's Gospel,* Cambridge, 1917.
Harris, J.R., *Fragments of Philo Judaeus,* Cambridge, 1886.
Hatch, E., and Redpath, H.A., *A Concordance to the LXX and the other Greek Versions of the O.T.* (including the apocryphal books), 2 Vols., Oxford, 1897.
Heinemann, I., *Philons griechische und jüdische Bildung,* Breslau, 1932.
Heinemann, I., 'Die griechische Quelle des Weisheit Salamos', *Jahresbericht des jüdisch-theologischen Seminars Frankelscher Stiftung für 1920,* Breslau, pp. 8–25.
Heinisch, P., *Die griechische Philosophie im Buche der Weisheit,* Münster, 1908.
Heinisch, P., *Das Buch der Weisheit,* Münster, 1912.
Heinze, H., *Der Lehre von Logos in der griechischen Philosophie,* Oldenburg, 1872.
Hengel, M., *Judaism and Hellenism: Studies in their Encounter in Palestine during the Early Hellenistic Period,* 2 Vols., London, 1974.
Héring, J., *L'Epître aux Hebreux,* Neuchâtel, 1954.
Héring, J., *The First Epistle of St. Paul to the Corinthians,* London, 1962.
Héring, J., *The Second Epistle of St. Paul to the Corinthians,* London, 1967.
Hesselgrave, C.E., *The Hebrew Personification of Wisdom,* New York, 1910.
Higgins, A.J.B., 'The Priestly Messiah', NTS, 13, 1966–1967, pp. 211–239.
Hill, D., *Greek Words and Hebrew Meanings,* Cambridge, 1967.
Holtz, T., *Die Christologie der Apokalypse des Johannes,* Berlin, 1962.
Hooke, S.H., 'The Spirit was not yet', NTS, 9, 1963, pp. 372–380.
Hoskyns, E.C., and Davey, F.N., *The Fourth Gospel,* 2 Vols., London, 1940.
Howard, G.E., 'The Letter of Aristeas and Diaspora Judaism', JTS, 22, 1971, pp.337–348.
Howard, W.F., Barrett, C.K., *Christianity According to St. John,* 4th ed., London, 1955.
Hull, J.H.E., *The Holy Spirit in the Acts of the Apostles,* London, 1967.
Hull, J.M., *Hellenistic Magic and the Synoptic Tradition,* London, 1974.
Hunter, A.M., 'Recent Trends in Johannine Studies', Exp.T., 71, 1959–1960, pp. 164–167, 219–222.
Hunter, A.M., *Paul and His Predecessors,* 2nd ed., London, 1961.
Jackson, F.J.F., and Lake, K., *The Beginnings of Christianity,* 5 Vols., London, 1920–1933.
Jackson, F.J.F., *The Acts of the Apostles,* MNTC, London, 1931.
James, M.R., ed., 'Apocrypha Anecdota II', *Cambridge Text and Studies,* Vol. V, No. 1, Cambridge, 1897.
James, M.R., *The Apocryphal New Testament,* 5th impression, Oxford, 1953.
Jaeger, W.W., *Die Theologie der frühen griechischen Denker,* Stuttgart, 1953.

164

Jellicoe, S., *The Septuagint and Modern Study*, Oxford, 1968.
Jewett, R., *Paul's Anthropological Terms*, Leiden, 1971.
Johansson, N., *Parakletoi*, Lund, 1940.
Johnson, S.E., *The Gospel According to St. Mark*, BNTC, London, 1960.
Johnston, G., *The Spirit-Paraclete in the Gospel of John*, Cambridge, 1970.
Jones, M., *The Epistle to the Philippians*, WC, London, 1918.
Jonge, M. de, *The Testament of the Twelve Patriarchs, A Study of their Text, Composition and Origin*, Assen, 1953.
Jonge, M. de, ed., *Testamenta XII Patriarcharum*, Leiden, 1964.
Jonge, M. de and Woude, A.S. van der, '11Q Melchizedek and the N.T.', NTS, 12, 1966, pp. 301–326.
Kahle, P., *The Cairo Geniza*, 2nd ed., Oxford, 1959.
Kallas, J., *The Significance of the Synoptic Miracles*, London, 1961.
Käsemann, E., *The Testament of Jesus*, London, 1968.
Käsemann, E., *Perspectives on Paul*, London, 1971.
Katz, P., *Philo's Bible: The Aberrant Text of Bible Quotations in Some Philonic Writings and its Place in the Textual History of the Greek Bible*, Cambridge, 1950.
Keck, L.E., 'The Spirit and the Dove', NTS, 17, 1970, pp. 41–67.
Kelly, J.N.D., *The Pastoral Epistles*, BNTC, London, 1963.
Kelly, J.N.D., *The Epistles of Peter and of Jude*, BNTC, London, 1969.
Kennedy, H.A.A., *The Theology of the Epistles*, London, 1919.
Kennedy, H.A.A., *Philo's Contribution to Religion*, London, 1919.
Kilpatrick, G.D., ed., Ἡ Καινὴ Διαθήκη, British and Foreign Bible Society, 2nd ed., London, 1958.
Kilpatrick, G.D., *The Origins of the Gospel According to St. Matthew*, Oxford, 1946.
Kilpatrick, G.D., 'What John tells us about Jn.', in *Studies in John* presented to Professor Dr J.N.D. Sevenster on the occasion of his 70th birthday, Leiden, 1970.
Kittel, G., and Friedrich, G., ed., *Theologisches Wörterbuch zum Neuen Testament*, Stuttgart, 1933–1973.
Kittel, G., ed., *Biblia Hebraica*, 7th ed., Stuttgart, 1961.
Klausner, J., *From Jesus to Paul*, London, 1943.
Knowling, R.J., *The Epistle of St. James*, 3rd ed., London, 1922.
Knox, W.L., *St. Paul and the Church of the Gentiles*, Cambridge, 1939.
Knox, W.L., *Some Hellenistic Elements in Primitive Christianity*, London, 1944.
Knox, W.L., 'Pharisaism and Hellenism' in *Judaism and Christianity, II The Contact of Pharisaism with Other Cultures*, ed., H. Loewe, London, 1937.
Knox, W.L., *The Acts of the Apostles*, Cambridge, 1948.
Knox, W.L., 'A Note on Philo's use of the O.T.', JTS, 41, 1940, pp. 30–34.
Knox, W.L., 'The Divine Wisdom', JTS, 38, 1937, pp. 230–237.
Kossen, H.B., 'Who were the Greeks of John 12:20?' in *Studies in John* presented to Professor Dr J.N.D. Sevenster on the occasion of his 70th birthday, Leiden, 1970.
Kraeling, C.H., *John the Baptist*, New York, 1951.
Kraus, H-J., *Worship in Israel*, Oxford, 1966.
Kümmel, W.G., *Man in the New Testament*, London, 1963.
Lagrange, M-J., *Saint Paul Epître aux Galates*, EB, Paris, 1950.
Lagrange, M-J., *Saint Paul Epître aux Romains*, EB, Paris, 1916.
Lagrange, M-J., *Evangile selon Saint Marc*, EB, 3rd ed., Paris, 1920.
Lagrange, M-J., *Evangile selon Saint Matthieu*, EB, 3rd ed., Paris, 1927.
Lampe, G.W.H., *The Seal of the Spirit*, 2nd ed., London, 1967.
Lampe, G.W.H., 'The Holy Spirit in the Writings of St. Luke', in *Studies in the Gospels*, Essays in Memory of R.H. Lightfoot, ed. D.E. Nineham, Oxford, 1955.
Lampe, G.W.H., 'Luke' and 'Acts', in *Peake's Commentary on the Bible*, ed. M. Black and H.H. Rowley, London, 1962, pp. 820–881, 882–926.
Langton, E., *Essentials of Demonology*, London, 1949.
Larcher, C., *Etudes sur le livre de la Sagesse*, Paris, 1969.

Laqueur, R., *Der jüdische Historiker Flavius Josephus,* Giessen, 1920.
Laurentin, A., 'Le pneuma dans la doctrine de Philon', *Ephemerides Theologicae Lovansienses* 27, 1951, pp. 390–437.
Leaney, A.R.C., *The Rule of Qumran and its Meaning,* London, 1966.
Leaney, A.R.C., *The Gospel According to St. Luke,* BNTC, 2nd ed., London, 1966.
Leaney, A.R.C., *The Letters of Peter and Jude,* Cambridge, 1967.
Leenhardt, F.J., *The Epistle to the Romans,* London, 1961.
Leisegang, H., *Der Heilige Geist,* Berlin, 1919.
Leisegang, H., *Hagion Pneuma,* Leipzig, 1922.
Lewy, H., *Sobria Ebrietas,* Giessen, 1929.
Liddell, H.G., Scott, R., Jones, H.S. and McKenzie, R., *A Greek-English Lexicon,* 9th ed., Oxford, 1940.
Lieberman, S., *Greek in Jewish Palestine,* New York, 1942.
Lieberman, S., *Hellenism in Jewish Palestine,* New York, 1950.
Lietzmann, H., *A History of the Early Church,* 2 Vols., 2nd ed., London, 1949.
Lightfoot, R.H., ed. Evans, C.F., *St. John's Gospel,* Oxford, 1956.
Lightfoot, J.B., *St. Paul's Epistles to the Colossians and to Philemon,* London, 1892.
Lightfoot, J.B., *St. Paul's Epistle to the Philippians,* London, 1903.
Lightfoot, J.B., *St. Paul's Epistle to the Galatians,* 7th ed., London, 1881.
Lindars, B. and Smalley, S., ed., *Christ and Spirit in the N.T.,* Studies in Honour of C.F.D. Moule, Cambridge, 1973.
Ling, T., *The Significance of Satan,* London, 1961.
Lock, W., *The Pastoral Epistles,* ICC, Edinburgh, 1924.
Lofthouse, W.F., 'The Holy Spirit in the Acts and in the Fourth Gospel', Exp.T. 52, 1941, pp. 334–336.
Lohmeyer, E., *Die Brief an die Philipper, an die Kolosser und an Philemon,* Göttingen, 1961.
Lohmeyer, E., *Die Offenbarung des Johannes,* 2nd ed., Tübingen, 1953.
Lohse, E., *Die Brief an die Kolosser und an Philemon,* Göttingen, 1968.
Longenecker, R.N., *The Christology of Early Jewish Christianity,* London, 1970.
Malatesta, E., *St. John's Gospel,* 1920–1965, Rome, 1967.
Manson, T.W., *The Sayings of Jesus,* London, 1949.
Manson, W., *The Epistle to the Hebrews,* London, 1951.
Marcus, R., 'Recent Literature on Philo (1924–1934)', in *Jewish Studies in Memory of George A. Kohut,* New York, 1935, pp. 463–491.
Marcus, R., 'Selected Bibliography (1920–1945) of the Jews in the Hellenistic-Roman Period', *Proceedings of the American Academy for Jewish Research* 16, 1946–1947, pp. 97–181.
Marcus, R., 'Hellenistic Jewish Literature', in *The Jews, Their History, Culture and Religion,* ed. L. Finkelstein, Vol. II, London, 1949, pp. 1077–1115.
Marcus, R., *Philo Supplement* (Questions and Answers on Genesis and Exodus), Loeb Classical Library, 2 Vols., London and Cambridge, Mass., 1953.
Marcus R., 'Divine Names and Attributes in Hellenistic Jewish Literature', *Proceedings of the American Academy for Jewish Research,* 1931–1932, pp. 43–120.
Marcus, R., 'Jewish and Greek Elements in the LXX', in the *Louis Ginzberg Jubilee Volume,* ed., S. Lieberman and Co., New York, 1945, pp. 227–245.
Marrou, H.I., *Histoire de l'Education dans l'Antiquité,* 3rd ed., Paris, 1955.
Marsh, J., *Saint John,* PGC, Harmondsworth, 1968.
Mattill, A.J., and M.B., *A Classified Bibliography of Literature on the Acts of the Apostles,* Leiden, 1966.
Mayor, J.B., *The Epistle of St. James,* 2nd ed., London, 1897.
Meeks, W.A., *The Prophet-King,* Leiden, 1967.
Merlan, P., 'Greek Philosophy from Plato to Plotinus', in *The Cambridge History of Later Greek and Early Medieval Philosophy,* ed. A.H. Armstrong, Cambridge, 1967, pp. 14–132.

166

Metzger, B.M., *Index to Periodical Literature on the Apostle Paul*, Leiden, 1960.
Metzger, B.M., *Index to Periodical Literature on Christ and the Gospels*, Leiden, 1966.
Michaelis, W., 'Zur Herkunft des johanneischen Paraklet-Titels', *Coniectanea Neotestamentica* XI (Friedricksen Festschrift), 1947, pp. 147–162.
Michel, O., *Der Brief an die Hebräer*, Göttingen, 1960.
Michel, O., *Der Brief an die Römer*, Göttingen, 1963.
Micklem, P.A., *St. Matthew*, WC, London, 1917.
Middleton, R.B., 'Logos and Shekinah in the Fourth Gospel', *Jewish Quarterly Revue* 29, 1938–1939, pp. 101–133.
Milik, J.T., *Ten Years of Discovery in the Wilderness of Judea*, London, 1959.
Milik, J.T., 'Le Testament de Levi en Araméen, RB, 62, 1955, pp. 398–406.
Minear, P.S., 'Luke's Use of the Birth Stories', in *Studies in Luke-Acts*, Essays presented in Honour of Paul Schubert, ed., L.E. Keck and J.L. Martyn, London, 1968, pp. 111–130.
Mishnah, ET, H. Danby, Oxford, 1933.
Mitton, C.L., *The Epistle of James*, London, 1966.
Moffatt, J., *The Epistle to the Hebrews*, ICC, Edinburgh, 1924.
Moffatt, J., *The General Epistles*, MNTC, London, 1928.
Montefiore, C.G., *Judaism and St. Paul*, London, 1914.
Montefiore, H., *The Epistle to the Hebrews*, BNTC, London, 1964.
Montgomery, J.A., 'The Religion of Flavius Josephus', *Jewish Quarterly Revue* 11, 1920–1921, pp. 277–305.
Moore, G.F., *Judaism in the First Centuries of the Christian Era: The Age of the Tannaim*, 3 Vols., Cambridge, Mass., 1927–1930.
Moore, G.F., 'Intermediaries in Jewish Theology', HTR, 15, 1922, pp. 41–85.
Moore, G.F., 'Fate and Free Will in the Jewish Philosophies According to Josephus', HTR 22, 1929, pp. 371–389.
Morton, A.Q., 'The Authorship of the Pauline Corpus', in *The New Testament in Historical and Contemporary Perspective*, Essays in Memory of G.H.C. MacGregor, ed. H. Anderson and W. Barclay, Oxford, 1965, pp. 209–235.
Morton, A.Q., and McLeman, J., *Paul, The Man and the Myth*, London, 1966.
Moule, C.F.D., 'Sanctuary and Sacrifice in the Church of the N.T.', JTS, 1, 1950, pp.29–41.
Moule, C.F.D., *The Epistles to the Colossians and to Philemon*, Cambridge, 1958.
Moule, C.F.D., 'A Neglected Factor in the Interpretation of Johannine Eschatology', in *Studies in John*, presented to Professor Dr J.N.D. Sevenster on the occasion of his 70th birthday, Leiden, 1970, pp. 155–160.
Moule, C.F.D., '2 Cor 3:18b', *Neues Testament und Geschichte* (Oscar Cullmann zum 70 Geburtstag) hg. von H., Baltensweiler, Bo Reiche, Zürich, 1972, pp. 231–237.
Moulton, W.F. and Green A.S., *A Concordance to the Greek N.T.*, 2 Vols., 2nd ed., Edinburgh, 1899.
Mowinckel, S., 'Die Vorstellungen des Spätjudentums von heilige Geist als Fürsprecher und der johanneische Paraklet', ZNTW, 32, 1933, pp. 97–130.
Müller, C. and T., *Fragmenta Historicorum Graecorum*, 4 Vols., Paris, 1885.
Murray, G.B., *Jesus and the Future*, London, 1954.
Mussner, F., *Der Jakobusbrief*, Freiburg, 1964.
McKenzie, J.L., 'Reflections on Wisdom', JBL, 86, 1967, pp. 1–9.
McNeile, A.H., *The Gospel According to St. Matthew*, London, 1915.
O'Neill, J.C., *The Theology of Acts in its Historical Setting* (2nd ed., London, 1970).
Parke, H.W. and Wormell, D.E., *The Delphic Oracle*, 2 Vols., Oxford, 1956.
Parratt, J.K., 'The Holy Spirit and Baptism. Part II The Pauline Evidence', Exp.T. 82, 1971, pp. 266–271.
Pauly, A.F. von, Wissowa, G., and Kroll, W., *Real-Encyclopädie in der classischen altertumswissenschaft*, 2nd ed., Stuttgart, 1913.
Perdelwitz, R., *Die Mysterienreligionem und das Problem des ersten Petrusbriefe*, Giessen, 1911.

Perrin, N., *Rediscovering the Teaching of Jesus,* London, 1967.
Pfeiffer, R.H., *History of N.T. Times with an Introduction to the Apocrypha,* London, 1949.
Plummer, A., *An Exegetical Commentary on the Gospel According to St. Matthew,* London, 1910.
Pohlenz, M., *Philon von Alexandreia,* Göttingen, 1942.
Pohlenz, M., *Die Stoa: Geschichte einer Geistigen Bewegung,* 2 Vols., Göttingen, 1948–1949.
Pulver, M., 'Das Erlebnis des pneuma bei Philon', *Eranos Jahrbuch* 13, 1945, pp.111–132.
Rackham, R.B., *The Acts of the Apostles,* WC, 12th ed., London, 1939.
Radford, R.B., *The Epistle to the Colossians and the Epistle to Philemon,* WC, London, 1931.
Rahlfs, A., ed., *Septuaginta,* 8th ed., Stuttgart, 1935.
Rankin, O.S., *Israel's Wisdom Literature,* Edinburgh, 1936.
Rawlinson, A.E.J., *St. Mark,* WC, London, 1925.
Reicke, B., *The Disobedient Spirits and Christian Baptism,* Copenhagen, 1946.
Reicke, B., *The Epistles of James, Peter and Jude,* New York, 1964.
Reider, J., *The Book of Wisdom,* New York, 1957.
Reitzenstein, R., *Die hellenistischen Mysterienreligion,* 3rd ed., Leipzig, 1917.
Rigaux, B., *Saint Paul les Epîtres aux Thessaloniens,* Paris, 1956.
Ringgren, H., *Word and Wisdom,* Lund, 1947.
Rissi, M., *Studien zum zweiten Korintherbrief,* Zürich, 1969.
Robertson, A., and Plummer, A., *The First Epistle of St. Paul to the Corinthians,* ICC, Edinburgh, 1911.
Robinson, J.A., *St. Paul's Epistle to the Ephesians,* 2nd ed., London, 1904.
Robinson, J.A.T., *The Body,* London, 1952.
Robinson, T.H., *The Epistle to the Hebrews,* MNTC, London, 1933.
Robinson, T.H., *The Gospel According to Matthew,* MNTC, London, 1928.
Rodd, C.S., 'Spirit and Finger', Exp.T. 72, 1960–1961, pp. 157f.
Ropes, J.H., *St. James,* ICC, Edinburgh, 1916.
Rostovtzeff, M., *The Social and Economic History of the Hellenistic World,* 3 Vols., Oxford, 1941.
Russell, D.S., *The Method and Message of Jewish Apocalyptic,* London, 1964.
Rust, M., 'The Revelation of St. John the Divine', in *The Interpreter's Bible,* Vol. 12, New York, 1957, pp. 347–365.
Rylaarsdam, J.C., *Revelation in Jewish Wisdom Literature,* Chicago, 1946.
Sanday, W., and Headlam, A.C., *The Epistle to the Romans,* ICC, 5th ed., Edinburgh, 1902.
Sanders, J.N. and Mastin, B.A., *The Gospel According to St. John,* BNTC, London, 1968.
Sandmel, S., *The First Christian Century in Judaism and Christianity: Certainties and Uncertainties,* Oxford, 1969.
Saunders, J.T., *The N.T. Christological Hymns,* Cambridge, 1971.
Schechter, S., *Some Aspects of Rabbinic Theology,* London, 1909.
Schlatter, A., *Die Korintherbriefe,* Stuttgart, 1962.
Schlier, H., *Der Brief an die Epheser,* 4th ed., Düsseldorf, 1963.
Schmidt, K.L., *Der Rahmer der Geschichte Jesu,* Berlin, 1919.
Schnackenburg, R., *Baptism in the Thought of St. Paul,* Oxford, 1964.
Schnackenburg, R., *The Gospel According to St. John,* Vol. I, London and New York, 1968.
Schnackenburg, R., *Die Johannesbriefe,* 2nd ed., Freiburg, 1963.
Schreckenberg, H., *Bibliographie zu Flavius Josephus,* Leiden, 1968.
Schürer, E., *Geschichte des jüdischen Volkes im Zeitalter Jesu Christi,* 3 Vols., and Index, Leipzig, 1911.
Schweitzer, A., *The Mysticism of Paul the Apostle,* 2nd ed., London, 1953.
Schweitzer, A., *Paul and His Interpreters,* London, 1912.

168

Schweizer, E., *Spirit of God,* Bible Key Words from TWNTE ed. G. Kittell and G. Friedrich, London, 1960.
Schweizer, E., *The Good News According to Mark,* London, 1971.
Scott, E.F., *The Epistles of Paul to the Colossians and to the Ephesians,* MNTC, London, 1930.
Scott, E.F., *The Spirit in the New Testament,* London, 1923.
Scott, E.F., *The Epistle to the Hebrews, its Doctrine and Significance,* Edinburgh, 1922.
Scott, R.B.Y., 'Wisdom in Creation', *Vetus Testamentum* 10, 1960, pp. 213–223.
Scroggs, R., 'Paul: ΣΟΦΟΣ and ΠΝΕΥΜΑΤΙΚΟΣ', NTS, 14, 1967, pp. 33–55.
Selwyn, E.G., *The First Epistle of St. Peter,* 2nd ed., London, 1947.
Sevenster, J.N.D., *Do You Know Greek? How Much Greek Could the First Jewish Christians Have Known?* Leiden, 1968.
Shoemaker, W.R., 'The Use of *Ruach* in the O.T. and of Πνεῦμα in the N.T.', JBL, 23, 1904, pp. 13–67.
Sidebottom, E.M., *The Christ of the Fourth Gospel,* London, 1961.
Smallwood, M., *Legatio ad Gaium,* Leiden, 1961.
Snaith, N.H., 'The Meaning of the Paraclete', Exp.T., 57, 1945, pp. 47–50.
Sowers, S.G., *The Hermeneutics of Philo and Hebrews,* Zürich, 1965.
Spicq, C., *L'Epître aux Hébreux,* EB, 2nd ed., 2 Vols., Paris, 1952–1953.
Stacey, W.D., *The Pauline View of Man,* London, 1956.
Strachan, R.H., *The Second Epistle of Paul to the Corinthians,* MNTC, London, 1934.
Strack, H.L. and Billerbeck, P., *Kommentar zum Neuen Testament aus Talmud und Midrasch,* 4 Vols., Munich, 1922–1928.
Swete, H.B., *The Gospel According to St. Mark,* London, 1898.
Swete, H.B., *The O.T. in Greek According to the LXX,* 3 Vols., 4th ed., Cambridge, 1934.
Swete, H.B., *An Introduction to the O.T. in Greek* (with an Appendix containing the Letter of Aristeas edited by H. St.J. Thackeray), 2nd ed., Cambridge, 1902.
Swete, H.B., *The Holy Spirit in the New Testament,* London, 1909.
Tarn, W., and Griffith, G.T., *Hellenistic Civilisation,* 3rd ed., London, 1952.
Tatum, W.B., 'The Epoch of Israel: Luke 1–2 and the Theological Plan of Luke–Acts', NTS, 13, 1967, pp. 184–195.
Taylor, V., *The Gospel According to St. Mark,* London, 1952.
Tcherikover, V.A., Fuks, A., and Stern, M., *Corpus Papyrorum Judaicarum,* 3 Vols., Jerusalem and Cambridge, Mass., 1957–1964.
Tcherikover, V.A., *Hellenistic Civilization and the Jews,* Philadelphia, 1961.
Teeple, H.M., 'Qumran and the Origin of the Fourth Gospel', NT, 4, 1960, pp. 6–25.
Thackeray, H.St.J., *The Relation of St. Paul to Contemporary Thought,* London, 1900.
Thackeray, H.St.J., *Josephus, the Man and the Historian,* 2nd ed., New York, 1967.
Thackeray, H.St.J., Marcus, R., Wikren, A., and Feldman, L.H., *Josephus,* Loeb Classical Library, 9 Vols., London and Cambridge, Mass., 1926–1965.
Thackeray, H.St.J., and Marcus, R., *Lexicon to Josephus,* Pts. I–IV, London and Cambridge, Mass., 1930–1956.
Thackeray, H.St.J., 'The Letter of Aristeas', in *Introduction to the O.T. in Greek,* H.B. Swete, 2nd ed., Cambridge, 1902, pp. 499–574.
Thackeray, H.St.J., *The Septuagint and Jewish Worship,* 2nd ed., London, 1923.
Thomas, K.J., 'The O.T. Citations in Hebrews', NTS, 11, 1965, pp. 303–325.
Torrey, C.C., *The Apocryphal Literature,* Yale, 1945.
Torrey, C.C., *The Apocalypse of John,* New Haven, 1958.
Unnik, W.C. van, 'Jesus the Christ', NTS, 8, 1961, pp. 101–116.
Unnik, W.C. van, *Tarsus or Jerusalem?* London, 1962.
Verbeke, G., *L'Evolution de la doctrine du Pneuma du Stoicisme à S. Augustine,* Louvain, 1945.
Vermès, G., *The Dead Sea Scrolls in English,* Harmondsworth, revised, 1968.
Vermès, G., 'Essenes, Therapeutai, Qumran', *Durham University Journal,* 52, 1960, pp. 97–115.

Vincent, M.R., *The Epistles to the Philippians and to Philemon,* ICC, Edinburgh, 1897.
Völker, W., *Fortschritt und Vollendung bei Philo von Alexandrien: eine Studie zur Geschichte der Frömmigkeit,* Leipzig, 1938.
Volz, P., *Der Geist Gottes,* Tübingen, 1910.
Waldron, R.A., *Sense and Sense Development,* London, 1967.
Wand, J.W.C., *The General Epistles of St. Peter and St. Jude,* WC, London, 1899.
Webster, T.B.L., 'Communication of Thought in Ancient Greece', in *Studies in Communication,* ed. A.J. Ayer, London, 1955, pp. 125–146.
Westcott, B.F., *The Epistle to the Hebrews,* London, 1889.
Westcott, B.F., *St. Paul's Epistle to the Ephesians,* London, 1906.
Whiteley, D.E.H., *The Theology of St. Paul,* Oxford, 1964.
Whybray, R.N., 'Proverbs 8:22–31 and its supposed prototypes', *Vetus Testamentum* 15, 1965, pp. 504–514.
Wikenhauser, A., *Die Offenbarung des Johannes,* 3rd ed., Regensburg, 1959.
Wilcox, M., *The Semitisms of Acts,* Oxford, 1965.
Wilder, A.N., '1 John', *The Interpreter's Bible,* Vol. 12, New York, 1957.
Williams, C.S.C., *The Acts of the Apostles,* BNTC, 2nd ed., London, 1964.
Williamson, R., *Philo and the Epistle to the Hebrews,* Leiden, 1970.
Wilson, R. Mc.L., 'Philo and the Fourth Gospel', Exp.T. 65, 1953, pp. 47–49.
Wilson, R. Mc.L., 'The Fourth Gospel and Hellenistic Thought', NT, 1, 1956, pp. 225–227.
Windisch, H., 'Jesus und der Geist nach synoptisches Überlieferung', in *Studies in Early Christianity,* ed., S.J. Case, London and New York, 1928, pp. 209–228.
Windisch, H., *Die Katholischen Briefe,* 3rd ed., Tübingen, 1951.
Windisch, H., 'Die fünf johanneischen Parakletsprüche', in *Festgabe für A. Julicher zum 70 Geburtstag,* Tübingen, 1927, pp. 110–137.
Windisch, H., 'Jesus und der Geist im Johannesevangelium', in *Amicitiae Corolla,* Essays presented to J. Rendel Harris on his 80th birthday, ed. H.G. Wood, London, 1933, pp. 303–318.
Wolfson, H.A., *Philo: Foundation of Religious Philosophy in Judaism, Christianity and Islam,* 2 Vols., Cambridge, Mass., 1947.
Wolfson, H.A., 'The Philonic God of Revelation and His Latter-Day Deniers', HTR, 53, 1960, pp. 101–124.
Würthwein, E., *The Text of the O.T.,* Oxford, 1957.
Yadin, Y., 'The Dead Sea Scrolls and the Epistle to the Hebrews', *Scripta Hierosolymitana* IV, 1958, pp. 36–66.
Yates, J.E., *The Spirit and the Kingdom,* London, 1963.
Zeller, E., *Die Philosophie der Griechen,* 5th ed., 3 Vols., Leipzig, 1923.

INDEX OF AUTHORS

174

|---|---|---|---|
Wilson, R.McL.	68 n.24	Xenophanes	26
Windish, H.	122f, 139	Yadin, Y.	66
Wolfson, H.A.	22, 32, 53 n.96, 54f, 57	Yates, J.E.	121 n.76, 142 n.259
		Zeller, E.	52 n.81
Wormell, D.E.W.	15 n.35, 50 n.76	Zeno	15 n.30
Würthwein, E.	5 n.16		

INDEX OF REFERENCES

1 Old Testament (Hebrew Canon)

Genesis
1. 35, 56, 61, 63
1.2 43, 55 n.108
1.26 32
2. 35, 56
2.7 35, 37, 61, 63
72 n.26
100 n.162
3. 33 n.117
6. 109
6.5 31 n.106
6.17 72 n.26
6.18 35
7.4 43
8.1 43
8.21 31 n.106,
31 n.108
15.9 117
21. 98
31.11, 13 112 n.258
35.18 72 n.30
41.8 11, 37 n.23
41.38 46 n.20

Exodus
3.2 112 n.251
3.14 23
6.9 11 n.10
8.19 121
10.13 10 n.3
14.21 10 n.3
17.1-6 138
25.8 25 n.62
25.9 23
25.40 23, 127
28.3 46 n.20
29.45f 25 n.62
31.2f 46 n.20
34.27-35 133 n.186
34.29-35 113
34.34 113
35.21 11
35.31 46 n.20
40.35 119 n.59

Leviticus
16.16 126
17.10f 37
20.7f 97
24.15f 141 n.253

Numbers
5.3 25 n.62
5.14 12
11.17 46 n.20,
47 n.37, 61
11.25 130
16.22 14
20.2-11 138
22. 47
23.6 12, 48
27.16 14, 29 n.86
27.18 47 n.44

Deuteronomy
2.30 12
4.12 112 n.252
9.10 121 n.77
10.16 134 n.194
18.18f 129
32.17 105 n.197
33.2 130
34.9 133 n.183

Joshua
5.1 11

Judges
3.16 73 n.41
8.3 12
9.23 12, 13 n.22
103 n.184
13.25 47 n.44
16.14 119 n.55

Ruth
3.9 119

1 Samuel (1 Kingdoms)
1.15 12
2.1-10 73 n.33
10.6 50
10.10-12 51 n.77
16. 48
16.14 13, 34 n.122
16.16 13, 103 n.184
16.23 13
18.10 13 n.22
19.4 33
19.9 33
22.15 48
28.7ff 104 n.193
28.13 33 n.121
30.12 37 n.22

2 Samuel (2 Kingdoms)
13.21 12
23.2 124 n.102

1 Kings (3 Kingdoms)
6.13 25 n.62
8.27 99 n.154
8.29 25 n.60
10.5 12
17.17 11 n.6
20(MT 21).4 12
20(MT 21).5 37 n.22
22.11 10 n.3
22.21 13, 14
22.22f 105 n.198

2 Kings (4 Kingdoms)
2.16ff 88 n.54
2.16 117 n.143

1 Chronicles
23.25 25 n.62
28.11f 23

2 Chronicles
15.1 47 n.44
21.16 12
24.20 47 n.44
36.22 37 n.23

176

Job
5.1 112 n.260
6.4 11 n.11
7.15 12 n.17
13.25 10
15.13 11 n.11
15.30 10 n.3
28.23-28 135

Psalms (MT in brackets)
1.4 10 n.3
8.3 121 n.77
22.10 119 n.56
30(31).5 71, 73
32(33).5 73 n.40
33(34).18 72
34(35).5 10 n.3
50(51).11 14, 20
67(68).6 102
67(68).19 131 n.63
85(86).21 25 n.62
94(95).7-11 125
103(104).4 111
104(105).30 72 n.26
109(110).1 124, 126
138(139).7 23 n.49
144(145).18 99 n.155

Proverbs
1.23 11 n.3
5.4 73 n.41
8.1-31 135
8.22-31 52 n.86
11.29 10 n.3
14.29 11 n.10, n.12
15.13 12 n.15
16.1f 12 n.15f
16.18 11 n.14
        12 n.15
16.19 11 n.12
16.32 11 n.13
17.22 12 n.15
17.27 11 n.12
        12 n.15
18.14 11 n.10
25.14 10 n.3
27.16 10 n.3
29.23 11 n.14

Ecclesiastes
2.23 23 n.44
5.17 23 n.44
6.4f 23 n.44

Ecclesiastes (contd)
7.8 11 n.12, 12
7.29 31 n.108
8.13 23 n.44
9.17 23 n.44

Isaiah
4.4 83, 115
7.14 120
11. 84
11.2 82
11.4 19 n.14,
        72 n.19, 83
13.21 16 n.36
29.10 71 n.12
30.1 19 n.15
31.3 98
31.21 102 n.183
32.15 83 n.7
34.14 16 n.36,
        102 n.183
38.12 11
38.16 11 n.5
40.7 12 n.16
40.13 11, 19 n.15,
        74
40.18ff 26 n.65
41.16 10 n.3
42.1 82
44.3 83 n.3
44.9-20 26 n.65
49.2 73 n.41,
        90 n.79
53.10 19 n.15
54.6 11 n.10
55.11 73 n.40
57.13 10 n.3
57.15 11 n.10
59.17 24 n.54
60.19f 21 n.24
61.1 13 n.20, 83,
        88 n.51
63.9 112 n.257
63.10f 14, 20,
        72 n.24
65.1-4 102
65.3 16 n.36
66.2 11 n.10
66.15 24 n.54

Jeremiah
3.4 120
4.4 134 n.194

Jeremiah (contd)
5.13 10 n.3, 11 n.4
23.24 23 n.49
23.29 73 n.40
28(MT 51).1 10 n.3
38(MT 31).
  31-34 132 n.175, 134
38(MT 31).
  33f 126

Ezekiel
2.2 13 n.20
3.24 13 n.20
5.10 10 n.3
8.3 117 n.43
11.1 117 n.43
11.19 83 n.4
12.14 10 n.3
13.3 11
13.13 11 n.5
17.10 11 n.3
19.12 11 n.3
32.26 134
36.26 83 n.5
37. 83 n.6
37.14 87 n.34,
        97 n.145
        119 n.55
38.18-22 24 n.54
39.29 11 n.11
43.7, 9 25 n.62

Daniel
5.13f 46 n.20
5.23 11 n.6
8.8 10 n.3

Hosea
6.6(MT 6.5) 90 n.79
13.15 10 n.3

Joel
2.28f 83, 88, 140
3.1f 13 n.20

Amos
7.14 51 n.78

Zechariah
1.6 13
1.12 112 n.260
2.14 25 n.62
4.2 111

2 Jewish Apocrypha and Pseudepigrapha

Song of the Three Holy Children			*Jubilees*			*Sibylline Oracles*	
63	36		1.25	110 n.233		III.30	26 n.72
(LXX Dan 3.86)			1.27	130		III.606-618	26 n.69
			5.	109 n.224		III.701	19 n.6
Susanna			6.21	130		III.738	38 n.29
42(Th.45)	46 n.21		11.3ff	26 n.64		IV.46, 189	82 n.1
54	46 n.20		12.3ff	26 n.64		V.260	38 n.29
			15.31f	26 n.64			
Bel and the Dragon			20.8			*Assumption of Moses*	
1-22	26 n.71					11.17	133
			Letter of Aristeas				
1 Maccabees			15f	27 n.76		*2 Enoch*	
1.11-15	2 n.5		134	26 n.66		12.1(B)	110 n.234,
			135ff	26 n.68			110 n.239
2 Maccabees			138	26 n.72		16.7	110 n.234
3.24	14 n.24		197	33		30.8(A)	35 n.1
			277	33, 76 n.66		30.14	111 n.240
3 Maccabees						31.4(A)	33
6.24	36 n.8		*Apocalypse of Moses*				
			(Life of Adam and Eve)			*2 Baruch*	
4 Maccabees			32.4	76 n.68		21.4	116,
1.18	41 n.66						119 n.55
2.22f	33		*1 Enoch* (excluding the			21.6	110
5.10	40 n.60		*Similitudes of Enoch =*			29.8	132
5.22	40 n.59		*1 Enoch 37-71)*				
5.23f	40 n.61		6.	109 n.224		*Psalms of Solomon*	
6.29	41 n.65		9.3	112 n.260		10.7	72 n.21
7.13	38, 40		10.11-14	109 n.224		17.37	84
7.17-23	41 n.67		15.2	112 n.260			
7.21	41 n.65		19.1	26 n.64		*Odes of Solomon*	
18.8	33 n.117		20.1-8	110 n.238		11.1-3	134 n.194
			90.21	110 n.238			
			91.1	116			

3 Dead Sea Scrolls

1QS *(The Community Rule)*			1QS *(contd)*			1QM *(The War Rule)*	
I.18, 23	85 n.19		IV.21	115		XIII.10	85 n.17
III.6f	107 n.206		IX.8-11	129		XVII.6ff	85 n.18
III.13–	85 n.20,						
IV.26	107 n.206		CD *(The Damascus Rule)*			1QH *(The Hymns)*	
III.20f	85 n.22		V.18	85 n.17		IV.30ff	85
III.25	85		VII.19	85 n.17		XII.19	84

4 Josephus and Philo

Josephus
Antiquitates Judaicae

I.34	35 n.6,		II.210-16	128 n.132		III.100,102	25 n.61
	37 n.24		II.218	128 n.133		III.200	46 n.20
II.75	37 n.23		II.229	128		IV.108	48 n.45,
II.87	46 n.20		II.230f	128 n.134			110 n.234
II.205	128 n.131		II.260	37		IV.118	50 n.69
			III.6f	111 n.242		IV.119f	48 n.46

182

De Vita Mosis (contd)

I.176	30 n.103	II.74ff	127 n.123	II.265	42 n.79,
II.14	25 n.58	II.102f	111 n.242		46 n.25,
II.37	48 n.51	II.108	99 n.156		55 n.111,
II.40	47 n.42,	II.144	25 n.58		108 n.217
	128 n.140	II.166	132	II.288-291	128 n.129
II.44	25 n.58	II.246	50 n.71		

5 Rabbinic Literature

Midrash

Tarqum

Tanhuma

On. Cant.

26C	131 n.161	II.11	116

6 New Testament

Matthew		*Mark (contd)*		*Luke (contd)*	
1.18-20	119 n.53	2.8	71, 73 n.34	2.26	88 n.48,
1.23	120 n.63	2.11	102 n.180,		89 n.70
3.11	114 n.16		103	2.27	88 n.48
3.16	116 n.27	3.28ff	102 n.177, 118,	2.29-32	89 n.69
4.1-12	117 n.46		139, 141	2.41-52	130 n.158
4.1	117 n.44	3.28	118	3.16	114 n.16
5.3	71 n.15	5.1-20	102 n.178	3.22	116 n.27
7.11	91 n.89	5.2, 8, 13	102f	4.1	88 n.46,
8.16	102 n.182	5.30	71 n.9		117 n.45,121
8.28, 30	102	6.7	102f	4.1-12	117 n.46
10.1, 8	102	7.25	102	4.14	89 n.63
10.20	118	7.30	100 n.164,	4.16-30	88 n.51
11.24ff	103		102 n.181	4.33	103
11.27f	141 n.254	8.12	72 n.22,	4.35	103 n.185
11.29	71 n.14		73 n.34	6.18	103
12.28	121	9.7	119 n.59	6.20	71 n.16,
12.32	118	9.17,20,25	102 n.180, 103		73 n.34
12.43ff	102	12.36	124	7.18-23	103
15.22	102	13.11	118, 139	7.21	103
17.5	119 n.59	14.38	73 n.34,	8.2, 26	103
26.41	76 n.71		76 n.71	8.30, 33	103 n.186
27.50	72	15.37	72 n.27,	8.55	72 n.28
28.19	87 n.38,		73 n.34	9.1	103
	91 n.82,			9.34	119 n.59
	113 n.7	*Luke*		9.39, 42	103
		1.15, 17, 35	119	10.1	130 n.160
Mark		1.41	88 n.47,	10.17-30	103 n.189
1.10	116		89 n.70	10.21	87 n.40
1.12	88 n.46,	1.47	71 n.10,	11.13	88 n.49,
	121 n.73		73 n.33,		122 n.84
1.18	114		89 n.69	11.19f	141 n.254
1.23	103	1.67	88 n.47,	11.20	121
1.26	102 n.180		89 n.70	11.24-26	102
1.27	102 n.176,	1.80	88 n.48	12.10	118
	102 n.180	2.25	88 n.48	12.12	119, 122 n.87

184

Romans
1.4 99
1.9 71 n.7
2.14ff 75
2.14 75 n.56
2.15 75 n.57
3.22 134 n.188
5.5 87 n.39, 97
5.12-19 78 n.80
6.1 47 n.33
6.9ff 109
7. 105
7.6 134 n.195
7.14 134
7.22 74
8.2 78 n.82, 134
8.4f 98, 134 n.191
8.5f 134
8.6 98 n.149
8.9f 93 n.103,
96 n.137,
96 n.139,
98, 113
8.10 78 n.82,
93 n.102, 134
8.11 93 n.106, 96,
113 n.1
8.13 77
8.14 91, 96 n.137
8.15 118 n.50
8.16 75 n.57,
137 n.230
8.23 87 n.33
8.26 118 n.50
9.1 75 n.57
9.16 87 n.33
11.18 71 n.12
11.34 74 n.54
12.1 97 n.144
12.11 71 n.13
14.17 87 n.43,
97 n.142
15.13 90 n.75,
97 n.142
15.16 87 n.38,
97 n.141
15.19 90
15.27 76 n.72
15.30 114
16.5 87 n.33

1 Corinthians
1.18-31 137 n.221
1.24 137 n.222
1.30 137
2.4 90
2.6-16 80
2.10 137 n.229
2.11 78, 80 n.95
2.12 96 n.137,
97, 105f
2.14 96 n.137, 98
2.16 74 n.54
3.1 77 n.77,
91 n.80
3.3 77 n.79
3.16 93, 196
4.2 71 n.14
4.20 90 n.72
4.21 87 n.39
5.3 75
5.4 71 n.8
5.5 76 n.61
6.11 113
6.19 93 n.103,
93 n.105
7.34 73 n.39,
76 n.62, n.70
7.40 96 n.137,
137 n.229
8.6 137 n.227
9.11 76 n.72
10.2f 138
12.1 87
12.3 92, 96 n.137,
97
12.4 83 n.108
12.9 125
12.11 87 n.37,
93 n.108
12.13 93 n.107
14. 75 n.58
14.1, 12 87 n.35
14.14 71 n.8,
75 n.59
14.32 90 n.77
14.37 90 n.76
15.24 105 n.200
15.44ff 77
16.18 71 n.8

2 Corinthians
1.22 87 n.31
2.13 71 n.8
3.3 96 n.137, 113,
134 n.193
3.6 113, 134
3.7-18 133
3.8 113, 133 n.187
3.17f 113 n.6
4.6 91 n.89
4.16 74
5.5 87 n.31
6.6 97
6.7 90 n.79
6.16 93 n.105
7.1 76 n.69
7.13 71 n.8
11.4 137 n.229
12.13 90 n.74
13.14 87 n.38, 114

Galatians
2.20 93 n.102
3.2 92
3.3 98
3.5 90 n.73
3.14 87 n.32,
92 n.95
3.19 130
4.5 92 n.92
4.6 118 n.50,
138 n.236
4.29 98
5.5 78, 92 n.94
5.16 77, 98 n.149
5.17 105
5.22 87 n.42,
97 n.142
5.25 92 n.93
6.1 71 n.14
6.18 70, 71 n.8

Ephesians
1.4 97 n.114
1.13 87
1.17 137 n.229
1.18 91 n.89
2.2 106
2.14-18 92 n.92
2.20ff 97 n.138

7 Jewish Christian Apocrypha

8 Church Fathers

9 Classical Works